Tyndale House Publishers, Inc.
Carol Stream, Illinois

The One Year® WOMEN of the Bible

Dianne Neal Matthews

Visit Tyndale's exciting Web site at www.tyndale.com

TYNDALE and Tyndale's quill logo are registered trademarks of Tyndale House Publishers, Inc.

The One Year is a registered trademark of Tyndale House Publishers, Inc.

The One Year Women of the Bible

Designed by Jacqueline L. Noe

Edited by Linda Schlafer and Susan Taylor

Library of Congress Cataloging-in-Publication Data

Matthews, Dianne Neal.
  The one year women of the Bible / Dianne Neal Matthews.
    p. cm.
  Includes index.
  ISBN-13: 978-1-4143-1194-4 (sc)
  ISBN-10: 1-4143-1194-X (sc)
  1. Women in the Bible. 2. Devotional calendars. 3. Women—Religious life. I. Title.
  BS575.M367 2007
  242′.643—dc22   2007014878

Printed in the United States of America

13 12 11 10 09 08 07
7   6   5   4   3   2   1

Dedicated to the memory of my grandmothers,
two women with different personalities but the same Savior

NETTIE DENNISON PICKENS
"Godliness with contentment is great gain."
1 Timothy 6:6 (NKJV)

BETSY REVELY NEAL
"A merry heart does good, like medicine."
Proverbs 17:22 (NKJV)

Thank you to the many people who contributed to this project:
Jon Farrar for his support and encouragement; women who shared their stories with me;
friends who read over material for me: Carrie Burns, Cindy Grabel, Mary Keeley,
Kathy Loutrel, Tonya Ruiz, and Sherry Schildt;
editors at Tyndale who helped polish the manuscript,
especially Linda Schlafer and Susan Taylor;
and Jackie Noe, for her exquisite cover design.

Introduction

Coming up with a year's worth of ideas based on women of the Bible was not easy. So many women get barely more than a mention, yet I would love to have *all* the details of their stories. It was also difficult trying to understand the women's motivations and feelings while trying not to interpret Scripture by my personal opinions or prejudices.

Once I made the effort to relate to these women from the perspective of my own experiences and emotions, they became more real to me than before. They also taught me some surprising things about myself. I never would have compared myself with Delilah, but her nagging showed me that sometimes I have a similar unspoken attitude toward God: *If you really loved me . . .* (April 23). Although I've never killed a man with a tent peg as Jael did, like Michal, I have been guilty of using killing words (September 24).

Most of the stories of contemporary women are based on real-life women that I have known, heard of, or read about. Unless I give first and last names or specifically refer to a woman as "my friend," the names have been changed and details have been fictionalized to guard identity. I also handled a few of my own experiences this way.

Growing up, I longed for a sister; as an adult, I've been blessed to find sisters in Christ to share my life journey. Now, in writing this book, I've discovered a new group of kindred spirits. Despite differences in lifestyle, biblical women faced the same basic struggles, problems, and needs that we do. I pray that as you read these devotions, you will see that the same heavenly Father who reached out to these women in the Bible still calls out to his daughters today.

> *All glory to God, who is able, through his mighty power at work within us, to accomplish infinitely more than we might ask or think. Glory to him in the church and in Christ Jesus through all generations forever and ever! Amen*
> *Ephesians 3:20-21*

January 1

The Crowning Touch
EVE

Genesis 2:15-25

The week between Christmas and New Year's Day had passed too quickly. We had enjoyed a wonderful time of visiting our families, filled with gift giving, good food, movies, laughter, and games. Still, there was something missing. Everyone cheered as my nephew positioned the last piece of the new six-hundred-piece jigsaw puzzle we had worked on so hard all week. We all admired the beautiful picture of a spring garden, copied from a painting by Monet, until someone noticed the tiny empty space near the center.

When God created the first man and placed him in the Garden to live, there was something missing there, too. Even after God had spent six days fashioning a world full of beautiful plants and a dizzying array of animals, his creation was not complete until he made the first woman. Eve was the crowning touch to God's perfect creation. Designed and shaped by God's hand, her femininity perfectly complemented everything else he had made. Adam took one look at Eve and exclaimed, "At last!" God surveyed his finished work and could now say that it was "very good" (Genesis 1:31).

God designed women to bring a special kind of beauty to the world. We are created in God's image, and we testify to his glory in a unique way as we embrace feminine traits of nurturing, sensitivity, compassion, and creativity. We are also fashioned to have a close relationship with our Creator. Until we know him personally, we are missing the vital piece that completes us, no matter how full our lives may seem. Even if we look as beautiful as a Monet painting, without a relationship with our Creator we have an empty space near the center of our being, right where our heart is.

> *You will be made complete with all the fullness of life and power that comes from God.*
> *Ephesians 3:19*

January 2

Putting a Spin on God's Word
EVE

Genesis 3:1-7

Marlene threw the newspaper down in disgust and started pacing back and forth. As a first-time candidate for mayor, she had jumped at the chance to share her views. The reporter, apparently, had his own agenda—changing a word here and there and leaving out some comments. Next time, Marlene would ask to see the article *before* publication, and she would go over it word for word.

When Satan wanted Eve to disobey God, his first step was to distort God's words. The serpent asked, "Did God really say you must not eat the fruit from any of the trees in the garden?" Eve corrected his misquote, and then added a phrase that was not in God's original command (see Genesis 2:16-17), saying that they must not "even touch" the tree in the middle of the Garden. Eve's careless misrepresentation of God's command encouraged Satan. He denied that disobedience would lead to death, and he questioned God's motives.

Today we have the awesome privilege of access to the entire Word of God in written form, yet it's easier than ever for Satan to make us question what God has said. Many people add to, water down, twist, or reinterpret the Bible to suit their personal opinions or desires. *Did God really say . . . that sex outside of the marriage relationship is wrong . . . that hell is an actual place . . . that Jesus is the only way to God?* Some people listen to speakers or read books about the Bible without ever studying it for themselves.

When Satan tried to get Jesus to distort God's Word, Jesus repelled his efforts by quoting appropriate Scripture back to him (see Matthew 4:1-11). If we want to live in a way that's pleasing to God, we need to have his Spirit living in us and we need to study his Word continually. When Satan comes to trick us, we can be ready to quote Scripture—preferably word for word.

> *I have hidden your word in my heart, that I might not sin against you.*
> *Psalm 119:11*

January 3

Defining Moment
EVE

Genesis 2:16-17; 3:4

In Eve's innocence, she didn't know that her conversation with the serpent was a decisive turning point in her life. Either Adam or God had told Eve about the commandment against eating fruit from the tree in the middle of the Garden. She had no reason to question God's word or his intentions, having known only her Creator's kindness and concern for her well-being. However, the serpent sounded wise too. The fruit on the beautiful tree looked delicious; how could it be harmful? What could be wrong about gaining more wisdom? As Eve decided whose advice she would follow, the fate of the world hung in the balance.

Similar scenes play out in countless lives every day. A teenager taught to abstain from premarital sex hears from his health teacher that it's perfectly natural and safe, as long as he uses protection. A college student has to listen as her professor daily promotes "the enlightened path to spirituality" while ridiculing the "old-fashioned" beliefs of Christianity. A woman struggles to hold her marriage and family together as her coworkers pressure her to consider her own needs first.

We all have defining moments in our lives when we have choices to make. Will we base our actions on the unchanging Word of God, or will we listen to other sources that sound reasonable or wise? Our decisions will determine the direction of our lives to some degree, and sometimes of the lives of others. It may not be a life-or-death situation, but the outcome can affect our health, a relationship, or our character. Whenever we have to choose between listening to God or some other voice, something precious hangs in the balance.

Whose voice will you listen to today?

January 4

Contentment 101
EVE

Genesis 3:6-7

My younger brother's first job was as a caseworker for the Department of Human Services in a small town. One day, a coworker's client reported that she had lost her food stamps. Since the woman wouldn't receive any more stamps for two weeks, the employees pooled what little money they could spare and bought groceries for her. The next day, the woman's caseworker brought back her response—she complained because the groceries didn't include enough meat.

This woman had a problem attitude that was first exhibited by Eve in the Garden of Eden. God had provided the perfect environment for meeting all of Eve's physical, emotional, and spiritual needs. She was surrounded by beauty and bounty, but when Satan drew her attention to the forbidden tree, Eve experienced discontent for the first time. Her focus shifted from all that she enjoyed to the one thing that God had withheld from her. Her happiness and well-being suddenly seemed to depend on eating fruit from the tree in the middle of the Garden. Nothing else would satisfy her.

We have all inherited the tendency to want more than what we have. When our eyes are drawn toward something that we don't have, suddenly our houses, furniture, marriages, or families don't seem to be quite enough. It's hard to stay focused on our blessings when something else is tempting us. This attitude insults God and inevitably leads us into sin. We can cultivate contentment by asking God to remove our desires for something more and then by trusting him to provide what is best for us. With his help, we will learn to be satisfied—even when we don't have as much meat or fruit in our diet as we might like.

I have learned to be content in whatever circumstances I am.
Philippians 4:11 (NASB)

January 5

The First Designer Dress
EVE

Genesis 3:7-11, 21

"What am I going to wear today?" That's one of the first questions we ask each morning—unless it's "What can I still fit into?" Clothing is a big part of a woman's life. We want to wear something that's comfortable, stylish, and flattering. Several times a year, clothing manufacturers introduce their new lines, and the stores' new merchandise can make us dissatisfied with our wardrobes. Many women rack up credit-card debt from spending more on clothing than their budgets allow. The billions spent on advertising make us forget that the purpose of clothing is basically to cover our naked bodies.

When Adam and Eve disobeyed God and felt shame for the first time, they made the first clothing—not Tommy Hilfiger, but fig leaves. God had something better in mind. Although their sin forced them to leave their perfect home and suffer painful consequences, God did not abandon them. He fashioned clothing for Adam and Eve from animal skins—garments that were more durable, protective, and less scratchy than leaves.

God's sacrifice of animals to cover Adam's and Eve's nakedness foreshadowed the day when Jesus would sacrifice his life to permanently cover our sin. We may try to make ourselves spiritually presentable by following rules or rituals or by being a good person, but that will leave us spiritually underdressed.

Only the robe of forgiveness provided by Jesus' sinless life, death, and resurrection is adequate to cover the shame of our sinful condition. Once we accept this incredible gift, our sin no longer separates us from the holy God who created us. We can draw near to him without thinking, *I don't have a thing to wear.*

> *Clothe yourselves with the Lord Jesus Christ.*
> *Romans 13:14 (NIV)*

January 6

Hide and Seek
EVE

Genesis 3:8-10

Eve's attempt to hide from God shows that she didn't get the results that Satan had promised her when she ate the forbidden fruit. She wanted to gain knowledge and wisdom but then was foolish enough to think that she could hide from an all-seeing God. Instead of joyfully running to meet him when he came to walk with them, Adam and Eve tried to avoid him. Their guilty consciences isolated them from the One who had created them, provided for their needs, and loved them.

We can't fully appreciate the loss that Adam and Eve experienced. We have never lived in a perfect environment or had God physically walk and talk with us in a garden, but we all suffer from the effects of their fall into sin. And people have been trying to hide from God ever since. Some hide behind philosophy, a false religion, or a destructive lifestyle. Christians play a more subtle game of hide-and-seek. We sometimes use church activities or spiritual busyness to avoid total openness and honesty with the Lord we are supposedly serving.

God knows us much more intimately than we know ourselves. He is fully aware of our actions, thoughts, feelings, and motives. No matter what we've done or how badly we've messed up, he seeks us and desires fellowship with us. His call of "Where are you?" is not a demand but an invitation to come clean and experience the joy of being unconditionally loved and fully accepted by our Creator.

God sent a Savior to take the penalty for our sin so that we could stand before him unashamed and free of fear. Once our guilty consciences are cleansed by Christ's blood, we never need to hide from God. We can come out from our hiding places and run to meet him.

Search me, O God, and know my heart.
Psalm 139:23

January 7

The Blame Game
EVE

Genesis 3:11-13

Adrienne eased out of bed and gently closed the door behind her. *I thought he'd never go to sleep tonight.* She frowned as she turned on the computer. Her heart raced as she saw *his* screen name. These late-night sessions were getting longer, but it was so nice to talk with someone who really understood her. Adrienne blushed as she wondered where the relationship would lead. *It's not my fault,* she sniffed. *If Jim weren't so wrapped up in other things, I wouldn't be looking for a soul mate.*

The blame game started in the Garden of Eden when God confronted Adam and Eve with their sin. Filled with fear over what they had done, each of them tried to pass the buck.

"It was the woman you gave me," responded Adam.

"The serpent tricked me," insisted Eve.

Did they really believe that God would fall for their excuses and not hold them accountable for their disobedience?

It's human nature to rationalize our behavior. As our own criminal defense attorneys, we look for ways to excuse our sinful choices rather than admit our fault. Society may encourage us to blame the environment or genetics, but that doesn't work with God. He accepts no plea bargains, and claims of temporary insanity get us nowhere.

Although we are influenced by many forces, the simple truth is that each of us answers to God for our attitudes, actions, and lifestyles. When we disobey God's laws, we have no one to blame but ourselves. We can't find forgiveness and release from guilt until we admit that we have done wrong. We can't be in a close relationship with God unless we are open and honest with him. That's when we will find our true Soul Mate.

I confessed all my sins to you and stopped trying to hide my guilt.
Psalm 32:5

January 8

The High Price of Disobedience
EVE

Genesis 3:14-19

She walked out of the lawyer's office in a daze. As the bookkeeper for a charitable organization, she had received a paltry salary. She'd seen nothing wrong with supplementing it out of donations from businesses. It didn't hurt anyone, since she took only small amounts. Besides, the center was doing fine, and no one else checked the records. As the years passed, she began to count on her "bonuses" as part of her income. Then one day she got a new supervisor, and suddenly she faced a choice of paying a large amount in restitution or spending time in prison.

Satan convinced Eve that there would be no consequences for disobeying God's commandment, but she soon learned the terrible truth. That one moment changed her life forever: She would experience pain in childbearing, conflict in her relationship with Adam, and eventually death. More important, she lost intimate fellowship with her Creator. Instead of becoming like God, as Satan had promised, she became alienated from him. Eve's choice also changed the world from a paradise to a hostile environment. Everyone who has lived since then has suffered from that first act of disobedience.

Today, Satan still uses the lie that we can break God's commands without suffering any negative consequences, and we still fall for it. We may think that we're getting away with something, but sooner or later we will pay the price for disobedience. All of God's commands are based on his desire for our physical, emotional, and spiritual well-being. Warnings against sexual impurity are to protect us from disease, heartache, and unhealthy relationships. Other commandments help us to live in a way that brings the greatest possible satisfaction and joy. When God forbids something, we can be sure that he has a reason and that there is a high cost for disobedience.

All your commands are trustworthy.
Psalm 119:86

January 9

Battle of the Sexes
EVE

Genesis 2:18; 3:16

Adam and Eve lost many blessings as a result of their disobedience, including the perfect marital relationship they had enjoyed. Before, the couple was as open and comfortable with each other as children running around naked with no sense of shame. After the disastrous choice to eat the forbidden fruit, they felt the need to cover up their bodies and their guilt. They were now at odds with God and with each other. God's pronouncement (see Genesis 3:16-19) indicated that no man and woman would ever again be able to achieve the perfect physical, emotional, and spiritual harmony that Adam and Eve had known.

Some women reinterpret the parts of the Bible that describe the role of women. Before God formed Eve, his stated intention was to make a helper for Adam. At first glance, this might seem like a secondary role, but the same term is used to refer to God in a number of verses, such as Psalm 70:5 and 115:9. God designed Adam to be the leader, but he and Eve functioned as equal partners until sin entered the picture. Ever since then, men and women have struggled with conflict in their relationships instead of fully enjoying the unity that God intended.

Political correctness has seeped into the church and caused many to avoid passages such as Ephesians 5 that discuss God's design for the family. Verses about submission seem outdated and make some women indignant. God's Word makes it clear that while men and women are equally important, we have different roles. When we submit to someone's leadership, we aren't demeaning ourselves; we are agreeing to God's plan for loving, harmonious relationships that include mutual respect. What we call "the battle of the sexes" is really a battle against the rebellious nature we inherited from our first parents.

> *Submit to one another out of reverence for Christ.*
> *Ephesians 5:21 (NIV)*

January 10

Living with Regret
EVE

Genesis 3:22-24

As Belinda opened her eyes, she immediately sensed the familiar heaviness in her spirit. In reality, it never left her, but certain conversations, events, holidays, and memories intensified it until she felt consumed. After last night's dinner party, Belinda knew what her day would be like. She would compare her friends' vibrant marriages and well-adjusted children with her own family. She would dwell on her past mistakes as a wife and mother and rehash the details of poor choices she had made. She would wonder how her life would be different—if only . . . *If only I could live the rest of my life free from this load of regret.*

Eve must have known the burden of living with regret. How many times did she think back to that fateful conversation with Satan and her decision to listen to him? Did she feel overwhelmed by the enormity of the consequences and imagine how her life would have been—if only? Although Adam and Eve's sin banished them from the perfect environment they had known, they looked toward the future and God's promise of a Savior.

As women, we have the tendency to replay a scene, conversation, or decision over and over in our minds for days, weeks, or even years. This can be beneficial if we prayerfully review our actions and decisions, asking God to show us our weak areas so that we can act in a more godly way the next time we face similar circumstances. Too often, though, we get stuck in guilt and regret that rob us of the joy of living. The Bible says that when we confess and turn away from our sins, they are taken so far away that God no longer considers them. He doesn't want us to live with a heavy burden of regret. No matter how dark our pasts may seem, the future looks bright if we belong to him.

I said to myself, "I will confess my rebellion to the LORD." And you forgave me! All my guilt is gone.
Psalm 32:5

January 11

The Good Old Days
WOMEN REMEMBERING THE ORIGINAL TEMPLE

Ezra 3:12; Haggai 2:1-9

She pulled a photo album from the bookcase and began listlessly turning the pages. The memories flooded her mind as she looked at the pictures that chronicled her marriage, her growing family, vacation trips, and frequent parties. Gazing at pictures of her former spacious home with its sprawling gardens and patios made her look around her small apartment in disgust. The albums only showed her what she no longer possessed. Her husband was long gone, the children grown and moved away. Once again she began her day by longing for the good old days.

Some of the Israelite women who watched the rebuilding of the Temple had similar feelings. Many people rejoiced to see progress being made, but the ones who remembered the original Temple wept aloud. The new version didn't compare to the riches and splendor of Solomon's Temple, which had been destroyed more than sixty years earlier. God understood their feelings of deep disappointment and discouragement, and he reminded them that he would always be with them, just as in former times. Looking ahead to Christ's reign, he promised that "the future glory of this Temple will be greater than its past glory" (Haggai 2:9).

When it seems that we have lost the things that gave our lives meaning, it's easy to fall into the trap of dwelling on "the good old days." Looking back at what we've lost makes us feel like weeping aloud. This comparison can plunge us into discouragement or depression and trick us into believing that our lives are no longer worthwhile. However, if we belong to God, he has a purpose for every stage of our lives. Focusing on God's love and mercy takes our minds off dissatisfaction with our circumstances. As long as we make it our first priority to seek and obey God, all the stages of our lives will be "good old days."

> *My heart is breaking as I remember how it used to be. . . . Why am I discouraged? Why is my heart so sad? I will put my hope in God!*
> *Psalm 42:4-5*

January 12

Eyewitness to a Miracle
AN AMAZING PICNIC

John 6:1-11

She shut the cabinet doors and leaned against the sink. Not much there to make dinner for a family. There was a time when she took food for granted—before she became the unemployed wife of a disabled husband. Public assistance helped, but it didn't always last until the end of the month. The kids would be home soon. How she would love to have a healthy, filling snack ready! She answered the doorbell and stared at the five sacks of groceries on her porch. Looking through the bags for a note, she found a grocery-store certificate for fifty dollars, which she could barely read through her tears.

A woman present when the Bible event in John 6 took place was also surprised by unexpected food that suddenly appeared. All afternoon she had ignored the growling of her stomach—it was worth going hungry to hear this rabbi. He healed people's diseases and taught like no one else. Now Jesus was thanking God for a little bread and fish. How could he be so cruel? Was he going to share a snack with a few of his disciples in front of this hungry crowd?

Later the woman rested on the grass, her mind as full as her stomach. She wasn't sure how it had happened exactly, but Jesus kept giving pieces of food to the disciples, who kept giving them to the people, who kept on eating. Tears filled her eyes as she vowed, *I will never forget this day as long as I live.*

All of us are born with a hunger that only God can fill. We may try to satisfy our spiritual hunger with possessions, pleasure, knowledge, or other people, but we won't be truly satisfied until we are in a close relationship with the One who created us. After God feeds us, we realize that we were starving and didn't even know it.

> *You satisfy me more than the richest feast.*
> *Psalm 63:5*

January 13

Eyewitness to a Miracle
PRECIOUS LEFTOVERS

John 6:12-14

"Could I please have a take-home box for my leftover steak?" Jan asked her server. *No need to leave this good food here for the restaurant to throw away.* This might be the most expensive place in town, but Jan had a reason to celebrate. After years of being lied to, verbally abused, and miserable, she had finally ended a very unhealthy relationship. Now she wondered how she could have been so blind. *At least I won't waste this food like I wasted the last four years of my life,* she thought.

A woman in the crowd that Jesus fed contemplated the miracle she had just witnessed. With just two fish and a few small loaves of bread, Jesus had fed a crowd of thousands, with everyone eating as much as he or she wanted. Then the woman heard Jesus tell his disciples to gather up the left-over pieces. With a large family to feed and little money, the woman knew about being frugal. She was glad to see that these "miracle scraps" wouldn't go to waste. After the disciples finished gathering the pieces, the woman counted twelve full baskets.

Jesus' instruction to gather the leftovers shows that although God has limitless resources, he does not waste things. We live in an extravagant society where people routinely squander food, money, and time. Sometimes our poor choices make it seem as if we have wasted years of our lives, but when we give God control, he will see that nothing goes to waste. He can use all our bad decisions, unhealthy relationships, and times of suffering to help us grow stronger spiritually. He will equip us to help others who are going through similar circumstances. When we let God gather up our broken pieces, our worst experiences can become our greatest assets.

> *Jesus told his disciples, "Now gather the leftovers, so that nothing is wasted."*
> *John 6:12*

January 14

Divine Multiplication
A MOTHER WHO PACKED A LITTLE LUNCH

John 6:8-9

Elaine raised her eyebrows as she looked at her checkbook. *I can't believe I made it through another month.* With no savings to fall back on when she was laid off, Elaine felt sure that she would have to borrow money to pay her monthly bills. But after five months of living on unemployment benefits, she still had a roof over her head, and she hadn't missed a meal. Her bills were all paid, although she wasn't sure how. *I never knew such a small amount could stretch so far,* Elaine marveled, and whispered, "Thank you, God."

Elaine's reaction pales in comparison with what I imagine a woman behind the scenes in John 6 felt—the mother who packed her son's lunch and then learned that it had fed five thousand men plus women and children. Her son must have burst through the door to share his news. The mother beamed with pride when she understood that he had shared his lunch, but her smile faded as she began to comprehend his excited words. There wasn't enough food in her entire village to feed a crowd like that, and Jesus had done it with the small lunch she had packed for her son? One thing she knew for certain—there was something different about this rabbi.

When we compare ourselves with others, we may feel as if we don't have much to offer to God. We imagine what great things we would do for him if we had a beautiful singing voice, powerful speaking ability, great talent, intelligence, or lots of money. But when we offer our time and resources to God in a spirit of loving service, he multiplies our small efforts into something great. If we place our lives in God's hands, someday we will be amazed at what he has done with our "little lunches."

[Jesus said,] *"To those who use well what they are given, even more will be given, and they will have an abundance."*
Matthew 25:29

January 15

Racial Prejudice
THE WIFE OF THE MAN HELPED BY A SAMARITAN

Luke 10:29-37

The elderly woman stood looking at her house and shaking her head. The tornado that had ripped through her town had been a shock, all right. And she had been surprised by the fourteen volunteers who had quickly shown up to put a new roof on her home and repair her front porch and windows. The speed with which they had completed the job was nothing short of amazing! But what shocked her most was the color of the group.

If the victim in the passage from Luke had a wife, she could have identified with the feelings of this elderly woman. In Jesus' parable, robbers beat a Jewish man and left him for dead. Although a Jewish priest and a Levite saw the man's condition, they offered him no help. Finally, a Samaritan came along and aided the injured traveler, even paying an innkeeper to care for him. Since Jews and Samaritans despised each other, we can imagine how surprised the victim's wife would have been to hear who had been willing to help him. They would have expected the priest and Levite to help a fellow Jew, but not a member of the Samaritan race.

Racial prejudice has been around for a long time. How sad that it often takes a disaster for people to look beyond skin color and simply see another person in need. In God's eyes we are all equal. We are all born as sinners who need a Savior. Rather than allow our differences to separate us, God wants us to concentrate on what we have in common. When he commands us to love one another, he doesn't mean for us to love only those who look, talk, and think as we do. If we treat one another as he intends, no one will be surprised when help comes in a different color.

> *My dear brothers and sisters, how can you claim to have faith in our*
> *glorious Lord Jesus Christ if you favor some people over others?*
> *James 2:1*

January 16

Betrayed and Used
THE LEVITE'S CONCUBINE

Judges 19

Janet threw down the newspaper in disgust. Last week she had seen the announcement about her ex-husband's promotion in the law firm; this week's paper included an account of his lavish wedding to the senior partner's daughter. *Quite a different lifestyle from our years together,* she thought bitterly, as she glanced around her sparsely furnished apartment. Janet had put her own education on hold and worked long shifts as a waitress while her husband finished school. Once he had passed the bar, he informed Janet that he no longer needed her.

The woman in Judges 19 knew about being betrayed and used by men. When a crowd surrounded the house and demanded that the Levite come out for sex, he used his concubine to protect himself. How terrified she must have been when her own husband pushed her out the door! We can only imagine the horrors she endured as the crazed mob took turns raping her all night.

The last verse in Judges explains this sad period in Israel's history: "All the people did whatever seemed right in their own eyes" (Judges 21:25). Today we live in a similar atmosphere. God's standards of right and wrong have been replaced with moral relativism and situational ethics. People do whatever seems right to them and expect others to tolerate it.

As a result of this moral decay, people selfishly use each other to get what they want, and they leave wounded, bitter men and women in their wake. But even when we feel betrayed by the very ones who should love and protect us, we can be sure that there is Someone who always puts our well-being first. When sin demanded the penalty of death, Jesus didn't push us out the door. He went out himself to face it—and died on a cross for us.

He personally carried our sins in his body on the cross.
1 Peter 2:24

January 17

Small Beginnings
LYDIA

Acts 16:11-15

Anne hung up the phone after listening to her friend rave about her church's holiday program with its special effects, orchestra, and large cast. Once again she had urged Anne to leave the tiny country church she had attended for forty-eight years. *We may not have the equipment and resources that many modern churches have,* thought Anne, *but we don't lack faith.* She mentally listed what their little group of fourteen members did have: meaningful Sunday services, special celebrations and meals together, and a commitment to meet for Wednesday-night prayer meeting—something that her friend's larger church had dropped.

Lydia also met with a small group for prayer. Although she was a Gentile, she worshiped the God of Israel. She must have longed to learn more about this God of the Jewish people, but in Philippi there was no synagogue. She faithfully met with a little group of women on the Sabbath to pray, and one day, God answered Lydia's prayers and hopes.

Paul had a vision of a man begging him to "come over to Macedonia and help us!" (Acts 16:9). Paul and Silas immediately sailed for northern Greece. The next Sabbath, they went outside the city and found the women gathered at the riverbank. Lydia responded to the gospel and became the first convert in that part of the world. She had a crucial role in the church as it spread throughout Europe.

It's easy for us to get caught up with numbers and play the comparison game. We may feel that our little church or Bible-study group is not as important as bigger ones, but God is concerned about the state of our hearts, not the size of our groups. God will respond to our desire to know and serve him, whether we're in a tiny country church or praying with a few women on a riverbank.

[Jesus said,] "Where two or three gather together as my followers, I am there among them."
Matthew 18:20

January 18

Miss Hospitality
LYDIA

Acts 16:13-15

When Jeannie and her husband built their beautiful, spacious home, they determined to use it to honor God. Their house has been used for youth group retreats, small-group meetings, Bible studies, ladies' luncheons, showers, and big potluck dinners. College kids working in the area for the summer and missionaries have stayed there. When someone doesn't have enough room for out-of-town visitors, they know that Jeannie's home is available. Each Thanksgiving, Jeannie's family hosts a large dinner for friends, work colleagues, and students from other countries.

Lydia exercised her gift of hospitality from the moment she became a follower of Christ. After she was baptized, she invited Paul and his fellow missionaries to be her guests if they considered her a true believer, and she urged them until they agreed. Lydia regarded the opportunity to play hostess to these missionaries as a privilege rather than a burden.

Many of us would like to be more like Jeannie and Lydia, but we think our houses aren't big enough, our furniture isn't nice enough, our cooking isn't impressive, or we don't have enough time. Usually the problem is that we have confused entertaining with showing hospitality. Showing hospitality simply means being focused on making another person feel at home. That doesn't have to resemble something in a magazine spread.

Like God's other commands, hospitality is a two-way blessing. Lydia's willingness to open her home played a key role in the growth of that first band of Christians in Philippi. Meanwhile, Lydia learned more about the truths Paul was sharing. Jeannie's family also receives joy from being able to share their resources with others. Only God knows how many people have been blessed by those two homes.

Always be eager to practice hospitality.
Romans 12:13

January 19

Godly Businesswoman
LYDIA

Acts 16:13-15; Proverbs 31:16-18

Stephanie groaned at the e-mail from her boss: It was time for another out-of-town business meeting. The professional side of the trip would be worthwhile, but her new supervisor's idea of fun clashed with Stephanie's ideas of right and wrong. Last time, she came up with an excuse to avoid going to the club that featured male strippers. Now she wondered how standing up for her beliefs would affect her career. Would she be respected for them or labeled a fanatic?

Lydia was a successful businesswoman who sold purple cloth. Her native Thyatira was known for the purple dye obtained from shellfish. Since the dye and the cloth were expensive, only the rich and noble dressed in purple. Lydia herself had become wealthy through her business and probably employed others. She must have felt great pride in her accomplishments and her business reputation, but something else was even more important to her.

A large number of Lydia's customers were involved in pagan worship. Some people would be hesitant to adopt a new religion that might affect their business, but not Lydia. She opened her heart to the gospel and immediately began using her resources to serve the Lord. Lydia's joy in her new-found faith gave her the courage to put God ahead of business. Her home eventually became the meeting place for the new church.

The ideal woman described in Proverbs 31 takes care of her family's needs and is also a successful businesswoman. Business skills can be used for great good in God's Kingdom if we keep our priorities in line. We can't use outside employment as an excuse to neglect our families or our personal relationship with God. We must always conduct our business dealings in a way that honors God and his principles. Like Lydia and Stephanie, our first business is to please our Lord.

Our purpose is to please God, not people.
1 Thessalonians 2:4

January 20

Don't Be So Gullible!
VULNERABLE WOMEN

2 Timothy 3:1-9

I can't believe it—I've done it again! Rita groaned as she read the e-mail. She had been deeply moved by the story of a little girl with a large brain tumor. The girl would die without medical treatment, but her family couldn't afford it. A well-known organization had agreed to donate seven cents each time the e-mail was forwarded. With so many names in her address book, Rita had been happy to do her part. Today, however, a friend had informed her that the story was a hoax. Rita pressed her lips together. *I won't be taken in again,* she vowed.

In today's Bible passage, Paul describes women who were susceptible to more than fake e-mails and urban legends. These spiritually immature and undisciplined women were easy targets for those who spread false teachings. They were so eager to learn, the women embraced every new idea presented to them, basing their opinions on their own emotional responses. As a result, they could not recognize the truth, and their lives were not transformed by God's power.

As in Bible times, there are plenty of people teaching their own ideas and proclaiming them as God's truth. It's easy to be taken in by stories that touch our emotions and by doctrines that sound right to us. That's why we need to evaluate new ideas against the standard of God's Word. If a teaching directly contradicts the Bible, then we know it is false. Only a thorough knowledge of God's Word will train us to distinguish between the real and the phony. It may be embarrassing to fall for an Internet hoax, but it's dangerous to be gullible about spiritual truth.

> *Dear friends, do not believe everyone who claims to speak by the Spirit. You must test them to see if the spirit they have comes from God. For there are many false prophets in the world.*
> *1 John 4:1*

January 21

Check It Out!
BEREAN WOMEN

Acts 17:10-12

Our society is saturated with deception. Every day, unsuspecting people fall prey to skillful con artists who convince them that they need to send money to claim a prize. Other people are tricked into paying for home repairs that are never completed. We buy products that don't come close to the claims made about them. We read "memoirs" that turn out to be fabricated. Our carelessness about checking things out makes us vulnerable to fraud.

The women in this passage from Acts were careful to check out their sources. Although they listened eagerly to the gospel message, they didn't take what Paul and Silas said at face value. Each day they searched the Scriptures to make sure that the two men were teaching the truth. Since the Bereans carefully verified the message as being based on the Scriptures, they recognized that the missionaries' claims about Christ were true and joyfully accepted God's gift of salvation.

Many people who claim to be Christians know little about the Bible except for the familiar stories they heard as children. Others attend Bible studies but only accumulate facts without applying the Scriptures to their daily lives. Still others study the Bible for years but then slack off, feeling that they have sufficient knowledge. We will never reach a point of having gained all the understanding, discernment, and wisdom that the Bible offers us.

Without consistent study of the Bible, believers can be taken in like anyone else by books and movies purporting to reveal the truth about Jesus or Christianity. The fact that it's a best seller written by someone with impressive credentials doesn't mean it's true. We will be protected from deception only when we follow the example of the Bereans and spend time in God's Word.

> *They searched the Scriptures day after day to see if Paul and Silas were teaching the truth.*
> *Acts 17:11*

January 22

Traumatized Women
"RACHEL" WEEPING FOR HER CHILDREN

Matthew 2:18

Hot tears stung her eyes as she looked at the calendar. It was six years ago today, and this year was no different from the rest.

First she remembered her friends' counsel: "This is not the right time—you need to finish college." "You have to think of what's best for you." "It's no big deal, really." "This is the only answer."

Then there were the familiar questions that she kept to herself: *Would I have had a son or a daughter in kindergarten? What color would his eyes be? Would she have my curly hair? What books would he like? How would her voice sound?*

Matthew 2:18 refers to two groups of women in Israel's history who mourned the loss of their children. Jeremiah originally uttered the prophecy to describe mothers whose children were carried off into captivity. Later, Matthew used the words to depict the grief-stricken mothers in the Bethlehem area whose sons age two or younger were slaughtered by Herod's soldiers. Imagine the deafening wails as women clutched the lifeless bodies of their baby boys, so suddenly struck down.

In our own nation, countless women mourn the loss of their children, often in silence. According to estimates from the Centers for Disease Control and the Alan Guttmacher Institute, more than 42 million abortions have been performed in America since the practice was legalized. Medical professionals have identified a range of symptoms in women who suffer from postabortion syndrome, including insomnia, eating disorders, alcohol and drug addictions, severe depression, and suicide attempts.

We are surrounded by millions of wounded women. Their only hope for healing is found at the cross, where Jesus suffered and died so that we could be made whole. However deep our secret pain, we can come to Jesus knowing that he was wounded so we can be restored.

He heals the brokenhearted and bandages their wounds.
Psalm 147:3

January 23

Comforting Words
BATHSHEBA

2 Samuel 12:7-25

She stumbled through the front door and collapsed onto the couch. The early morning light cast an eerie glow on the framed ultrasound picture on the mantel. Had it all been just a bad dream—the onslaught of cramping, the trip to the emergency room, the hours of frantic activity followed by sudden stillness? As she put her hand gently on her abdomen, her numb mind abruptly filled with questions. *Where is my son? Will I ever see him again? Will he know me as his mother?*

Bathsheba also knew the pain of losing a baby. When King David got Bathsheba pregnant and then had her husband killed, God's judgment on this sin included the death of their infant. David fasted and prayed while his son struggled with his illness, but he stopped mourning after the baby died. David explained that he couldn't bring his child back from the dead, but he would be with his son one day in the future. These words must have soothed Bathsheba's aching heart. Despite the pain of loss, and grief for her sin, Bathsheba held on to the promise that her child rested safely in God's hands. She would see him again.

Through the ages, David's words have brought solace to countless mothers who have lost a baby or a young child. Regardless of how a child is conceived or dies, we can cling to the hope that if we accept Christ as our Savior, someday we will be with our babies who were lost to miscarriage, abortion, illness, or accidents. The Bible doesn't answer all our questions about these situations, but God does promise that these babies are safe in his hands. Those are the most comforting words that any mother could hear.

> [David said,] *"I will go to him one day, but he cannot return to me."*
> 2 Samuel 12:23

January 24

Choosing Life
A TRUE MOTHER

1 Kings 3:16-28

Allie hesitated, bit her lip, and then signed the paper. It was heartrending to think that in just a few seconds she had given up her rights to the baby girl she had delivered three days earlier. Allie knew that she needed to finish school and grow up before she would be ready to be a parent. She felt grateful that she had been able to choose the couple who would adopt her daughter—she knew that the Fosters already loved the baby and would give her the life that Allie couldn't provide. But as her parents drove her home, Allie ached as she remembered holding that warm little bundle for the very last time.

Allie showed love for her child in a similar way to one of two women who came before King Solomon. When both women claimed the same baby, the king ordered that the child be cut in half with a sword so the women could share him. Solomon knew that the woman who was willing to give up her baby was the real mother. No matter how painful it would be to relinquish her son, she would put his safety first. She would abandon her rights to him so that he could live.

Girls and young women who give up their babies for adoption are some of the most devoted, courageous mothers who have ever lived. Our society offers women in unplanned pregnancies a supposedly easy way out through abortion. But in reality, abortion means death for a child and physical and emotional health risks for the mother. Even after making the choice to give birth, women have to struggle against their natural maternal instincts as they give their baby to another couple. No matter how good a home the adoptive couple provides, young women like Allie have already given their children a precious gift that no one else could give them—the gift of life.

Choose life, so that you and your children may live.
Deuteronomy 30:19, NIV

January 25

No Disguise
JEROBOAM'S WIFE

1 Kings 14:1-6

Jackie sat waiting in the dean's office, wondering how on earth anyone recognized her during that stupid prank. When she and her friend decided to push over the bicycles in front of the dorm, Jackie had a foolproof disguise. She wore a red wig, dark glasses, a surgical mask, and a hospital gown. What Jackie didn't remember was that she also wore sweatpants with her last name emblazoned across the seat.

The disguise of King Jeroboam's wife didn't work any better. Her husband had led Israel into idol worship and persecuted God's priests, but when their son became gravely ill, Jeroboam sent his wife to ask a prophet if he would recover. Following her husband's instructions, she removed her jewels and queenly clothing and disguised herself as an ordinary woman. She walked through the streets toward Ahijah's home, confident that no one would recognize her. Imagine her shock at hearing the blind old prophet call out before she even knocked on his door, "Come in, wife of Jeroboam!"

Many of us go through life trying to wear a disguise, whether intentionally or subconsciously. Some people desperately try to look more virtuous or smart than they are. Others act one way during the week and then put on their Sunday disguises to attend church. Whether we're trying to impress people or are merely fooling ourselves, God sees through any masquerade. He knows our words before we speak them and our thoughts before they enter our minds. If we don't understand God's love and mercy, this seems frightening, but those who know his mercy and acceptance are set free. Whatever our faults may be, we don't have to pretend to be someone else with our loving heavenly Father.

Why are you pretending to be someone else?
1 Kings 14:6

January 26

Sing Your Song
WOMEN WHO SANG

Judges 5:1-5; 1 Samuel 2:1-2; Luke 1:46-49

Twila hung up the phone and marked the date on her calendar. Although she had always avoided public speaking, she couldn't turn down being a part of the dinner to honor Mr. Shelton. It was his generosity and business savvy that had put her family and others back on their feet after the factory closed. He had made it possible for Twila to fulfill her dream of going to college, and now he was helping her through medical school. After Twila's dad died, Mr. Shelton had become her mentor, even walking her down the aisle at her wedding. Sure, she got nervous about giving a speech, but how could she pass up the opportunity to share how this kind man had made what seemed impossible happen?

The Bible contains three beautiful examples of women testifying to what God had done for them. After seeing God help Israel conquer a powerful army, Deborah praised him with a victory hymn. When God gave Hannah a son after years of barrenness, she poured out her gratitude in a poem. Mary's awe at being chosen to give birth to the Messiah caused her to burst into song. Three different women in three different situations all experienced God's mercy and goodness, and they all freely expressed their joy, wonder, and gratitude.

Each of us has a unique life story, and each of us can testify to God's goodness and love. We may not be able to sing on key, write moving poetry, or sound like professional speakers, but God wants us to be ready to talk about him whenever we have the opportunity. There might be a relative, friend, coworker, neighbor, or stranger who needs to hear what God has done in our lives. Our one-of-a-kind story might be just what encourages that person to grow closer to God or to meet him for the first time. That's worth testifying about!

> *Come and listen, all you who fear God, and I will tell you what he did for me.*
> *Psalm 66:16*

January 27

Feeling Ignored
THE MOTHER OF A DEMON-POSSESSED DAUGHTER

Matthew 15:21-23

Becky sat stiffly in the hard plastic chair and rocked her toddler back and forth. Dylan had finally cried himself to sleep, and now she was fighting back tears of her own. The accident had happened so quickly. One minute he had been laughing on top of the slide, then suddenly he was on the ground, holding his arm tightly to his chest and screaming if she touched it. Now they had been in the emergency room for more than two hours, and still no one had attended to them. As Becky looked at the women behind the desk, she felt like screaming, "Can't you see my child needs help?"

The woman in today's Bible passage knew the feeling of being ignored. She had heard stories about Jesus' miracles and healings. Now he had come to her city, and her heavy heart felt the first ray of hope in a long while. The woman cried out to Jesus, begging him to help her daughter, who suffered terribly from demon possession, but he ignored her cries. When she kept pleading for help, Jesus' disciples urged him to make her go away. The woman felt confused. Was this the same man who had a reputation for reaching out to the needy?

It doesn't feel good to be ignored, especially when we need help. It's frustrating enough to feel overlooked by people, but when it seems that even God isn't responding to us, we don't know what to think. Sometimes our prayers for help seem to bounce back off the ceiling. At those times, it's tempting to question whether God really cares about us and our pain. When God seems to be ignoring us, we can be sure that he is fully aware of our situation and that there is a purpose for his delay in responding. Like the Gentile woman with the demon-possessed daughter, we must continue crying out to the One who is our only hope.

> *The eyes of the LORD watch over those who do right; his ears are open to their cries for help.*
> *Psalm 34:15*

January 28

Stubborn Faith
THE MOTHER OF A DEMON-POSSESSED DAUGHTER

Matthew 15:24-28

The Gentile woman who asked Jesus to heal her demon-possessed daughter must have been surprised when Jesus rebuffed her. Most people would have been hurt or offended or would have become angry and walked away. If I had been in her sandals centuries ago, I would immediately have said, "But Jesus, you healed this man's daughter, this woman's son, that blind person, and that deaf person. Why not my daughter?" Instead of giving up, the woman stubbornly continued to plead for Jesus' help.

Scripture doesn't explain why Jesus treated this woman so differently from his usual manner of responding to needy people. It is a difficult passage to understand. God had clearly given Jesus the mission of calling Israelites back to God (later, God sent apostles such as Paul to tell the Gentiles about God's love). Throughout history, God demonstrated his faithful love and extraordinary patience to the world by how he treated the Jews.

Jesus was clearly focused on God's purpose during his time in human history. Perhaps Jesus wanted to stretch the woman's faith or reveal his disciples' prejudice. Maybe he wanted to make the point to the people watching him that he knew that this woman was a Gentile and that God accepted all people who believed in him, not just the Jews.

Whatever the reason, this passage shows that at times we may feel as if God is rejecting us while meeting the needs of others. During those difficult times when God's actions are confusing, we need to remind ourselves that God has a good plan for us. We need to have a stubborn faith that trusts that God always has a purpose and that he will answer us at the right time. Like the desperate mother who demonstrated stubborn faith so long ago, we may see our confusion suddenly turn to joy.

> *"Dear woman," Jesus said to her, "your faith is great."*
> *Matthew 15:28*

January 29

The Sight of Blood
WOMEN AND THE SACRIFICES

Exodus 24:5-8

I stared up at the ceiling as the nurse drew blood from my daughter's arm. I recalled the day when I discovered my problem with seeing blood. My fiancé and I had just had blood taken, and I was walking stiffly out of the building, pretending that I didn't have a strange feeling all over my body. Within minutes, I crumpled to my knees in the parking lot. Since then, I have learned to look down during gory battle scenes in movies, close my eyes when television doctors are operating, and hope that no one needs my help after an accident.

It's hard to imagine how Jewish women in the Old Testament felt about blood. Animals were continually being sacrificed for the people's sins. The altar, the articles of worship, and the high priest's clothes were all purified with blood. After Moses read God's commandments to the people, he even sprinkled the Israelites with blood and water to confirm the covenant they had made with God. Did any of the women feel queasy about the blood involved in their worship, or were they used to it?

How glad the women in New Testament times must have been to know that the bloody sacrifices and purifying rituals were no longer necessary. How joyful we feel when we remember that Jesus' blood did what the repeated sacrifice of animals failed to accomplish. Only the sacrifice of the sinless Christ was good enough to bring forgiveness for our sins. One perfect sacrifice for all time replaced centuries of slaughtering, cutting, and sprinkling. When I think of the blood of Christ, spilled for me, I don't feel nauseated—I feel grateful beyond words.

> *Our guilty consciences have been sprinkled with Christ's blood to make us clean.*
> *Hebrews 10:22*

January 30

Beauty *and* Brains
ABIGAIL

1 Samuel 25:1-20

"Why I Went Blonde and Skinny!" "So Ugly, I Paid $90,000 for a New Face!"

As I stood in the checkout line at Wal-Mart, the magazine titles screamed at me that I didn't measure up as a woman. I felt that I needed to leave my paper towels and toilet cleaner behind and rush to the nearest beauty salon. The women's magazines on either side of me wanted to improve my appearance, and the content seemed designed to make me feel stupid. For intellectual stimulation, one of the periodicals offered, "Is Your Star Sign Ruining Your Love Life?" and "Catch Him, Kiss Him, Keep Him: Your Ultimate Boy-Pulling Bible."

Abigail also lived in a culture that based the value of a woman on her appearance, but the Bible notes that she had beauty *and* brains. In a time of danger, the servant went to Abigail not because of how she looked but because he knew that she had common sense and practical wisdom. After Abigail's husband, Nabal, insulted David, the servant approached Abigail, explained what had happened, and urged her to figure out how to deal with the trouble ahead.

Many of us are buying the lie that beauty is all-important. That can make us depressed, obsessed, and broke. Data from the American Society for Aesthetic Plastic Surgery show a 444 percent increase in cosmetic procedures from 1997 to 2005. People may admire us for a beautiful face, but good judgment and wisdom will have a lasting effect on our lives and the lives of others.

The book of Proverbs reveals that to acquire wisdom, the first step is to cultivate a correct attitude toward God and his character (see Proverbs 9:10). As we get to know God better, we grow in wisdom that comes to our aid in difficult times. Not even a ninety-thousand-dollar face can compete with that.

> *Charm is deceptive, and beauty does not last; but a woman who fears the* Lord *will be greatly praised.*
> *Proverbs 31:30*

January 31

Love for the Undeserving
ABIGAIL

1 Samuel 25:20-38

Susan stared out at the rain as she and Sean began the three-hour trip to her sister's home. Although Susan loved catching up with Emily and the rest of their siblings, she dreaded how the day would end. Sean would be loudly telling the same old obscene jokes. While Sean remained oblivious to how this affected her family, Susan caught every sarcastic glance from her mother, and for days afterward rehearsed her sisters' whispered remarks.

It's never easy to endure the rude behavior of those closest to us. Abigail knew the same embarrassment and frustration that Susan felt and that many of us feel when we live with the consequences of foolish behavior. Scripture describes Abigail's husband, Nabal, as a rude, ill-tempered drunkard. Abigail had undoubtedly experienced many days of wincing at inappropriate comments, but when Nabal insulted David's men after they had generously protected Nabal's flock, his behavior crossed the line from embarrassing to dangerously foolish. Abigail could have let her husband's behavior depress and paralyze her. Instead, she swallowed her frustration and acted decisively to save Nabal and her family, even if it meant accepting blame for her husband's actions.

It's hard to love and serve people who clearly don't deserve such treatment. That kind of unselfish love never comes naturally, but it's the kind of love that God calls us to. When we're in a difficult marriage or a problem relationship with a relative, boss, or coworker, it's easier to think of what the other person deserves than of how we can lovingly correct the situation.

Our response to people shouldn't be determined just by how they treat us. We can resolve to love others when we remember that Jesus is at God's right hand interceding for us (see Romans 8:34). And, we can be thankful that God doesn't give us what we deserve, even though we, too, sometimes act like fools.

> [Love] . . . does not demand its own way. It is not irritable, and it keeps no record of being wronged.
> 1 Corinthians 13:5

February 1

Paid in Full
WOMEN SOLD FOR DEBT

Matthew 18:25; Nehemiah 5:5

Cathy cringed at the sick feeling in the pit of her stomach. It was that time of the month—time for the credit-card bill, and she'd just seen Sam striding toward the mailbox. Doing some quick math in her head, Cathy realized that she had gotten a little carried away during this cycle. But then again, look at how much she had saved by shopping the after-Christmas sales. *Why couldn't he still be at the hardware store?* she thought angrily. *Then I could have paid the bill without his seeing it, and we would have avoided a nasty argument.*

As Israel interacted with the nations around them and moved away from God's principles, debt became a serious problem with serious consequences. Instead of demonstrating leniency toward those in poverty, creditors sometimes sold the debtor, his wife, or his children as payment. Women were sometimes separated from their husbands or had to watch their children be taken away as slaves. Jesus referred to this practice more than once in his parables—and his listeners were all too familiar with the anguish caused to families that were torn apart by debt.

We were all born with a debt that we can never repay—the penalty for our sinful condition. Rather than selling us off, God took care of the bill by having Jesus die on the cross for us. Our accounts were paid in full. Once we accept that transaction, however, we assume another debt. For the rest of our lives, we owe it to God to show his love to everyone around us. When we remember the great debt that God paid on our behalf, we will find joy in meeting others' needs. We don't get a monthly bill for our debt of love, but we have a chance to make a payment every day.

Let no debt remain outstanding, except the continuing debt to love one another.
Romans 13:8 (NIV)

February 2

Lying Lips
SAPPHIRA

Acts 5:3-11

"Five feet, three inches?" asked the man filling out my driver's license renewal form.

"Yes," I answered.

"Blue eyes?"

"Yes."

"Still 130 pounds?"

I nodded. He started typing, then stopped and peered at me over his reading glasses. "What's that look for?" he demanded.

"Well . . .," I stammered, "just how important is it to be totally accurate here?" I knew I wouldn't be standing behind the high counter forever.

Lying often has serious consequences, as Sapphira and her husband Ananias found out. When the couple sold a piece of property, they pretended to give all the money to their group of believers, but they secretly kept some for themselves. No one would be any the wiser—or so they thought.

Sapphira came in to see the apostles without knowing that her husband had been struck dead a few hours earlier for lying. When Peter asked if the money Ananias had contributed was the amount they had received for their land, she answered, "Yes, that was the price." Sapphira expected to be commended for such generosity; instead, she was horrified to hear Peter denounce her and Ananias for lying to God. He told her that she would die for this sin as her husband had.

God struck Sapphira and Ananias down to purge the developing church of destructive forces such as lying and hypocrisy. Thankfully, he doesn't always judge lying so severely, but he still hears every lie that we tell, and he despises this sin. Each time we are less than truthful, we are building a habit of dishonesty. We are also acting like Satan, whom the Bible calls "the father of lies" (John 8:44). Eventually, we will suffer the consequences of disobeying God's command to avoid lying. We may be able to fool others, but we will never fool God—not even standing behind a high counter.

The Lord detests lying lips, but he delights in those who tell the truth.
Proverbs 12:22

February 3

Impure Motives
SAPPHIRA

Acts 4:32-37; 5:1-2

My friend closed her car door and sat staring at the clinic, wondering if and when she would return. As a college student, she had welcomed God's call to become a physician and help hurting people. Years passed as she maintained her busy career while also being a wife, mother, and church volunteer. One day during her quiet time, she realized that her main motivation had become the recognition and praise of other people. God was now calling her to relinquish her career until she could honor him rather than seek admiration.

Sapphira, the woman in today's passage, did not examine her motives, and she paid dearly for it. The bond of love and unity in the early church led many wealthy believers to sell property and give the money to be distributed to the poor among them. Sapphira and her husband followed this example, but unfortunately, their motives were not pure. Although they sold some land out of desire to help the needy, the couple decided to keep part of the money for themselves. This would have been perfectly acceptable if they hadn't pretended to donate the full amount to the church in order to be admired for their generosity.

Even when our actions seem honorable, our motives can dishonor God. Other people may not question our sincerity, but God sees deep into our hearts and knows what really motivates us. Are we doing volunteer work out of a desire to help others, or because it looks good? Did we pick up the check because we wanted to treat our friends, or because we wanted them to owe us? As long as we're in our earthly bodies, we'll struggle to maintain pure motives. With God's help, we can learn to base our actions on our desire to love and honor him—the kind of actions that he can reward.

> *I, the LORD, search all hearts and examine secret motives. I give all people their due rewards, according to what their actions deserve.*
> *Jeremiah 17:10*

February 4

Testing the Limits
SAPPHIRA

Acts 5:3-4, 9

I watched my eighteen-month-old granddaughter slowly back up, her eyes glued to her mom's back. Lacey knew that she wasn't allowed to sit on or lean against the rough brick hearth that jutted out from my fireplace. She knew that sooner or later, her mom would turn around, tell her no, and pull her away, but that didn't stop her from trying to get away with it. Suddenly, Holly turned around. Lacey locked eyes with her and started jabbering, as if that would distract her mom from noticing her disobedience.

The woman in today's passage acted in a similar way. Ananias and Sapphira knew God's commandment against lying. They understood that he is all-knowing. Yet they still thought that they could get away with lying about the money they had donated to their group of believers. Peter asked Sapphira how she could dare to test the Holy Spirit in such a way. Her desire to appear righteous in the eyes of others had led her to presume on God's mercy. Was this a habit in her life or an isolated event? In either case, Sapphira never dreamed how seriously God would deal with this testing of his limits.

Sometimes we act like little children in our relationship with God. Although we clearly understand his instructions, we still test the boundaries. We may convince ourselves that we're following God's ways, but in some little area that seems so insignificant, we push our toe over the line. When nothing disastrous happens, we step over a little further. It's easy to fool ourselves by concentrating on God's love and mercy and ignoring his need to judge sin. Eventually, we reap the consequences of seeing how far we can push him. God wants us to be obedient so that we will be open to his blessing. He doesn't want us to find out how dangerous presumption can be, as Sapphira did.

> *Peter said, "How could the two of you even think of conspiring to test the Spirit of the Lord like this?"*
> *Acts 5:9*

February 5

Complete in Him
SINGLE WOMEN

1 Corinthians 7:7-8, 34

Lindy grimaced as she looked over the flyer about her fifteenth high-school reunion. Should she go or skip it? It was just another chance for her to hear the dreaded questions, "Over thirty and still not married? What are you waiting for?" Lindy *really* despised it when people followed up their questions with some clever comment such as, "You're not getting any younger, you know." *Very original. Oh well,* she sighed, *at least the form for the dance has a "stag or drag" box.*

Single women during Bible times were pressured by society to marry and have a family. At a time when it was rare for women to have careers, their worth was tied up in their roles as wives and mothers. Paul's letter to the believers at Corinth painted a different picture of singleness. He explained that without the demands that marriage places on a woman's time, energy, and resources, it's easier for her to be wholeheartedly devoted to God. She is free to focus on serving God without being distracted by the concerns of a husband and children.

While being a single woman now doesn't carry the stigma that it used to in our society, many women still feel that they need a mate to complete them. Popular speaker and author Michelle McKinney Hammond encourages women to stop focusing on their marital status and learn to find joy in an intimate relationship with God. The fact that the animals boarded the ark two by two doesn't mean that a single woman can't enjoy a fulfilling life. Our happiness does depend on our being part of a couple—it comes from a one-on-one relationship with the Lover of our souls. Without that, nothing can complete us.

> *God gives to some the gift of marriage, and to others the gift of singleness.*
> *1 Corinthians 7:7*

February 6

Never Rejected
DIVORCED WOMEN

Matthew 19:3-8

As she slipped into the back pew just as the service began, Roxanne quickly glanced around. Was it her imagination, or had the woman next to her avoided eye contact? Roxanne blushed as she grabbed a hymnal. Three months had passed since her divorce, and she still felt uncomfortable in public. Even her close friends seemed uneasy, as if they didn't know what to say to her. Roxanne could certainly understand that—she didn't know what to say about the breakup of her marriage, either. After thirty years as a wife, almost overnight she had joined the ranks of divorced women.

We tend to think of divorce as a modern issue, but it was a hot topic in New Testament times as well. The Pharisees tried to embroil Jesus in a theological debate about divorce, and women would have had a keen interest in his answer. At the time, people were divided between two opposing interpretations of the regulations in Deuteronomy 24:1-4. One group believed that a man could divorce his wife for nearly any reason; the other group supported divorce only in cases of infidelity. Jesus avoided the conflict by focusing on God's original intention for the marital relationship to be permanent.

Divorce has become widespread in our society, but that doesn't lessen the pain of its consequences. Divorced women often struggle financially, especially when they have children to care for. Some women feel like failures after their marriages break up. Even if some divorces end unhealthy relationships, women usually find the transition into single life difficult. God planned for marriage to be a lifetime commitment, but he doesn't love us any less if we're divorced. We are not less valuable in his eyes, and he still has a purpose and plan for our lives. We don't need to worry that God will reject us, even if someone else does.

He will never abandon the godly.
Psalm 37:28

February 7

Never Alone
WIDOWS

1 Timothy 5:3-6

Irene slipped on her house shoes and padded down the hallway, chuckling. She couldn't wait to tell Max about her crazy dream. *Why hasn't he made the coffee yet?* Suddenly, it all came flooding back—the sudden heart attack, two days in the intensive-care ward, the memorial service just one week ago. Irene sank down at the table, thinking back over their sixty-nine years of marriage. She and Max had outlived their son, their siblings, and most of their friends. Now she'd lost her best friend and life partner. How could she go on without him?

In the Bible, God instructs his people to pay special attention to widows. As the early church ministered to women who had lost their husbands, Paul defined the true widows who were in need of the congregation's support. These women were alone in the world, without children or grandchildren to care for them. If these widows served God and sought his help, the other believers owed them respect and support.

It's always traumatic to lose someone with whom we have shared our lives. The loneliness is intensified when a widow has no children, family, or lifelong friends. It can be especially frightening for an elderly woman who was dependent on her husband in many ways. Other life experiences besides widowhood can also make us feel isolated—moving to a new area, dealing with an empty nest, or dealing with a serious illness, for example.

God understands all that we go through, including our feelings. Although he wants to comfort us, we have to receive his care through praying, reading his Word, and keeping our thoughts fixed on him. Our best cure for loneliness is spending time with the One who is always watching over us. We may feel lonely at times, but we are never really alone.

Your Creator will be your husband.
Isaiah 54:5

February 8

Wholehearted Love
WIVES OF PHARISEES

Matthew 23:25-26; Luke 18:9-12

Haley watched her husband as his eyes scanned the crowded restaurant for business colleagues or potential clients. As usual, she wouldn't get much of his attention during their anniversary dinner. He'd sent her the usual dozen roses and given her an expensive diamond bracelet, but how long had it been since they had shared more than superficial conversation? When was the last time he had held her hand, listened to her, or looked into her eyes? Haley's friends thought that she had it made, but if he was such a model husband, why did she feel unloved?

In Jesus' day, the Pharisees were a powerful religious/political party and were considered model Jews. They took great pride in following the laws down to the slightest detail, but Jesus condemned them as hypocrites for their lack of love. What was it like to be married to a Pharisee? Did these men love their wives as they loved God, with an outward show of ritual that bypassed their hearts? The Pharisees' wives may have felt the same lonely frustration as Haley, whose husband concentrated more on how the marriage looked to outsiders than on building a mutually fulfilling relationship.

God doesn't desire an empty relationship any more than a woman does. It's easy to slip into a pattern of going through the motions of worshiping God while neglecting or even ignoring him. Our claim to love him rings hollow if we're not taking time to talk with him in prayer, listen for his voice, obey his Word, and talk about him to others. Love Pharisee-style means nothing to a God who looks past our outward show of affection and sees the condition of our hearts.

> *They honor me with their lips, but their hearts are far from me.*
> *Isaiah 29:13*

February 9

The Greatest Love Story
YOUNG WOMAN IN SONG OF SONGS

Song of Songs 1:1-4

Paula spun the rack of paperbacks at the library. It was getting harder to find one that she hadn't already read. So many of the covers looked the same—a muscular, handsome, shirtless man grasping a woman with flowing hair and a dress that was slipping off her shoulders. No wonder Paula felt the need to hide the books from her kids. But how she loved those hours of escape into a dream world of passion, pursuit, and happily ever after. *If only my life could be like one of these books,* she sighed.

How did the women in Bible times react when they heard the Song of Songs read? Did they blush at the graphic descriptions of love between a man and a woman? Did they envy the way the young man wooed his lover? Did they daydream of being cherished like the young woman in the text?

Although Solomon had seven hundred wives and three hundred concubines, many people believe that he wrote the Song of Songs as a protest against the practice of polygamy. The book depicts a model relationship between a man and a woman who enjoy romantic love within the marriage relationship as God intended. On a deeper level, many see it as a picture of God's intense love for believers.

In an imperfect world filled with imperfect people, we will never experience a perfect romantic relationship. Boyfriends and husbands will always disappoint us in some way. But God's love is "more wonderful than any other." If we want to find love that truly fulfills, we have to get to know the One who loved us enough to die in our place. Then we discover that the greatest love story of all is in the Bible. And we never have to be embarrassed about the cover.

I am my beloved's and my beloved is mine.
Song of Songs 6:3 (NASB)

February 10

Feeling Less Than Desirable
YOUNG WOMAN IN SONG OF SONGS

Song of Songs 1:5-11

Looking around at the pretty, well-dressed women near her, Alexis wished that she had skipped the party. She wore bags under her eyes and fifteen extra pounds on her body. Her hair desperately needed a cut and highlights, and her face needed more than the quick dab of lip gloss she had managed. *She's really taken a toll on my looks, but it's all worth it,* Alexis thought, as she looked down at the seven-week-old baby sleeping in her arms. Alexis had no idea how beautiful she looked at that moment to her husband, who gazed at her from across the room.

Is there a woman on earth who hasn't compared herself with others and felt that she came up short? The young woman in Song of Songs was no exception. As a country girl, she had suntanned skin from working in her family's vineyards. When she looked at the refined complexions of the city women in Jerusalem, she felt embarrassed about her appearance. Her insecurity made her turn to the one person that she knew would see her as beautiful. Her betrothed thought that her skin was lovely.

We all feel less than desirable at times. If we compare our appearances to digitally retouched photos of professionally made-up models, we don't stand a chance. But even in everyday settings, there is always someone who has shinier hair, clearer skin, whiter teeth, and a better figure. During those times, it helps to remember that there is Someone who looks past our stringy hair, acne, and extra weight. He sees us as worth dying for just as we are—which is why he did. God gazes at his daughters with eyes of unconditional love, and we have no idea how beautiful we look to him.

> *When my lover looks at me, he is delighted with what he sees.*
> *Song of Songs 8:10*

February 11

Giving Compliments
YOUNG WOMAN IN SONG OF SONGS

Song of Songs 4:1-7; 5:9-16

Justine took a final look in the mirror before heading downstairs to meet her husband and leave for the restaurant. In the past two weeks, she'd had her gray roots touched up, bought a new dress, and started on a new skin-care program. Not that she expected Harry to notice. How long had it been since he had commented on her appearance? Still, she couldn't help wondering if he still found her attractive after thirty years of marriage. Justine stopped abruptly when she saw Harry smoothing his thinning hair in front of the hall mirror. *Is he thinking the same thing?*

The young couple in Song of Songs didn't hesitate to lavish compliments on each other. Although some of the metaphors sound strange to us, both the man and the woman went into great detail in describing the beauty of each other's hair, teeth, mouth, cheeks, neck, and body. The young Shulamite woman must have felt prized by her betrothed as he declared her "beautiful beyond words." In turn, she said that he was "desirable in every way."

How sad that many couples drop the habit of giving each other compliments as they grow older. Parents often stop praising their children when they reach their teen years and the parent-child relationship becomes more challenging. Old friends may neglect to share words of appreciation with each other. None of us ever become so secure that we no longer need to hear words of affirmation from those we care about.

God also wants to hear words of affirmation from us. All too often, we spend our prayer time listing our needs without expressing our appreciation for who he is. Praising God for his love, mercy, and kindness does more than acknowledge how much we value him; it changes our attitude as we focus on him rather than on our problems. Although God is truly "beautiful beyond words," the least we can do is try to describe him.

I will praise You, O Lord my God, with all my heart.
Psalm 86:12 (NKJV)

February 12

Love Is Indestructible
THE YOUNG BRIDE

Song of Songs 8:6-7

The elderly woman stroked her husband's arm as his vacant eyes stared out the sunny window. How she ached to hear him say her name, to feel his hand gripping hers, to get any response at all. Although her friends told her that she was wasting her time, somehow she managed to get to the nursing home several times a week. She had watched helplessly as Alzheimer's disease stole his memory, his personality, his speech, and his dignity. But she refused to allow this enemy to steal her love from him.

This woman chose to live out the words spoken by the bride in today's Bible passage. Her declarations about the permanent nature of love contain some of the most beautiful verses about love in the Bible. Enraptured with devotion for her husband, the young woman asserted that love is "as strong as death." Although it "flashes like fire," even rivers cannot quench or drown it. The bride's love for her husband had matured beyond physical or emotional feelings and desires. She had chosen to make a lasting commitment that would endure through time and triumph over obstacles and problems.

In today's society, many people know only a cheapened substitute for love instead of the real thing. How sad to settle for a relationship based on physical attraction, emotional feelings, or a self-centered desire to get our own needs met. The Bible teaches that genuine love for others is one of the proofs that we belong to God. That means making a lasting commitment to have their best interests at heart. When we treat others in this way, we reflect the indestructible love that God has for us—an unconditional love that lasts through eternity. You can't get a more lasting commitment than that.

> *Three things will last forever—faith, hope, and love—and the greatest of these is love.*
> *1 Corinthians 13:13*

February 13

Love Is a Gift
THE YOUNG BRIDE

Song of Songs 8:7

Backing out of the driveway, Mara glanced down at the box beside her—the biggest chocolate assortment the gourmet shop offered. She had already sent roses and made dinner reservations. *Why do I even bother?* Mara wondered. Nothing she did ever seemed quite good enough for her mom—not her career choice, the way she raised her kids, or even her hairstyle. After months of counseling, Mara finally understood why she pushed herself so hard. She was still trying to earn the one thing she craved most—her mother's approval. "No more!" Mara shouted, as her right hand ripped the cellophane from the box of chocolates.

Mara did not experience love as the young woman in Song of Songs did. As she praised her relationship with her husband, the young wife pointed out that love cannot be bought at any price. Even if people tried to purchase love with all the wealth they owned, their offer would be scorned. The woman knew that the love between her and her husband was a priceless gift that they willingly shared with each other.

Sometimes women find themselves in relationships in which they feel compelled to keep striving to earn someone's approval. If we could just look better or cook better, get smarter or work harder, then maybe our parent/sibling/boyfriend/husband would love us. But in these relationships, the problem is with the other person's emotional development, not our performance.

Many people think of God's love as performance based, but nothing could be further from the truth. Jesus died for our sins simply because he loves us, not because we deserve it. Salvation is offered to us as a gift, and once we accept that gift, there is nothing we can do to make God love us more. His love can't be bought—not with good deeds and not with gourmet chocolates.

It is by grace you have been saved, through faith—and this not from yourselves, it is the gift of God—not by works, so that no one can boast. Ephesians 2:8-9 (NIV)

February 14

Purity Vow
THE YOUNG BRIDE

Song of Songs 8:4

Since the nationwide "True Love Waits" movement began in 1993, more than two million high-school and college students have committed themselves to waiting until they are married to have sex. The teens sign a pledge card that states, "Believing that true love waits, I make a commitment to God, myself, my family, those I date, and my future mate to be sexually pure until the day I enter marriage."

Today's Bible verse sounds like the original purity vow. Three times in the book, the young woman urges other women "not to awaken love until the time is right." As the narrative progresses, the young woman expresses her joy and delight with her beloved. In spite of intense physical attraction, she and her groom have respected the boundaries God set for physical intimacy; now they are free to enjoy this gift fully. The young woman desires this same fulfillment and joy for other women.

With our society's emphasis on romantic love, it can be tempting for us to rush into a relationship with the wrong person. With our society's obsession with sex, it can also be tempting to ignore God's guidelines for the physical aspects of a relationship. God's Word emphasizes reserving sex for marriage so that we can fully enjoy physical intimacy as he intended.

God's Word also urges us to keep ourselves spiritually pure by imitating him in every aspect of our lives. Although we will always struggle with temptations while we live on earth, some day we will be freed from all traces of sin. Until then, we'll find our greatest joy and fulfillment by living according to his guidelines. It's never too late to commit to sexual *or* spiritual purity.

> *All who have this eager expectation will keep themselves pure, just as he is pure.*
> *1 John 3:3*

February 15

The Most-Precious Jewels
THE HIGH PRIEST'S CHESTPIECE

Exodus 28:15-29

Michelle fingered the gold chain around her neck and wished that she never had to take it off. It had to be the best birthday present she would ever receive—a Mother's necklace with three jewels set in gold. The amethyst, the ruby, and the blue sapphire represented three of the most important dates in her life. "It's a Mommy necklace," little Adam had explained. "You wear it so we'll always be close to your heart."

Aaron and the high priests who followed him wore a sort of "Father's jewelry" as they ministered before God—an exquisite, one-of-a-kind piece designed by God. The chestpiece, or breastplate, contained twelve precious gems, each one set in gold filigree and representing a tribe of Israel, with the name of the tribe engraved on it. Israelite women knew that their tribe's jewel shining in the high priest's chestpiece represented them, too. The high priest carried their tribe's name over his heart as he approached God to remind them that God kept each one of them close to his heart.

Jewelry is nice, but the best kind to wear isn't found in stores. God advises us to wear loyalty and kindness like a necklace (see Proverbs 3:3) and to tie our parents' teachings around our necks (see Proverbs 6:20-21). He compares common sense and discernment to jewels on a necklace (see Proverbs 3:21-22). In contrast, a description of wicked people says that "they wear pride like a jeweled necklace" (Psalm 73:6). We may not realize it, but people see the outward evidence of what's going on inside us. If we hold God's teachings close to our hearts, the gems of his wisdom will be evident in our lives. Then, everyone will see that we're wearing our Father's jewelry.

Common sense and discernment . . . are like jewels on a necklace.
Proverbs 3:21-22

February 16

Finding a Family
WOMEN IN THE EARLY CHURCH

Acts 2:42-47

Gwen sat in the restaurant parking lot and fiddled with her keys. What a difference one phone call could make! Although she had enjoyed a wonderful childhood with her adoptive parents, a vague feeling of loneliness had always tugged at her heart. It intensified when her parents died thirteen years ago. Now, at age thirty-four, Gwen discovered her birth family. It included seven brothers and sisters, who were all waiting in the steak house with her biological mother and maternal grandparents. As Gwen stepped out of her car, she laughed. *One thing's for sure—I'm not an only child anymore.*

Women in the early church also discovered a family, one united by a shared belief in Jesus. The early believers enjoyed a close-knit fellowship as they met in one another's homes to eat, pray, and worship God together. Joy in their newfound faith spilled over into joy in one another's company. Those who already had families were happy to find new sisters in Christ. Believers without a family were blessed to gain a network of friendship and support. Besides growing in number, the believers found that their faith matured and that their closeness strengthened them to face the coming persecution of the church.

Once we become children of God, we gain a worldwide network of brothers and sisters in Christ. This new family is based on more than biology or shared childhood memories. Love and gratitude for our salvation binds us together more tightly than any earthly relationship. As with siblings we grow up with, we sometimes have trouble getting along with one another. But it's important not to neglect our relationships with fellow believers, especially since we'll spend eternity together. One thing is for sure—in God's family, there's no such thing as an only child.

God places the lonely in families.
Psalm 68:6

February 17

Don't Give Up!
ICHABOD'S MOTHER

1 Samuel 4:12-22

Within a period of seven years, best-selling author and speaker Barbara Johnson lost one son in Vietnam, had a second son killed by a drunk driver, and discovered that a third son had adopted a homosexual lifestyle. She admits that she thought about driving off a California overpass; instead, she began a ministry that has offered words of hope and joy to thousands of heartbroken women.

In one message, Ichabod's mother learned of the deaths of her husband and father-in-law and the loss of the Ark of the Covenant. This bad news caused her to go into labor and into despair. The midwives tried to comfort her, because the Israelites regarded the birth of a son as a great blessing, but she named her son Ichabod ("Where is the glory?"). Before she died, she said, "The glory has departed from Israel, for the Ark of God has been captured."

Israel had treated the Ark as a magic charm that would ensure a military victory instead of revering it as the testimony of God's presence and provision. Ichabod's mother also seemed to depend more on the symbol than on God. The name that she chose for her son reflected her hopelessness. Her final words make us wonder if she died from physical complications or because she simply lost her will to live.

Trials and losses can make us feel that God's glory has departed from our lives. It may be that God wants to wean us from dependence on visible evidence of his working so that we can learn to trust in him alone. Galatians 6:9 urges us not to get tired of doing good and promises that "we will reap a harvest of blessing if we don't give up." We will experience disappointment in life, but we should never be hopeless if we have the glory of God's Holy Spirit living within us.

> To [His saints] God willed to make known what are the riches of the glory of this mystery among the Gentiles: which is Christ in you, the hope of glory.
> Colossians 1:27 (NKJV)

February 18

Dangerous Dabbling
THE MEDIUM OF ENDOR

1 Samuel 28:3-14

The talk show *Crossing Over* ran for four years, launching host John Edward to fame. On each episode, the psychic/medium tried to connect audience members with the spirits of loved ones who had died. Edward remains a best-selling author and a much sought-after speaker and talk show guest. His clients often spend two years on a waiting list for private sessions with him.

When God didn't answer King Saul's inquiries by the usual means, Saul found a medium who supposedly possessed the ability to contact the dead. Bible scholars have suggested three possible explanations for what happened next: (1) The woman used deception to trick Saul; (2) she tapped into demonic power to conjure a counterfeit Samuel; or (3) God brought Samuel's spirit back to prophesy one last time.

Although the medium seemed confident in her abilities, she screamed when Samuel's spirit appeared, so she must have been taken by surprise. Perhaps she saw that this time God's power was at work, not her own dark arts. She was not the one in control.

Some people become obsessed with the idea of contacting the spirit of a loved one who has died. Our society feeds that desire through articles, books, and shows featuring stories of people who have supposedly contacted someone "on the other side." These people are either deceiving us or have been deceived.

Contacting spirits may seem harmless, but this practice is forbidden by God (see Deuteronomy 18:10-11), for good reason. Occult practices are based on the powers of Satan and his demons. We may experience initial "success" for the purpose of luring us in. But eventually, we will discover that *we* are the ones being controlled. Attempting to "cross over" is contrary to what God commands.

> *When men tell you to consult mediums and spiritists, who whisper and mutter, should not a people inquire of their God? Why consult the dead on behalf of the living?*
> Isaiah 8:19 (NIV)

February 19

Naughty *and* Nice
THE MEDIUM OF ENDOR

1 Samuel 28:15-25

Erin was shocked to realize that she had just been chatting and laughing with a woman she had planned to avoid for the rest of her life. This couldn't be the head of the local atheists' group, the woman whose vocal protests had led to the removal of Christmas carols from the school's winter concert, the leader of the petition drive to ban the traditional Easter cross from the courtyard square. How could this woman be so nice? *Must have left her horns and pitchfork at home,* Erin mused.

Saul visited a medium who engaged in practices condemned by God as detestable and punishable by death, yet she also displayed a different side. When Saul fell on the ground, paralyzed by the bad news he had just heard, the woman showed concern for him. She pleaded with him to eat so that he could regain his strength. Then she hurriedly killed and prepared a calf, baked bread, and served a meal to Saul and his men. They couldn't have asked for a more generous, kind, or attentive hostess.

However, being nice is not the same thing as being godly. Even those who actively fight against God may have loving, empathetic personalities, but that's not enough to get people into heaven. It's not a matter of our nice deeds outnumbering our naughty ones. We all fail to live up to God's standard of perfection. That's why we need a Savior.

Being nice will never cover up deliberate disobedience. It may make other people want to be around us, but niceness can be superficial and even self-centered. Godliness results when God's Spirit controls us. Even our best efforts at being nice are meaningless apart from a foundation of trust in God. They can never make up for a sin, whether it's practicing necromancy or refusing to believe in God.

Everyone has sinned; we all fall short of God's glorious standard.
Romans 3:23

February 20

Generous Women
WIDOW WITH TWO COINS, MARY OF BETHANY

Mark 12:43-44; John 12:1-3

The college president made no attempt to hide his excitement during the interview as he talked about the school's unexpected windfall. Just as the small private college faced its worst financial crisis ever, it received the largest donation in its history. A widowed heiress had died, and since she was childless, she willed her entire fortune to the small college she had attended many years earlier.

The two women in today's verses came from different financial circumstances, but both displayed extreme generosity. The widow probably lived in poverty, barely managing to feed herself. According to Jesus, her offering of two coins was all the money she had to live on. Many people would have called the widow crazy for giving the money to the Temple instead of keeping it for her own needs.

Mary of Bethany probably enjoyed much more wealth than the poor widow, but a large jar of pure nard certainly didn't fit her budget either. The cost of the rare perfume she poured over Jesus' feet was equal to a laborer's wages for an entire year. Jesus understood that Mary's generosity overflowed from her love and gratitude to him. When some observers criticized her for wasting money, he defended her gesture.

God wants us to be wise in handling our finances, but he also expects us to be generous in giving to others and in giving some of our resources back to him. Anything we put in the offering plate originally came from his hand. We don't have to worry about giving him more than we can afford. If we're obedient children living for him, then our heavenly Father has committed himself to meeting all our needs. Even if others think we're wasting our money, God will reward our giving and make it possible for us to be even more generous.

Yes, you will be enriched in every way so that you can always be generous.
2 Corinthians 9:11

February 21

Deeply Loved
RACHEL

Genesis 29:10-20

There wasn't a dry eye anywhere as Stephen and Cassandra exchanged their wedding vows. Stephen had longed to marry her since kindergarten, so this day had been a long time in coming. He had waited patiently during her disastrous first marriage shortly after high school. Later, he had supported her financially and emotionally through a long illness, eventually giving her one of his kidneys. Now, watching Cassandra beam at her groom, I wondered what her life would be like with a husband who loved her enough to sacrifice so much. I wouldn't have to wait long—the second half of the miniseries would air the next night.

Today's Bible passage describes a real-life example of a woman loved by a man who was willing to sacrifice for her. Jacob loved Rachel from the first moment that he laid eyes on her. Since he had fled from his home and had no material possessions to offer her father, Jacob promised to work for seven years in exchange for Rachel's hand in marriage. Rachel must have felt a wonderful security and joy in knowing that Jacob loved her so deeply that seven years of hard work as a shepherd seemed like just a few days to him. Later, he even agreed to work an additional seven years to secure her as his bride.

What woman doesn't dream of being loved that deeply? Yet what woman hasn't already been loved far more than that? Whether we know it or not, there is a Man who loves us so much that he willingly died on a cross to save our lives. That kind of selfless love is amazing enough, but in reality, Jesus was God, taking human form to lay down his life on our behalf. The same God who created us made the ultimate sacrifice for us, and we'll never find a love deeper than his.

> This is real love—not that we loved God, but that he loved us and sent his Son as a sacrifice to take away our sins.
> 1 John 4:10

February 22

Starved for Affection
LEAH

Genesis 29:21-35

Cindy frowned as she glanced at her husband across the room, absorbed in the sports pages. *Funny how he remembers the batting averages of every Cubs player but forgot my birthday last week,* she mused. The coming weekend, he would be glued to the bleachers at the stadium or to the television for the big game. Cindy sighed and returned to her romance novel, in which the heroine was admired and valued.

Like Cindy, Leah felt like a second-place wife. After being overshadowed for years by her beautiful younger sister, Leah experienced the ultimate humiliation when her father tricked Jacob into marrying her. To add to her disgrace, Jacob married Rachel just one week after he married Leah. She must have dreaded the years ahead as she shared her husband with a woman he loved enough to work fourteen years to marry.

God saw that Leah was unloved and gave her children, while Rachel remained barren for several years. Leah gave birth to three sons, all the while hoping that their births would cause Jacob to love her. When the fourth son was born, she exclaimed simply, "Now I will praise the LORD!" Leah's focus had shifted from her yearning for a husband's affection to faith in God.

Many wives feel that they have been replaced in their husbands' hearts by a job, television, hobbies such as fishing or hunting, or even by a ministry. Other women are hurt by parents who treat them as less important than a sibling. Whenever someone on earth doesn't love us as much as we would like, we can know that Someone in heaven cherishes us more than we can imagine. He will take care of us as he did Leah, who had the great privilege of giving birth to Judah, through whom God's own Son would come to earth.

> *I have loved you with an everlasting love.*
> *Jeremiah 31:3 (NIV)*

February 23

Sibling Rivalry
LEAH AND RACHEL

Genesis 30:3-20

Cutting the price tag off her new dress, Janelle sighed. She would have worn her blue silk dress to the family wedding if Beth hadn't recently bought one similar to it, only fancier. Her sister always had to one-up her by taking the most impressive dish to holiday dinners and buying the most expensive Christmas gift for their parents. She even compared their salaries and their children's grades. Her parents liked to repeat three-year-old Beth's comment after Janelle's birth: "I'm Daddy's girl, not her!" It didn't seem funny to Janelle.

Leah and Rachel knew about sibling rivalry. Rachel's grief over her barrenness was intensified by her jealousy at sharing her husband with a sister who had delivered four sons. In desperation, Rachel gave her maid to Jacob. When Bilhah had two sons, Rachel named the second one Naphtali to reflect her competition with Leah. Not to be outdone, Leah gave Jacob her maid, who also had two sons. After that, Leah gave birth to two more sons and a daughter, and Rachel delivered two sons. The need to keep score must have marred the normal joy and pride of motherhood for the sisters.

Competition can be a good thing when it pushes us to strive for excellence. It becomes destructive when spurred by jealousy or selfish ambition. Rivalry can make a home, a work environment, or a church a miserable place to be when people compete with each other rather than work together as a team. Jealous rivalry can take away our joy of accomplishment or even tear a family apart. Whenever we feel pressured to compare our performance with someone else's, we need to remember that God's opinion is the one that truly matters. When we focus on pleasing him, we no longer feel the need to keep score.

> *Wherever there is jealousy and selfish ambition, there you will find*
> *disorder and evil of every kind.*
> *James 3:16*

February 24

Let's Make a Deal
LEAH AND RACHEL

Genesis 30:14-16

The rivalry between Leah and Rachel reached a new low when Leah's son found some mandrake plants, which were believed to be aphrodisiacs. When Rachel begged for the plants, Leah bitterly asked if it wasn't enough that Rachel had already stolen her husband. So Rachel agreed to give up her turn for being with Jacob that night in return for some of the plants. Leah met Jacob as he came from the fields and informed him that she had "paid" for him with mandrakes. The sisters were so caught up in their envy and competition that they treated their husband like a male prostitute.

Many people enjoy haggling over prices and relish the satisfaction of getting a good deal. But this attitude causes problems when it moves out of the business world and into relationships. Thinking that "everybody has a price" causes some people to manipulate others rather than interact with them in honest, healthy ways. No one wants to be treated like a commodity to be bought and paid for.

Sometimes people even try to make deals with God. When we're in trouble, it's tempting to promise God that we will change our ways or give up a bad habit if he will help us out. If someone we love is seriously ill, we may vow to serve God for the rest of our lives if only he will heal our loved one. But God doesn't work that way. We can make requests, but there is nothing we can pay him to make him do what we want. God's love and mercy are graciously offered; they are not to be haggled over like these two jealous sisters haggled over their husband.

There is joy for those who deal justly with others and always do what
is right.
Psalm 106:3

February 25

Our Hidden Idols
RACHEL

Genesis 31:17-35

Sandra rushed up the stairs and shoved the envelope in the bottom of her underwear drawer. *Just in time,* she thought as she heard the garage door open. Lately, Matt had been wondering why their bank account stayed so low, but she knew how to disguise her spending. He'd be furious if he discovered that she played the lottery every week, but someday he would thank her. She just knew that any day now she would have a winning ticket.

During the time period of Genesis 31, many people kept small wooden or metal idols, or "gods," in their homes. These were thought to afford protection and guidance, and they also had legal significance connected with passing on the family inheritance. When Jacob decided to leave his uncle's home, Rachel secretly stole her father's idols. Did she hope that the idols would bless their journey, or was she afraid that Laban could use them to find out where they had gone? Perhaps she stole them to ensure that she would inherit her father's estate.

Whatever her reason, the theft soon put Rachel's life in danger. When Jacob was confronted by Laban, he promised to kill anyone who was found in possession of the gods. Laban searched, but he never found his idols because Rachel was sitting on them the whole time.

We may not have statues or objects in our homes that we bow down to, but we may have idols in our hearts. Anytime that we give something other than God first place in our lives, it becomes an idol. It may be a relationship, a job, a habit, a hobby, materialism, or the pursuit of pleasure. God wants us to be fully devoted to him. He is the only One worthy of our worship and adoration. We can't hide our idols from him, even by sitting on them.

> *[Jesus replied,] "You must love the Lord your God with all your heart, all your soul, all your mind, and all your strength."*
> *Mark 12:30*

February 26

First-Class Women
CONCUBINES

As Patsy listened to her friends gush about their plans to enjoy a spa day, her mind frantically searched for an excuse not to join them. Why set herself up for more embarrassment and shame? She could experience that any day. No matter where she went with her two best friends, Patsy felt the sting of discrimination. In restaurants and shops, they received attention while Patsy felt overlooked or ignored. Her friends meant well, but they were oblivious—and they were skinny. *I'm tired of being treated like a second-class person just because of my size,* Patsy thought.

Concubines in Old Testament times knew how it felt to be second-class citizens. Although God did not condone the practice, it became acceptable in Israelite society for a man to take female slaves, bondservants, or foreign prisoners of war as secondary wives. Becoming the master's concubine meant a rise in status for a slave or servant, but she still remained inferior to his wife. A concubine's children were considered the legal children of her mistress but had no inheritance or property rights unless their father chose to adopt them.

Many women struggle with feelings of inferiority and see themselves as second-class people. These feelings may be based on social or economic status, ethnic origin, family background, level of education, or even appearance. Although the world may encourage these perceptions, in God's eyes there are no second-rate people. No matter what circumstances we're born into, we are equally guilty of the sin that separates us from him. Fortunately, God sees each of us as someone worth dying for. Once we are born into his family by believing in Jesus, we are equally accepted and forgiven. God has no second-rate children in his family.

> *There is neither Jew nor Greek, slave nor free, male nor female, for you are all one in Christ Jesus.*
> Galatians 3:28 (NIV)

February 27

Out of Control
A SLAVE GIRL HEALED BY PAUL

Acts 16:16-19

Rosemary slammed her bedroom door and flung herself facedown on the comforter. She'd done it again! Why did she get so worked up? Michael had been considerate enough to let her know that he would be working late again, and they *did* need the extra money. So why did she start screaming into the phone and throw her coffee cup against the wall? After each outburst, Rosemary vowed to control her temper, but it was no use. She always seemed to be at the mercy of her emotions.

The slave girl in Acts 16 was at the mercy of her masters and also a demonic spirit. This young woman was not a con artist; she was possessed by an evil spirit that enabled her to predict the future. Her affliction had made her owners rich, but what a miserable, degraded life she must have lived. Shunned by everyone except paying customers, she must have longed to be valued for who she was as a person, not just for her performances.

One day, an encounter transformed the girl's life. When Paul commanded the demon to leave her, she was instantly set free from the evil spirit that controlled her. The girl's owners were furious because they had lost their means of making money, but through the power of Jesus' name, she was restored to emotional and mental health.

We all struggle with our emotions, but some people are mastered by them. The Bible teaches that outbursts of anger, rage, and jealousy are part of our sinful nature. Only God's Holy Spirit living in us can set us free from these demons. We must make the choice to let him control us. The only way to avoid being at the mercy of our emotions, like Rosemary, is to be at the mercy of God.

Those who belong to Christ Jesus have nailed the passions and desires
of their sinful nature to his cross and crucified them there.
Galatians 5:24

February 28

Talking with God 24/7
ANNA

Luke 2:21-38

Julie opened her e-mail account and found a long list of prayer requests waiting. *Oh well,* she sighed, *it's not as if I haven't got the time.* She adjusted the wheelchair that had carried her since the accident that paralyzed her thirty years before. Sometimes she couldn't help thinking how things might have been different, but not this morning. Today, Julie was determined to live up to her nickname, "Prayer Warrior on Wheels."

Anna the prophetess also had a powerful prayer ministry. She was widowed after only seven years of marriage, so she stayed at the Temple day and night, worshiping God through fasting and prayer. Many scholars believe that Anna was more than one hundred years old. God richly rewarded her dedication to serving him through prayer. She was one of the first people to see and recognize the Messiah, when he was a little over a month old. Her joy and excitement over this privilege spilled out as she immediately began telling others about Jesus.

Believers today have God's Spirit living in them. Since our bodies are God's temple (see 1 Corinthians 6:19), we are like Anna in living at this temple day and night. Like Anna, we are also called to be in continual prayer. At first, this sounds impossible, since many of us define prayer as an extended period of time alone or something we do only in a certain place.

Having a consistent quiet time is important, but God wants prayer to be a natural part of our day-to-day lives, like breathing. He is with us at every moment in our joys, petty annoyances, and serious problems. No matter where we are or what's happening around us, we can develop the habit of an ongoing conversation with God. He is looking for an army of prayer warriors like Anna and Julie.

Never stop praying.
1 Thessalonians 5:17

March 1

A Strong Tower
WOMEN OF THEBEZ

Judges 9:42-51

Most of us have horrifying images from September 11, 2001, burned into our minds. How can we forget seeing people jump to their deaths from the top of the World Trade Center? The 110-story towers represented an engineering innovation, but when terrorists crashed their jets into the buildings, the towers became fiery traps for the people inside. Rescuers worked feverishly, but for many there was no escape.

When a bloodthirsty madman attacked the ancient town of Thebez, the entire population fled to their tower for safety. It was strong, with thick walls built for protection from their enemies. At that moment, however, they wished they were anywhere else. Had they heard that Abimelech had just destroyed his own town of Shechem and burned down the temple of Baal-berith with all the people in it? From the top of their tower, the people of Thebez could see the smoke still rising from the direction of Shechem. Panic must have gripped the women's hearts as they watched in horror from the roof, unable to escape as Abimelech approached.

We all want to feel safe, but we'll never find anything on earth that can truly guarantee our security. Without realizing it, some people place their confidence in a person, the government, their money, or their wisdom. Sometimes the very things we depend on for protection end up putting us in danger. Since God holds ultimate control over the universe, he is the only One who can protect us. When a crisis hits, we often don't think of God until we realize that we have nowhere else to run. Trusting in God every day and calling on his name before danger threatens wraps us in his power and strength. Then, no matter what happens around us or to us, we know that we are in his hands, which is the safest place to be.

> *The name of the LORD is a strong tower; the righteous run to it and are safe.*
> *Proverbs 18:10 (NKJV)*

March 2

A Powerful Weapon
A WOMAN OF THEBEZ

Judges 9:52-53
As Abimelech attacked the tower in Thebez, one quick-thinking woman on the roof discovered an unusual but effective weapon. When she saw Abimelech getting ready to set fire to the entrance below, she grabbed a nearby millstone, used for grinding grain, and dropped it. The millstone landed on Abimelech's head and crushed his skull. While the men in the tower were probably wishing for bows and arrows, spears, or other traditional weapons, this woman used what was at hand.

We tend to admire certain strong people who look like spiritual giants, but God has given all his children everything they need to fight any battle that comes their way. Our faith and obedience protect us from Satan's attacks as he tempts us to turn aside from following God. Our offensive weapons—prayer, God's written Word, and his Holy Spirit within us—give us the power to do spiritual battle.

Although God has designated specific spiritual weapons, he also wants us to think creatively when doing his work. Sometimes we feel ill-equipped to do a certain job, when what we need is right at hand. Instead of wishing that we could accomplish more for God, a self-inventory might reveal overlooked skills, talents, connections, or material possessions waiting to be invested in God's Kingdom. God used an ordinary wooden staff in Moses' hand to perform miracles before the Egyptian pharaoh. God used a millstone and a woman to kill an evil madman. In God's hands, common things can accomplish uncommon feats.

The LORD asked [Moses], "What is that in your hand?"
Exodus 4:2

March 3

The Strength of Weakness
A WOMAN OF THEBEZ

Judges 9:54-57

Abimelech knew that the blow to his head was fatal. He could face death, but not the humiliation of being killed by a woman. Abimelech commanded his armor bearer to run him through with his sword. He died, but his tactic didn't work, as Scripture records the manner of his death not once, but twice, here and in 2 Samuel 11:21. While Abimelech died in humiliation, the woman who threw down the millstone lived with the victory of having saved the entire population of her town from a horrible fate. The Bible doesn't record her name, but she stood out as a heroine on that day.

Compared to Abimelech and his forces, the woman on the roof looked weak and powerless, yet she became a conqueror. God has a history of making heroes out of unlikely characters—choosing younger, weaker candidates to become leaders and using small forces to conquer mighty armies. He often put the Israelites in situations where they had to realize that they had prevailed through God's power, not their own.

Human frailty provides the perfect backdrop for displaying God's power. When we have no resources of our own, we are forced to depend totally on God. Then he works through us in amazing ways. To the world, Jesus looked weak and powerless during his trial and crucifixion, but in reality, the Cross displayed God's power more than any other event in history. If we feel weak and foolish, that can be a good thing. That's just when God can use us for something great.

> *God chose the foolish things of the world to shame the wise; God chose the weak things of the world to shame the strong.*
> *1 Corinthians 1:27 (NIV)*

March 4

Don't Worry
JESUS' TEACHING

Luke 12:22-31

Miko walked down the aisle of blouses and tops. After being out of the job market for so long, she felt nervous about her upcoming interview. She had been worried about not owning an appropriate outfit, and she had no money to spend on new clothes. Thank goodness her friend had suggested this thrift store. Glancing at the tailored tweed blazer in her cart, she thought, *What are the chances of matching that shade in my size?* A few minutes later, her mouth dropped open as she pulled out a turtleneck in the perfect color and size—with her initials monogrammed on the neck!

The women who heard Jesus teaching his disciples in today's passage had the same everyday concerns that we do. They could easily relate when Jesus spoke about worry over food and clothes, since their lives largely revolved around feeding and clothing their families. They listened as he reminded them that if God fed the ravens, he would certainly feed them. They watched with rapt attention as he gestured at some nearby lilies, beautifully "dressed" by God. Did they feel a burden lift from their shoulders as Jesus assured them of their heavenly Father's continuous care?

God commands us not to worry about our everyday lives for good reason. Worrying wastes our time and energy without changing the situation. It contributes to poor physical and emotional health, and it interferes with our relationship with God. We can't trust in God and worry about our needs at the same time.

Faith is the only antidote to the harmful habit of worry. If we truly believe that our heavenly Father knows our needs and will provide for us, then we can train our minds to substitute a prayer for every anxious thought that crops up. God wants us to concentrate on spiritual matters and leave the details of everyday life to him.

Don't worry about anything; instead, pray about everything.
Philippians 4:6

March 5

Transient Lifestyle
SARAI

Genesis 12:1-6

Melinda hung up the phone and dropped her head in her hands. Another move—when they had just settled into the neighborhood, and the kids were doing so well in school. She had known that life with a military husband would mean occasional transfers, but twelve moves in sixteen years of marriage? As their family and possessions had grown, each relocation had become a little more difficult. Melinda felt drained just thinking about the days ahead.

Many women in the Bible had transient lifestyles. Because of God's call, Sarai had to leave her home, her relatives, and her country. Sarai didn't even know where they were going—God simply instructed the couple to leave and go to the land that he would show to Abram. Her heart surely ached as she left all that was familiar to join her husband on this journey. As Sarai adapted to a seminomadic lifestyle, we can imagine that her thoughts often returned to the city life she had always known.

It's never easy to leave the security of what is familiar and comfortable. Even if we're excited about a move, a new job, or a change in lifestyle, the uncertainty of what lies ahead can fill us with doubt and fear. How comforting it is to know that wherever our life journey takes us, God is right there with us. Even more, he has already gone ahead of us and made arrangements for the changes to be used for our good, however painful they may seem at the time. Abram and Sarai's obedience to God's call brought blessings to them and to the rest of the world. When God calls us to leave something behind, we can expect to find blessings ahead.

"I know the plans I have for you," says the LORD.
Jeremiah 29:11

March 6

Unfair Situations
SARAI

Genesis 12:10-20

As Sonia finished labeling the last packing box, she sat back on her heels and looked around. There were so many memories in this family room. It seemed unreal that tomorrow she and Stan would leave the house where their children had grown up, the home where she had expected to grow old. If only she hadn't agreed to Stan's harebrained investment scheme. She had had doubts about it from the beginning, but Stan had seemed so sure that it would pay off. Now Sonia fought back tears. *This is just so unfair,* she fumed.

Sarai must have thought that her situation was unfair when she ended up in a harem. Abram had passed Sarai off as his sister rather than his wife out of fear that an Egyptian would kill him to take her. Sarai had consented to his scheme; after all, it was only a half lie and she did want to protect her husband. Now, it must have seemed like an unreasonable request. The pharaoh planned to take her as his wife, and there seemed to be no way out. How overjoyed Sarai must have been when God intervened to free her from the ruler's harem.

We have all known the feeling of being in an unfair situation. It may develop because of our own choices or foolish behavior, or we may find ourselves trapped through the choices of other people. Regardless of the cause, we can look to God for deliverance. He delights in justice and often intervenes in our problems in unexpected ways. At other times, he doesn't change the circumstances but gives us the strength to endure them. He promises to right all wrongs someday. No matter how unfair our situation seems, we can be sure that we will be vindicated, sooner or later.

> *The LORD will vindicate his people and have compassion on his servants.*
> Psalm 135:14 (NIV)

March 7

Looking for Shortcuts
SARAI

Genesis 16:1-6

We all love shortcuts and quick fixes. Some of these, such as curling irons, microwaves, computers, and drive-through windows, save time and make life more efficient. Others create more problems than they solve. Too many fast-food meals can wreck a balanced diet and our figures. An online quickie degree does not substitute for years of college study. Online dating services may not be the best route to finding a committed life partner. Some things just take time, and they're worth the wait.

Sarai also looked for a shortcut. For years, God had promised that Abram would have a son and heir. Now Sarai was long past child-bearing age, and she was tired of feeling disappointed year after year. Why keep waiting for something that obviously wasn't going to happen? So she took matters into her own hands and gave her servant to Abram. According to the custom, Hagar's child would be regarded as Sarai's. Perhaps this was how God intended to provide Abram's heir.

Sarai's idea was not part of God's plan, and she soon regretted her rash decision. Hagar's pregnancy created conflict between Sarai and her husband, and jealousy between Sarai and her servant. It also began a hostility that continued through the descendants of Hagar's son and Sarai's son, the Arab people and the Jewish nation.

God's plan often includes something that is very difficult for us to do—waiting. As we anxiously watch months or years go by with no sign of God's acting to fulfill his promises, we may despair. We begin to wonder if he has forgotten us, or if we have missed something. It's tempting to intervene and "help God out." That is always a mistake. Human efforts to fulfill divine promises only complicate matters, as Sarai learned the hard way.

I watch in hope for the LORD, I wait for God my Savior.
Micah 7:7 (NIV)

March 8

Attitude Adjustment
HAGAR

Genesis 16:7-16

Once again, the new supervisor was the topic of conversation at break time.

"Ever since she got promoted, she barely speaks to me."

"Yeah, she thinks she's too good to associate with us now—you should have seen how she turned up her nose when I asked her about being on the bowling team this year."

"What she forgets is that she *needs* us—if we don't do our jobs, then she doesn't look good with *her* boss."

"Hmmm, anybody got any ideas?"

When Sarai had Abram sleep with her Egyptian servant, Hagar was elevated to the position of secondary wife. At first, Hagar probably felt honored and grateful for her unexpected change in status, but she soon became arrogant. After Hagar became pregnant, she treated Sarai with contempt. Hagar rubbed it in that she could do something that her mistress could not do—bear Abram's child.

Sarai responded to Hagar's insolence by mistreating her. Rather than admit her fault and apologize, Hagar ran away. The angel of the Lord came to Hagar in the wilderness and told her that she would have a son and more descendants than she could count. He also instructed her to return and submit to Sarai's authority. Hagar returned home with a new attitude and a new name for God—"the God who sees me."

It's easy to be humble when we're surprised with an honor, whether it's an award, a promotion, or just verbal praise. But as time goes by, we may start thinking that we deserve even more. We may begin treating others with contempt or develop a rebellious attitude toward authority. God sees our thoughts as well as our actions. He knows when we are headed for a fall, and he recommends an attitude adjustment. Hopefully, we won't wait until we're in a wilderness caused by our own arrogance.

Pride goes before destruction, and haughtiness before a fall.
Proverbs 16:18

March 9

New Name, New Woman
SARAH

Genesis 17:15-16; 18:1-12; 21:1-7

"Have you seen Tina lately?" Bethany asked her friend as they started their morning walk. "I met her in the store and almost didn't recognize her. She actually had a smile on her face instead of a scowl, but the most amazing part was hearing her talk without her usual bitterness and sarcasm. Something has definitely happened to her!"

"You're wrong," Emily answered, smiling. "I found out from her sister that Tina has started going to Bible study. Some*thing* didn't happen to her—Some*one* did."

Sarai had many bitter experiences in her life. Although she had a devoted husband, she remained barren in a culture that based a woman's importance on her ability to bear sons. As God prepared for Isaac's miraculous birth, he changed Sarai's name to Sarah. Both names mean "princess." The change in Sarah's name was slight, but she soon went through a dramatic transformation.

Abraham was ninety-nine when the angel of the Lord confirmed the promise that he would have numerous descendants. This time, God gave a more specific prediction: Sarah would have a son within one year. Sarah overheard the conversation, and she laughed silently at the ridiculous idea that she might become pregnant. Later, when she delivered a son as prophesied, she declared, "God has brought me laughter." Something, or rather, Someone had changed Sarah's attitude from laughing in disbelief to laughing with joy.

The Bible teaches that when we become God's children, we are new creations. God's Spirit living in us begins to transform our thoughts, attitudes, and actions to conform us to the image of Christ. God's love and grace flow through us to others. Our names may not change, but like Tina and Sarah, our lives will show that we have had an encounter with the King of kings. And he can make princesses out of us all.

Anyone who belongs to Christ has become a new person.
2 Corinthians 5:17

March 10

God of the Impossible
SARAH

Genesis 18:1-15

Sarah faced an impossible situation. She and Abraham had set out from their home twenty-four years earlier, trusting in God's promise that they would have countless descendants. Abraham had fathered a son by Hagar, but God insisted that Abraham's heir would come from Sarah. As she neared the age of ninety, Sarah's hope must have worn thin. At times, the promised blessing may have felt to her like a cruel joke.

When God visited Abraham and confirmed that Sarah would have a baby the next year, God asked, "Is anything too hard for the LORD?" This is a question we need to ask ourselves when we face impossible situations. God often expects us to believe what seems unbelievable. We may wonder how we can stay in such an unfulfilling marriage, or if we will ever see the fruit of our spiritual training in our children. He may ask us to give up a lifelong habit or to serve him in some way that seems far beyond our abilities.

By waiting to fulfill the promise until Sarah was far beyond normal childbearing years, God displayed his power for everyone to see. No one could deny that Isaac's birth was miraculous. The Bible gives many accounts of God's revealing himself by accomplishing the impossible. He conquered powerful armies with a small band of faithful followers, parted a sea, and raised the dead. His most "impossible" feat was to become human and die for our sins so that we wouldn't have to.

Our society spouts positive-thinking clichés such as, "If you believe it, you can achieve it," but we do better to believe in God than to rely on our own mental powers. Is anything too hard for the Lord? Our faith may sometimes waver, but we know the answer. We can be positive that God will keep his promises—even when it means doing the "impossible."

> *[Jesus said,] "Humanly speaking, it is impossible. But with God everything is possible."*
> *Matthew 19:26*

March 11

Never Abandoned
HAGAR

Genesis 21:8-21

Ashley stared at the note in her hand, trying to comprehend the words. She had fallen head over heels for Todd even though he was still legally married. Soon he moved into her apartment. Whenever Ashley asked about the lengthy divorce proceedings, Todd reassured her and talked of their future life together. Now Ashley had come home to find a note informing her that he had decided to reunite with his wife—and wanted nothing to do with the two-month-old baby girl beside her, crying to be fed.

Hagar also felt abandoned and hopeless. During the feast to celebrate Isaac's weaning, Hagar's teenage son had mocked Isaac. Abraham's wife Sarah had demanded that Abraham get rid of his concubine and her son. Since Isaac was the son through whom God's covenant with Abraham would be fulfilled, God approved the separation, but he didn't forsake Hagar and Ishmael.

Abraham sent Hagar away with some food and a container of water. She and Ishmael wandered aimlessly in the wilderness until the water ran out, and then Hagar separated herself from her son. She couldn't bear the anguish of watching him die. But the same God who instructed Hagar to name her son Ishmael ("God hears") heard his cries. The God whom Hagar called "the One who sees me" (16:13) opened her eyes to see a well of water. God continued to be with her son as he grew up and fathered a great nation of people.

Sometimes we feel abandoned by the very people who should love and protect us. Whether we're a single parent raising children with no help or estranged from someone with whom we once had a close relationship, it can be frightening. It may seem at times that no one on earth cares for us, but God hears our cries and sees our needs. He will protect and provide for us—whether we're alone in our apartments or in the middle of a wilderness.

God has said, "I will never fail you. I will never abandon you."
Hebrews 13:5

March 12

Acceptable but Not Advisable
SARAH

Genesis 16:4-5; 17:20

Catching a glimpse of the clock on her nightstand, Mary groaned. She had been looking forward to turning twenty-one and enjoying her special evening at the hottest bar in town, but she had forgotten the custom of drinking a toast with every sorority sister present. After a night of throwing up, she had missed her interview appointment. Mary knew that she wouldn't get another shot at the internship. *I missed my big chance, and all for the sake of a campus tradition,* she thought as she ran to the bathroom.

Sarah's decision to have Abraham sleep with her servant was perfectly acceptable according to the customs of that time. If Hagar had a male child and Abraham adopted him, he could become the legal son and heir. Since Sarah was barren and approaching eighty years old, it seemed obvious to her that God didn't intend for the promised son to come from her. After so many years of waiting, perhaps she felt relieved that she had figured out a solution to their problem. Sarah soon learned that although the world considered her "solution" morally sound, God did not approve of it. The bitter consequences affected her and the history of two nations.

The fact that something is legal doesn't mean that it's a good idea. The world considers acceptable many things of which God doesn't approve. Premarital sex, homosexuality, and abortion may be sanctioned by society, but they are not part of God's plan for us. These choices can result in serious consequences that will plague us for the rest of our lives, much as Sarah's decision affected her. When deciding on a course of action, it's not enough to ask whether or not our choice is legal or acceptable in the world's opinion; a far wiser decision is to make sure that it's godly. If we allow God to guide our decisions, we can expect positive consequences, which can also have lasting effects.

> You say, "I am allowed to do anything"—but not everything is good
> for you.
> 1 Corinthians 6:12

March 13

Busy Hands
DORCAS

Acts 9:36-42

The teenage girl brushed the soft baby afghan against her cheek. She had found the pink-and-white blanket in a bag of gifts that her mentor from the Crisis Pregnancy Center had just dropped off in her hospital room. As a single mom on public aid, the girl couldn't afford to buy even the necessities. Her eyes filled with tears as she thought of her sweet baby girl wrapped up in the pretty, hand-knit afghan. Meanwhile, across town, an elderly, homebound woman sat knitting and praying for young women she would never meet.

Dorcas, or Tabitha, was another believer with busy hands. Seeing the poor and needy in her town stirred her compassion and spurred her to use her sewing ability to help clothe them. Dorcas developed a reputation for doing kind things and for helping the poor. When she died, the other believers were so heartbroken that they sent for Peter.

The widows showed Peter the clothing and coats that Dorcas had made for them. They probably wouldn't have had adequate clothing except for this special woman's kindness. Each one wept as she remembered things that Dorcas had done especially for her. Peter sent them out of the room and prayed, and God brought Dorcas back to life.

Too often in the church, attention tends to focus on the more visible ministries. If we aren't involved in speaking, teaching, or performing, we may feel that we don't have much to offer. But God has given his children all kinds of gifts and abilities. Practical skills such as sewing, cooking, decorating, and organizing may not be flashy, but they can have a tremendous impact on other people's lives. Whatever ability we have can bless others if we dedicate it to God. We can't all sew clothes, but we can all sow seeds of kindness—using whatever tool God has given us.

Each one should use whatever gift he has received to serve others, faithfully administering God's grace in its various forms.
1 Peter 4:10 (NIV)

March 14

Ready for the Truth
RAHAB

Joshua 2:1-11

"Mommy, why didn't my birth mother want to keep me?"

Roberta looked down at her little girl's brown eyes and wrinkled forehead. *How should I answer this?* she wondered. Maggie had always known that she had been adopted as a newborn, that God had chosen her as a special gift for a family with no children. But lately, she had been asking more probing questions.

"Let's go out on the deck, sweetheart," Roberta said. She knew that Maggie was ready to hear the truth.

Rahab was also ready to receive the truth. She had heard reports of how the God of Israel miraculously parted the Red Sea for his people, and how they later conquered two powerful Amorite kings. Perhaps she had mulled these stories over in her mind, filled with curiosity about the God who proved himself so much more powerful and merciful than the pagan gods of her Canaanite people. Then, amazingly, two men who worshiped Yahweh walked into her house. Along with the rest of her people, Rahab dreaded Israel's inevitable attack on Jericho, but despite her fear, Rahab embraced the little that she knew about Yahweh and declared her belief in him as the one true God.

In all the evil, violent city of Jericho, God found only one person receptive to his truth. When he saw Rahab's heart probing for him, he directed the spies to her house. Yahweh deals with people in the same way today. When he sees someone searching for him, he provides an opportunity for that person to connect with him. We don't have to understand everything in the Bible to become God's children; we just have to accept the truth that God sent Christ to die for our sin. As we grow spiritually, God reveals further truth to us as long as we are faithful to what we already understand. He will always send the truth that we are ready for.

> *You received the Spirit because you believed the message you heard about Christ.*
> *Galatians 3:2*

March 15

Defining Moment
RAHAB

Joshua 2:3

When the two Israelite spies chose to stay in Rahab's house overnight, it triggered a defining moment in her life. The king of Jericho soon learned about the men's presence in the city and their mission to spy out the land. He immediately sent soldiers to demand that Rahab turn over the men. If Rahab complied, she would probably be generously rewarded for protecting her city. If the king learned that she had hidden the men on her roof, she would be executed for treason. Would Rahab obey her king or act on the little knowledge she had of Israel's Yahweh?

Many of us have faced a defining moment similar to Rahab's. We may be offered a promotion and a nice raise, but the extra hours would force us to neglect our family's needs. Or we might be confronted with a situation where our boss expects us to do something that contradicts God's ways, and our refusal might mean being fired. We may have to decide between pursuing our own interests and making a commitment to care for a parent with Alzheimer's.

Sometimes our circumstances force us to choose between turning down something in order to follow God more fully or just going along with the status quo. Rahab's choice would determine whether she placed her allegiance with her own pagan city or with Israel's God, who had demonstrated his powerful protection of his people. In a similar way, our daily choices determine whether we will follow the earthly kingdom around us or God's Kingdom, which represents a better way of living. It's always hard to turn down something that looks valuable or necessary to our happiness, but in the long run, obeying God is always the better choice.

What is God asking you to turn down in order to follow him more fully?

March 16

Risking Everything
RAHAB

Joshua 2:11-16

In January 1956, five American missionaries made contact with a previously unreached tribe of Auca Indians in Ecuador. After an initial friendly encounter, five violent Waorani men returned to spear the missionaries to death. Some time later, a representative from the tribe invited Rachel Saint and Elisabeth Elliot to live with them. Because these women risked their lives by staying with the killers of their brother and husband, the Waorani opened their hearts to God's forgiveness and broke free from their lifestyle of fear and revenge killings.

Rahab also took a risk for God. She believed that Yahweh was the one true God, and she wanted to be on the winning side in the coming battle. Her faith emboldened her to risk her life to protect the Israelite spies, hiding them on her roof and sending the king's soldiers on a wild goose chase. The next day, Rahab helped the spies escape down a scarlet rope through the window of her house. Rahab knew that if the soldiers figured out that she had deceived them, she would be executed for helping enemy spies. She must have suffered some anxious moments, but her belief in God's power overcame her fear of what might happen to her.

Living for God can be risky business. He asks us to turn over complete control of every aspect of our lives to him. Sometimes he even expects us to do things that appear dangerous or life threatening. Whatever dangers we face, we can trust him to control every circumstance. We can also rest secure in knowing that even after death, we will remain safe in his hands. When we understand God's goodness and power, we understand that following him is never really a risk—it's the only sure thing.

> *I know the one in whom I trust, and I am sure that he is able to guard what I have entrusted to him until the day of his return.*
> *2 Timothy 1:12*

March 17

Faith in Action
RAHAB

Joshua 2:17-24

June watched the car pull out of her driveway, then walked back toward the house with a heavy heart. She wished that she had never introduced her coworker to her brother. After just three months of dating, Dan was hopelessly in love and had already proposed. Hallie claimed to love Dan, but June had her doubts. Their relationship looked more like that of a queen and her subject than two people in love with each other. All the affection seemed to be on one side. June wondered if Hallie understood that love requires more than words.

Rahab declared her belief in the true God, and she was required to demonstrate her belief by taking action. In return for helping the Israelite spies escape, they agreed to spare her and her family on the condition that she leave the scarlet rope hanging from her window. As the days dragged on, did she anxiously wonder if the spies would keep their word to a prostitute in an enemy city? Did she frequently check the rope to make sure that it was still in place, reassuring herself that she had done what was necessary to save her family?

In the Bible, God tells about people who honor him with their lips while their hearts are far from him (see Isaiah 29:13). Genuine faith demands more than words—it calls for action. Rahab acted on her belief in God by aiding the spies and following their instructions. We prove our faith in God by how well we follow his instructions, which results in our spiritual growth and in loving service to others. If we truly believe in God, our faith will be as visible as a scarlet rope hanging from a window.

Just as the body is dead without breath, so also faith is dead without good works.
James 2:26

March 18

A Promise Kept
RAHAB

Joshua 6:1-25

The elderly woman sat in front of her house, her eyes fixed on the dirt road that wound toward the village. She smiled as she fingered the well-worn note in her pocket. Eight years had passed since her son had left for America in search of a better life. People in the village predicted that he would forget his promise to come back for her, but she knew better. Suddenly, she noticed a cloud of dust in the distance.

Rahab didn't have to wait long to see if the spies would keep their promise. Less than a month after the spies' visit, all of Jericho watched the Israelite forces silently march around the walled city. For six days, Rahab's family huddled together in her house, watching and wondering what would happen. Nothing could have prepared them for the dramatic events of the seventh day. When the Israelites shouted, Rahab must have watched in amazement as the thick, fortified walls fell flat. Was the section that included her house left standing? She must have still been stunned as the two former spies escorted her family to safety.

God's children live with a promise more powerful than the one that Rahab clung to as she waited for the attack on Jericho. We have God's pledge that someday we will begin glorious new lives with him that will last forever. We can get so caught up in our busy lives that we forget that this earth is marked for destruction. Although God desires everyone to come to him, he will eventually judge the world for rejecting him, just as he judged Jericho when its time had come. We don't know when this will happen, but no matter how bad things get, we have God's promise that he will one day escort us to safety.

> *Let us hold tightly without wavering to the hope we affirm, for God can be trusted to keep his promise.*
> *Hebrews 10:23*

March 19

A Transformed Life
RAHAB

Matthew 1:5; Hebrews 11:31

Rahab's step of faith did more than save her life—it transformed it. After the former spies moved Rahab to a safe place near their camp, she seems to fall out of the picture—until we reach the New Testament and discover that she played a key role in Israel's history. Even before Jericho's destruction, Rahab believed in the power of Israel's God. As she lived among the Israelites and learned more about their God, she also experienced his forgiveness, mercy, and grace.

This former prostitute's shameful past disappeared just as surely as the city of Jericho went up in smoke. She dedicated herself to living in a way that would please God. As she became a godly woman, eventually a prince from the tribe of Judah chose her to be his wife. Rahab and Salmon became the great-great-grandparents of King David. Their names are included in Matthew's genealogy of Jesus Christ. Any memories of her old life as a prostitute in a pagan city must have renewed Rahab's wonder and gratitude that God's grace had given her a new life.

God also honored Rahab by including her as one of two women mentioned by name in the Hebrews chapter that lists some heroes of the faith. He wants each of us to become a faith hero. Part of this process involves giving up things, which can be painful. Leaving a life of crime or blatant immorality to follow Christ is a no-brainer, but sometimes God calls us to abandon habits that seem harmless or activities that are good in themselves. The things that we balk at relinquishing are the things that keep us from experiencing the transformed life that God desires for us. Before we fully become what he wants us to be, we may have to watch some things go up in smoke, as Rahab did.

> *Some of you were once like that. But you were cleansed; you were made holy; you were made right with God by calling on the name of the Lord Jesus Christ and by the Spirit of our God.*
> *1 Corinthians 6:11*

March 20

Dying in Order to Live
WITNESSES TO JESUS' TRIUMPHANT ENTRY

Matthew 21:1-11

In spite of the chilly temperatures, the calendar assured Madison that today was the first day of spring. Throwing on a sweater, she stepped outdoors to look for further evidence. Sure enough, straight green shoots pushed out of the soil in her flower bed. Madison smiled as she closed her eyes and envisioned how her yard would soon look, filled with blooms from bulbs that had rested underground for months. Shrubs that now looked dead would be covered with blossoms. *I wish we could just take winter out of the year,* she thought.

The women in the crowd who accompanied Jesus into Jerusalem must have felt that a new season had begun. By riding into Jerusalem on a colt, Jesus fulfilled a prophecy that revealed him as the Messiah. The crowds followed along, spreading garments and branches in his path and shouting praises of their long-awaited King. They believed that a new day had dawned for the nation groaning under Roman oppression.

As Jesus rode toward Jerusalem that day, it seemed that his ministry was blossoming. The people recognized his glory and followed him. But Jesus foresaw that in a matter of days one of his disciples would betray him, the crowds would turn against him, and he would be humiliated and suffer a painful death. Jesus also knew that without his death, there would be no resurrection and no payment of the price that our sin demanded.

Death is necessary in the natural and the spiritual worlds. We have to die to our sinful nature in order to experience new life as believers in Christ. Becoming more like him requires that we make this choice daily. Eventually, our physical deaths will open the door to eternity, and we will live in a season that has no darkness, no cold, and no end.

> *Those who live only to satisfy their own sinful nature will harvest decay and death from that sinful nature. But those who live to please the Spirit will harvest everlasting life from the Spirit.*
> *Galatians 6:8*

March 21

Mob Action
WOMEN IN THE CROWD

Matthew 27:20-26

The girl sat between her parents at the police station, staring at the floor. It all seemed unreal—she had never even hit anyone before. She went to the park only because her friends said they needed her. Then the other group showed up, and things got out of hand. The next thing she remembered was holding a baseball bat, with a girl lying at her feet.

The same people that adored Jesus when he made his triumphant entry into Jerusalem turned into a hateful mob only a few days later. Since Pilate believed Jesus to be an innocent man, he offered the crowd a choice between releasing Jesus and releasing Barabbas, a murderer. At the religious leaders' urging, the crowd chose Barabbas. Each time Pilate asked a question, the crowd shouted, "Crucify! Crucify!" The chanting whipped the crowd into such a frenzy that they screamed for the responsibility for Jesus' death to fall on them and their children.

I can only imagine how sickened any women who participated in this scene felt the next day, wondering how they could have been so cruel and bloodthirsty. History reveals that people will do things as part of a crowd that they would never dream of doing individually, even to the point of attacking someone. When people get caught up in group emotions, they tend to follow along even when a rash action conflicts with their values.

We also face the danger of being led astray by our culture. Every day, we're surrounded by the loud voices of the media urging us to behave in ways that go against God's values. If we aren't careful to listen to God's voice, we may wake up one day and find that we have done something we never dreamed we were capable of doing.

[The Lord said,] "You must not follow the crowd in doing wrong." Exodus 23:2

March 22

Surprising Courage
WOMEN AT THE TOMB

Matthew 28:1-5

Lois held her whimpering toddler close and rocked him. If it hadn't been for their dripping clothes, she would have thought she had dreamed the last few minutes. She and Jacob had stopped at the house of their vacationing neighbor to feed the cat and water the flowers on the deck. When Lois heard a sudden splash, she jumped into the deep end of the pool without a second thought. Now she wondered how she had managed to pull Jacob out. Lois didn't know how to swim, and she had been afraid of deep water since childhood.

The women who went to Jesus' tomb two days after his crucifixion also displayed surprising courage. When an angel rolled the stone away from the tomb and sat on it, his face shone like lightning and his clothing was a brilliant white. The Roman guards shook with fear and fainted when they saw him, but the women listened to what the angel had to say. How did these women, already weakened by grief at witnessing Jesus' crucifixion, stand up to such a terrifying sight when Roman soldiers, trained for hardship and combat, fainted?

The soldiers considered Jesus a criminal and stood guard to prevent his followers from stealing his body and pretending that he had risen from the dead. The women came to tend the body of the leader they had loved and served. Although the angel's appearance alarmed them, their pure motives gave them the courage to face the situation despite their fear. When we concentrate on loving and serving God, we find surprising courage just when we need it. Even when fear would be a natural response, our faith will help us to face whatever comes our way—rather than faint like a Roman soldier.

Be strong and courageous, all you who put your hope in the LORD!
Psalm 31:24

March 23

Come and See
WOMEN AT THE TOMB

Matthew 28:5-6

A hush fell on the room as Gina described the week she had spent helping to repair homes hit by Hurricane Katrina. We all had been affected by news of the disaster. When we saw television images of flattened buildings and homeless families, our hearts went out to the victims. But Gina spoke as an eyewitness. She had seen for herself the vast piles of debris where homes, churches, and schools once stood. She had looked into the hopeless faces of people who had lost everything they owned in a matter of seconds. For her, the tragedy was real in a way that the rest of us could only try to comprehend.

God planned for the women at the tomb to be eyewitnesses of the Resurrection. The angel's word would have been sufficient to convince the women that Jesus had been raised from the dead, but the angel encouraged them to come inside the tomb and see for themselves that Jesus' body was no longer there. Instead of anointing his body as they had intended, the women had the privilege of being the first to hear the news that he had risen. As they stepped through the opening as into a dream, did they understand that the rock had not been rolled away to let Jesus out, but to let them in?

God still invites people to see the truth. He lovingly calls each of us to come to that place in faith where we can see for ourselves the reality of the sacrifice he made for us. We may not enter the physical tomb where Jesus' body was laid, but we can read the account of his death, burial, and resurrection in the Bible. Through receiving and believing the gospel, we can have a personal relationship with God. Then, when we talk about him, we'll be reporting what we have seen and experienced, not just repeating hearsay.

[The angel said,] "Come, see where his body was lying."
Matthew 28:6

March 24

Go and Tell
WOMEN AT THE TOMB

Matthew 28:7

Melissa hung up the phone and laughed out loud. Such wonderful news! For six long years, her daughter and son-in-law had hoped to adopt a newborn. Now they had connected with a pregnant teenage girl who was trying to place her baby. Melissa beamed as she picked up the phone to call her friends, and then she froze. Maybe it was too early in the process to tell everyone. Maybe her daughter wanted to be the one to make the announcement. After all, Melissa didn't have their permission to spread the news. *Maybe this isn't the right time to talk about it,* she thought.

The women at the tomb didn't have to ponder this question as Melissa did. Standing inside the empty tomb, they must have struggled to take in the meaning of it all. How long would they have stood there, frozen in place, as they stared at the burial cloths where Jesus' body had been placed? The angel spoke again, jolting them back to the present moment. "Go quickly and tell his disciples that he has risen from the dead," he instructed them. The women had the most important message of all time to deliver—Jesus Christ was alive.

We all love to share news, especially when it's something joyful. But when it comes to sharing the good news about Jesus, we hesitate and make excuses. We don't want to force our beliefs on others, or invade their privacy, or offend them by being too pushy. But how can we even think of keeping the most wonderful news of all time to ourselves? God's Word reminds us that we have the privilege and responsibility of sharing the gospel with others. To truly celebrate Easter, we need to make sure that we not only "come and see" but also "go and tell" that Jesus is alive.

> [The angel said,] "And now, go quickly and tell his disciples that he has risen from the dead."
> *Matthew 28:7*

March 25

Instant Obedience
WOMEN AT THE TOMB

Matthew 28:8-10

"One, two, . . ." *Why do we have to go through this same routine every night?*
Dana wondered. Her four-year-old daughter knew the rules. ". . . three,
four, five, . . ." Ten minutes before bedtime, Stacey was supposed to put
away her toys. ". . . six, seven, . . ." If she didn't do it, she got a warning.
". . . eight, nine, . . ." After the second warning, Stacey had until a count of
ten to finish her chore, or she would forfeit *The Wiggles* and *Dora* the next
day. ". . . ten!" Stacey slowly rolled off the couch and began picking up tiny
Barbie shoes.

The women who went to Jesus' tomb give us a beautiful picture of
obedience and its rewards. The angel's appearance and words bewildered
them, and they didn't yet understand the full implications of the empty
tomb. But when the angel told them to take the news to Jesus' disciples,
they immediately ran, rather than walked, to follow his instructions. On the
way, the women had an even greater surprise when Jesus suddenly greeted
them. If the empty tomb had filled them with joy, how wild their emotions
must have been at this unexpected meeting with their beloved Master.

Most of us can be slow at times in following God's commands. When
we discover a new truth in his Word, we may spend time thinking it over
instead of immediately applying it to our lives. If his Spirit urges us to do
something, we can come up with lots of excuses to put it off or avoid it.
True obedience is doing something when we're told to do it, no matter
how fearful, confused, or tired we are. Just as the women's obedience was
rewarded with unspeakable joy, God rewards us when we obey him. And
he doesn't want to have to count to ten.

I will hurry, without delay, to obey your commands.
Psalm 119:60

March 26

Believing without Seeing
EYEWITNESSES OF THE RESURRECTED JESUS

John 20:19-29; 1 Corinthians 15:6

In 1998, a Congressman announced to his colleagues in the House of Representatives that comedian Bob Hope had died. Within seconds, media outlets across the world rushed to prepare tributes to the entertainer. Bob Hope's daughter Linda had quite a different perspective. She immediately phoned news agencies to deny the reports. At her home in Pasadena, California, Linda was watching her father eat his breakfast.

The women in the passage in John had a different perspective on Jesus' death. It's hard to imagine the emotions of the women who saw Jesus after his resurrection. They had witnessed his slow, agonizing death on the cross. Some of them had watched Joseph of Arimathea wrap his body in linen and place it in the tomb. When Jesus first appeared to the women, they must have wondered—were they dreaming now, or had the past few days just been a nightmare? Jesus came to them in a body that they could touch, yet he could appear and disappear at will. The women's ecstasy must have exceeded anything they had ever experienced, a deep joy that would stay with them for the rest of their lives.

Some people think that faith requires miraculous signs and angelic appearances. When Jesus appeared to his disciples, he pronounced a special blessing on those who would believe without seeing him. This blessing includes everyone who accepts the evidence that God has given us. The Bible and other historical accounts establish Jesus' life, death, and resurrection. When we investigate Jesus through the biblical account of his life, God lets us see Jesus with eyes of faith. Then we discover the special joy that comes from knowing that Jesus is alive, not because we saw his body with our own eyes, but because God has revealed him to us.

> *You love him even though you have never seen him. Though you do not see him now, you trust him; and you rejoice with a glorious, inexpressible joy.*
> *Peter 1:8*

March 27

Is That All There Is?
THE WIVES OF SADDUCEES

Matthew 22:23-33

"Mommy, will I ever see Grandma again?"

The question haunted Jessie long after she had tucked Emma into bed. Her pat answer, "She'll live in our hearts as long as we remember her," didn't fully satisfy her daughter—and now Jessie had doubts of her own. She had always considered herself too "enlightened" for her mom's old-fashioned beliefs about heaven and life after death. But to think of her mother's vibrant spirit and loving nature being snuffed out like a flame, with nothing left but memories? Jessie began to wonder. . . .

The Sadducees were religious leaders in Jesus' day who did not believe in angels, spirits, or life after death. When they designed a question to ridicule the idea of resurrection, Jesus answered that they did not know the Word or the power of God.

Did the Sadducees' wives accept their husbands' beliefs, or did some of them secretly believe that life goes on after death? As they attended the funerals of family members and friends, did they struggle with the idea that their loved ones had simply ceased to exist? When they heard about the confrontation between the Sadducees and Jesus and heard his answer, perhaps some of them embraced the assurance that they had been longing for.

Our beliefs about death help to determine how we live. The Bible teaches that we will continue to live for eternity, with God or without him. Now is the time to get to know God, to do his will, and to share the truth about him with others. If we think that life ends when our bodies die, then it doesn't matter much how we spend our brief time on earth. To think that God would create us and then snuff us out would make anyone sad, even someone who wasn't a Sadducee.

Yes, we are fully confident, and we would rather be away from these earthly bodies, for then we will be at home with the Lord.
2 Corinthians 5:8

March 28

Hurting God
WOMEN WHO SAW JESUS' WOUNDS

Luke 24:35-40

Heather watched the door and fidgeted with the hospital sheets. Her mind still struggled to piece the last few weeks together. She remembered stepping off the subway after the late shift. After that, she depended on others to fill in the details of the robbery attempt, the stranger who stepped in to stop the vicious attack, the head injury that had kept her in a coma for twelve days. Heather answered the gentle knock and gasped. A man limped in with one arm in a sling, a patch over his right eye, and deep cuts still healing across his cheekbone. Tears filled Heather's eyes. *He got those injuries while saving my life.*

Tears must have also filled the eyes of the women who saw Jesus after his resurrection. Although he had a glorified body capable of appearing and disappearing, the marks of his crucifixion remained visible. The loving hands that had reached out to comfort and heal people now bore the imprints of cruel Roman nails. The feet that had walked miles to teach and minister to hurting people displayed deep gashes. The image of Jesus' hands and feet burned into the women's minds for the rest of their lives and gradually took on deeper meaning as they understood that he had suffered to save them.

A mental image of the wounds in the resurrected Jesus' hands and feet serves as a powerful reminder of the ordeal he suffered for us. What we *can't* see are the wounds that we inflict on God by loving other things more than him. He grieves anytime we turn away from him to seek comfort or fulfillment in another source. Since God wants what is best for us, it hurts him when we refuse to let him meet our needs. If we could see how our rebelliousness affects God, our eyes would be full of tears as well.

> *How I have been hurt by their adulterous hearts which turned away from Me.*
> *Ezekiel 6:9 (NASB)*

March 29

Access to God
THE TORN CURTAIN

Exodus 26:31-33; Mark 15:37-38

The woman stared at the pile of rubble where the concrete wall had once stood, topped with barbed wire and guarded by watchtowers. All her life, the Berlin Wall had cut through her city, separating East from West. After seeing the television images of the barrier coming down, she had wanted to see it for herself. She didn't fully understand all the ramifications of the wall's removal, yet she felt a surge of excitement.

A barrier also went down more than two thousand years ago. As Jesus took his last breath on a cross outside Jerusalem, the thick curtain in the Temple ripped in half from top to bottom. How did the Jewish women feel when they heard about this bizarre event? They knew that God had given instructions for the curtain to be hung in front of the Most Holy Place as a symbol of the separation between the people and his presence. They knew that only the high priest could pass through the curtain, and then only on the annual Day of Atonement. As Jesus' followers grasped the meaning of the torn curtain, their minds must have filled with awe that the barrier between them and God had been removed.

Although the New Testament explains the relationship between Jesus' death and the ripping of the Temple curtain (see Hebrews 10:19-22), it is still hard for us to grasp the significance of the event. We're all affected by the barrier that went up between God and every human being at the moment when sin entered the world. But since we haven't lived with that constant visual reminder, it's difficult for us to fully comprehend its removal. Jesus' perfect sacrifice opened up access to God and provided a way for sinful men and women to be united with their heavenly Father. Like the Berlin Wall, the barrier has been removed; now we are free to enter God's presence.

> *By his death, Jesus opened a new and life-giving way through the curtain into the Most Holy Place.*
> *Hebrews 10:20*

March 30

Someone's Already There
JESUS' ASCENSION

Acts 1:6-11

Barb yawned and turned onto the long gravel driveway that led to her parents' lakeside cabin. Glancing at her watch, she grimaced. *Maybe I should have waited 'til tomorrow to come. It'll be two in the morning by the time I get things set up.* Barb was surprised to see her sister's car in front of the cabin and felt relieved to know that the heat would already be turned on. More surprises greeted her as she lugged her bag to the bedroom. The bed looked inviting, with new, turned-down flannel sheets. On the nightstand stood her favorite roast beef sandwich, with a note that said "ENJOY."

When Jesus physically ascended into heaven, his followers didn't immediately grasp all the implications of his leaving them. Their minds strained to comprehend recent events: Jesus had been arrested and executed, three days later he rose from the dead, and for forty days he appeared to groups of his followers to comfort and teach them. Now Jesus had risen into the skies in a cloud. Only later, through the help of the Holy Spirit, would believers fully understand what it meant to them personally that Jesus had returned to heaven.

Whatever we face in life, we can know that Jesus has already been there ahead of us. He willingly took on a human body and suffered the same temptations and trials that we go through so he could identify with us. If we experience loneliness or rejection, we can find strength and compassion from One who endured those same things on our behalf. If we struggle with grief and troubles, the Man of Sorrows offers us comfort. Jesus has gone ahead of us into heaven. Someday, we'll arrive to find the new home he has prepared for us and really learn the meaning of "ENJOY."

> *I am going there to prepare a place for you.*
> *John 14:2 (NIV)*

March 31

Be Prepared
THE TEN BRIDESMAIDS

Matthew 25:1-13

As I stood in the kitchen looking over my menu, I felt uneasy but not panicked. I had estimated the time it would take my husband's family to drive from Memphis to central Illinois. Taking into account that they probably wouldn't leave as early as they planned, I figured that I still had an hour and a half. We probably wouldn't eat until midafternoon. But as always, I wished I had done more preparation ahead of time. *I could have made those pies a day earlier,* I thought. Just as I picked up a knife to peel potatoes, our guests walked in.

Jesus' parable of the ten bridesmaids waiting to join the wedding procession illustrates the danger of not being spiritually prepared. Five women took extra oil for their lamps, and five didn't bring enough. When the groom finally showed up at midnight, the bridesmaids who needed more oil panicked and begged the others to lend them some. When their request was denied, the women rushed out to try to buy oil. They arrived late to the wedding feast and pleaded to be admitted, but the groom refused. Only the bridesmaids who had thought ahead enjoyed the privilege of participating in the festivities.

Many people are living like the foolish bridesmaids, going through life without giving a thought to their eternal destinies. When we're healthy and happy, it's tempting to ignore our spiritual needs. It's easy to get so caught up in the present that we don't prepare for the future. We forget that a day is coming when we'll stand before our Creator to account for our lives. When that moment comes, we don't want to be like the bridesmaids who heard the groom say, "I don't know you!" We want God to find us spiritually prepared so we can enjoy the festivities with him.

> *[Jesus said,] "You also must be ready all the time, for the Son of Man will come when least expected."*
> *Luke 12:40*

April 1

Delayed Answers
MARTHA AND MARY

John 11:1-6

Janice rubbed her swollen ankle and stared at the clock. *What on earth could be taking him so long?* she wondered again. When she had called Steve to tell him she'd sprained her ankle, he readily agreed to leave work early. Now there had been more than enough time for him to get home, and the kids were clamoring for dinner. Finally, the back door opened and Steve walked in with a bag from their favorite Mexican restaurant, a bouquet of roses, and a box of chocolates.

The two women in today's Bible passage also waited and wondered. When their brother became seriously ill, Martha and Mary naturally turned to Jesus for help. The three enjoyed a close friendship with Jesus, who often stayed at their home. The sisters had seen Jesus perform miracles and knew that he had the ability to heal Lazarus. Martha and Mary were heartbroken when Lazarus died soon after the messenger left. As the next few days dragged by, their grief must have mingled with disappointment and confusion at Jesus' delay in responding to their message.

God's children naturally cry out for his help in times of sudden trouble or sorrow. We know that he loves us enough that he died for us. We also know that he has the power to control any situation in our lives. But when he doesn't respond to our pleas right away, we may become confused, despondent, angry, or bitter.

It's hard to remember that God has a plan and that he will answer our prayers according to *his* timing. When his answer comes, it is often better than what we requested. Jesus delayed in responding to Martha and Mary's message because God had something far greater than a healing in mind. When God seems slow to move in our situations, we can be sure that he has something greater in store for us.

> *The Scriptures give us hope and encouragement as we wait patiently for God's promises to be fulfilled.*
> *Romans 15:4*

April 2

Limited Understanding
MARTHA

John 11:17-26

My friend Lisa's son always preferred academics over sports. One day when he was in the fourth grade, his PE class played baseball. While Mark was on base, a batter hit the ball. Seeing that Mark was daydreaming, the teacher and his friends all began shouting, "Run home, Mark! Run home!" Mark immediately took off—in the direction of his house, which was a few blocks from the school.

Sometimes we don't fully comprehend what someone is saying to us. When Jesus told Martha that her brother would rise again, she assumed that he was referring to the final resurrection of the dead. Martha had no idea that Jesus was about to perform a miracle. Filled with grief over the loss of her beloved brother, she thought that Jesus meant to comfort her by reminding her of a future event. Martha's understanding was limited to the familiar teachings about the resurrection of the dead. Although she acknowledged Jesus as the Messiah and Son of God, her mind could not conceive what he had in mind.

We all struggle with limited understanding of God. We have no trouble believing that he controls the universe, but it may be harder to accept that he is involved in the details of our lives. We understand that Jesus died to secure eternal life for us, but we don't quite understand the abundant life that he promised his followers. It's easier to embrace the idea of going to heaven someday to be with God than it is to understand that he lives in us right now. Like Martha, we don't always fully comprehend what God is saying to us, but he will help us grow until the day in heaven when there are no limits to our understanding.

All that I know now is partial and incomplete, but then I will know everything completely, just as God now knows me completely.
1 Corinthians 13:12

April 3

The Most Important Answer
MARTHA

John 11:27

Martha may not have understood the full meaning of Jesus' comment that her brother would rise again, but she knew the right answer to his next question. Jesus said, "I am the resurrection and the life. Anyone who believes in me will live, even after dying" (John 11:25). When he asked Martha if she believed that, her response revealed her deep faith. Without hesitation, Martha affirmed that Jesus was the Son of God, the promised Messiah whom God had sent into the world.

Like Martha, each of us must answer the question that Jesus posed to his disciples in Luke 9: "Who do you say I am?" Our relationship with God and the eternal destiny of our souls depend on what we believe about Jesus' identity. Was he simply a good, moral man who taught God's ways to his followers? Was he deceiving people or himself when he claimed to be the Son of God? Or was he who he claimed to be—God in human form, who came to earth to die for our sins so that we could have a personal relationship with our Creator?

Once we know the answer to the all-important question, "Who do you say I am?" we have a rock-solid foundation for our lives. There will always be times when we don't know what God is doing. We will always struggle with some aspects of the spiritual life and find some parts of the Bible hard to understand. But even when we're confused or disappointed, we can hang on to what we do know—that Jesus Christ is Lord of our lives and that he is always trustworthy. When we face questions we can't answer, it isn't *what* but *whom* we know that counts.

> *I know the one in whom I trust.*
> *2 Timothy 1:12*

April 4

The Heart of God
SEEING JESUS WEEP

John 11:28-37

During a wedding ceremony, all eyes are usually on the bride, but during Keisha's wedding, everyone's attention shifted to the groom. Before that day, many people wondered what had attracted Keisha to Jack. Keisha was a petite, dainty bookworm, and Jack was a big, burly outdoorsman, several years older than she was. Halfway through the ceremony, the guests discovered what Keisha saw in him—a tender heart. This former football player and ex-marine cried like a baby as he softly repeated his vows.

The women present in today's Bible passage must have been moved by Jesus' tears. Jesus had been deeply moved by the sight of Mary and the other mourners crying for Lazarus. Their grief had filled him with compassion and with anger over the anguish and death that sin had brought into the world. As he asked to be shown Lazarus's tomb, Jesus wept. Some interpreted his tears as a sign of how much he loved Lazarus; others asked why he couldn't have kept Lazarus from dying, since he had healed a blind man. None of the observers understood what they were seeing—the all-powerful God of the universe crying over the fallen state of the human race.

"Then Jesus wept." Those three short words reveal so much about God's heart and character. God is not a cold, stern taskmaster waiting to zap us when we mess up. As a loving Father, he chose to enter our world and share in human suffering. Sin and its consequences anger him, but he always has compassion on his children who come to him needing comfort and reassurance. When we're in pain, he hurts with us. When we mourn, he grieves too. When we cry, God sheds tears along with us. In the book of John, God gave us a touching picture of his compassion to help us remember that.

> *Then Jesus wept.*
> *John 11:35*

April 5

Rolling the Stone Away
MARTHA

John 11:38-40

My stomach felt queasy as I heard the story on the evening news. When neighbors complained about bad odors coming from a ramshackle house, authorities went to check on the elderly woman who lived there. She refused to answer the door or let the policemen in the house. When they finally opened the door, the smell almost knocked them down. Inside they found an unbelievable mess—cats crawling all over the place, furniture soaked with urine and feces, and piles of old garbage everywhere.

Since Lazarus had already been dead for four days, Martha knew that there would be a terrible smell from his decaying body. She recoiled at Jesus' instruction to roll the stone aside from the cave. Her brother was past the point of being healed. What possible good could come of opening his tomb and subjecting the mourners to the foul odor? When Jesus gently chided her for protesting, Martha relented and gave permission for the stone to be pushed aside. She trusted Jesus even when she didn't understand him.

We all have smelly things in our lives that we try to keep hidden from other people. Past events may fill us with shame, or we may struggle with an impure thought life, secret temptations, or a habit that we know displeases God. If people ever found out, they would be disgusted with us. So we seal off a part of our lives and try to ignore it.

God wants to renew every area of our lives. There is nothing too messy or repulsive for him to tackle, but he can't deal with those areas as long as we hold back. He waits for our permission to roll the stone away so that he can go in. Once we open up our secret areas to him, we'll be amazed at how fresh the air becomes.

> *"Roll the stone aside," Jesus told them.*
> *John 11:39*

April 6

Unexpected Joy
SEEING LAZARUS RISE

John 11:41-44

The distraught wife leaned against her father's strong shoulder. How much time had passed since the company spokesperson quietly shared the news with the group of relatives and friends? Rescue workers had confirmed that all the trapped miners were dead. Suddenly, the woman heard a commotion. Pushing through the crowd, she saw a man being helped out of the entrance. She caught her breath—could it be . . . ? The man looked into her face, and her knees buckled.

Martha and Mary received a similar shock four days after their brother died. When Jesus had the stone rolled away from the tomb, they had no clue as to what was in his mind. Perhaps he wanted to go into the cave and take one last look at his friend's body. They didn't expect Jesus to shout for Lazarus to come out of the grave. And they certainly didn't expect to see their brother walk out of the tomb, his head and body wrapped in burial cloths! The sisters, who had been mourning for four days, must have erupted into uncontrollable joy at the sight of their brother restored to life.

Since loss is a normal part of life, we all go through periods of mourning. During those times, we may feel that we will never laugh again, but when we grieve in a healthy way, we eventually move through the process and embrace happiness again. If we're in a close relationship with God, unexpected joy sometimes surprises us even in the midst of sorrow. Remembering that God can bring good out of any heartbreak helps us find comfort in his loving arms during the most painful times of our lives. It also helps to remember that a time is coming when everything that hurts us now will be replaced by everlasting joy.

You have turned my mourning into joyful dancing.
Psalm 30:11

April 7

An Innocent Man
PILATE'S WIFE

Matthew 27:11-19

Jane waited in her car, her eyes focused on the gate. Her brother was finally getting out of prison. The nightmare had begun eight years earlier, when Larry was accused of shooting a coworker. Another man testified against him, but Larry maintained his innocence. Only Jane stood behind him as their family and friends turned away, one by one. As the years passed, Jane clung to her trust in her brother's character and integrity. Now, new evidence had reopened the case and established his innocence.

Pilate's wife is mentioned only once in the Bible, but she has the distinction of being the only person who testified to Jesus' innocence during his trial. As the Roman governor sat in the judgment seat, she sent him a message urging him to "leave that innocent man alone." The passage tells us that she was deeply troubled by a nightmare she had about Jesus. We aren't given any details about the dream, and we don't know how it affected her life later. All we know is that Pilate's wife insisted on Jesus' innocence when his enemies falsely testified against him and the crowd turned on him.

According to polls conducted in 2002 by the Barna Group, 40 percent of American adults believe that Jesus Christ committed sins while living on the earth. That directly contradicts what the Bible teaches. Although Jesus faced the same temptations that we do, he never sinned (see Hebrews 4:15). Only a perfect, unblemished animal was acceptable for the Israelites' sacrifices, and only the perfect Son of God could bear the sins of the world. It's only because of Jesus' innocence that we can be freed from guilt. The Bible is the only evidence we need of that.

> *God made Christ, who never sinned, to be the offering for our sin, so that we could be made right with God through Christ.*
> *2 Corinthians 5:21*

April 8

Watching as Jesus Is Mocked
WITNESSES OF THE CRUCIFIXION

Matthew 27:27-44

In the crowd attending Jesus' trial and sentencing, his followers saw their beloved leader being mocked and tortured. When the Roman soldiers finished their cruel treatment of him, Jesus was so disfigured that he could hardly be recognized as a man. This fulfilled a prophecy from Isaiah 52:14. As Jesus hung on the cross, the mocking continued. The people passing by; the leading priests, religious teachers, and elders; and even the criminals crucified beside him all ridiculed Jesus.

Each scornful word must have cut deep into the heart of the women who had loved and served Jesus. The leaders got what they wanted, but they weren't satisfied with Jesus' death sentence. Now they taunted and mocked him as he suffered the painful execution. The women watched helplessly, unable to defend the man they had come to respect and honor.

People have never stopped mocking Jesus since that day on Calvary two thousand years ago. Some people dismiss any notion of a God and choose to worship themselves instead. Others accept the idea of a Supreme Being but scorn the idea that Jesus was anything but a good man and teacher. Our society grows bolder about openly mocking God in music lyrics, books, art, movies, and television shows.

Those of us who understand Jesus' sacrifice are wounded whenever we hear his name derided or used as profanity. We shouldn't be surprised when the world ridicules Jesus or when it ridicules us for believing in him. He warned his followers to expect the same type of treatment that he received. Jesus said we should welcome persecution because it means that we are faithful. When someone makes fun of us for believing in Jesus, we can look back to what he endured for us, then look ahead to our reward.

> *[Jesus said,] "God blesses you when people mock you and persecute you and lie about you and say all sorts of evil things against you because you are my followers."*
> *Matthew 5:11*

April 9

A World of Sorrow
DAUGHTERS OF JERUSALEM

Luke 23:26-31

Mandy took one look at the sunshine pouring through the window and pulled the comforter over her head. Each day, she had to fight a little harder just to get out of bed and get dressed. *Why bother?* Mandy groaned. *Something bad is sure to happen.* First, there had been the two miscarriages; then, both of her parents had been diagnosed with terminal cancer. Just days after the second funeral, Mandy learned that while she was dealing with her parents' illnesses, her husband had been having an affair with a family friend. A year later, Mandy still felt numb and wondered just how much pain one person could bear.

Even as Jesus faced his own excruciating pain, he showed compassion for women in sorrow. The large crowd that followed him to the cross included many women. They cried and stumbled along the road, overcome with grief at his death sentence. Jesus knew the anguish that awaited him on the cross, and he also knew the fate of Jerusalem. In about forty years, the Romans would destroy the city. Women with young children would suffer most from the violence. His heart ached for them even as he walked toward his death.

We all want to live happily ever after. We may think that God owes us a trouble-free life if we're doing our best to follow him. But as long as we live among imperfect people in a world corrupted by sin and Satan's evil influence, we can expect trials and sorrows. Disease, divorce, death, and other painful experiences can make us wonder if life is worth living. The only place where we can find comfort and strength is the cross, where Jesus voluntarily suffered pain and anguish so that he could share ours.

> [Jesus said,] *"Here on earth you will have many trials and sorrows. But take heart, because I have overcome the world."*
> *John 16:33*

April 10

Till the Very End
WOMEN AT THE CROSS

Matthew 27:45-61

As Jesus hung dying on the cross, a large group of women kept watch. Matthew identifies three of them: Mary Magdalene; Mary, the mother of James and Joseph; and the mother of James and John. In his gospel, John tells us that Jesus' mother and aunt, along with Mary Magdalene, stood near the foot of the cross (see John 19:25). These women, along with many other women, followed Jesus from Galilee to care for his needs. Even when events spun horribly out of control, they stayed with Jesus to the bitter end.

These women had witnessed Jesus teaching with undeniable authority, healing the sick, and even raising the dead, and they had devoted themselves to serving him. Now, the terrible turn of events left them frightened and stunned. It seemed that their hopes and dreams were dying along with their beloved Master as he gasped for breath. What strengthened these bewildered, heartbroken women and allowed them to stick with Jesus through the bitter end when others fled in fear? They stayed because of their love for him.

Sooner or later, each of us will face a moment when it seems that our hopes and dreams are dying. We may have crippling health problems, broken relationships, the loss of a loved one, or a child who chooses the wrong path. How will we react when, despite our desperate prayers, there is no visible sign of God's hand working in our lives? Will we give up our faith and walk away, or will we stay out of love for our Master? The women near the cross couldn't foresee the wonderful event that was coming in a couple of days. When we feel that we've reached the end of the road, we need to remember that we can't yet see what God has in store for us, either.

> *If we are faithful to the end, trusting God just as firmly as when we first believed, we will share in all that belongs to Christ.*
> *Hebrews 3:14*

April 11

Hope in the Midst of Grief
WOMEN MOURNING JESUS' DEATH

Rebecca dropped to her knees by the new tombstones glinting in the spring sunshine, one large and two small ones. It still seemed so unreal. . . . She had stayed home to get ready for the twins' birthday party, not knowing that a drunk driver would change her life forever. Doubling over, Rebecca exploded into tears once again. *If only I hadn't been so busy that morning. . . . If only I had known that it was the last time I would see them, the last chance to say "I love you."* . . . *If I could just tell them good-bye and hug them one last time. . . . If only . . .*

Jesus' sudden arrest and crucifixion must have seemed unreal to the women who loved and followed him. This was not how they expected things to turn out. The Messiah of Israel, who had taught them God's Word, healed their diseases, and loved them, was cruelly murdered. They had devoted themselves to serving Jesus; now he had been taken away from them. *If only I had known that it was the last time I would get to talk with him. . . . If only I had done more to show him that I loved him. . . . If I could just look into his eyes once again and say thank you.*

We never know when we will see someone for the last time. After the death of a loved one, our minds may dwell on things that we wish we had said to them or things we could have done differently. If the death came suddenly, we ache to tell them good-bye. The normal grieving process takes time, but if our loved ones believed in Jesus, we have the comfort of knowing that we will see them again. We can cling to the promise that they are safe in God's hands and that we will join them someday. Then our "if onlys" will disappear, and we will spend eternity together.

> *Dear brothers and sisters, we want you to know what will happen to the believers who have died so you will not grieve like people who have no hope.*
> *1 Thessalonians 4:13*

April 12

A Comforting Voice
MARY MAGDALENE

John 20:11-18

As Macy stared at the wall opposite her, she felt as if a crushing weight bore down on her. A rush of adrenaline had carried her through the phone call about her parents' accident and the long airplane flight. Now, with both of them in intensive care, a deep sense of grief gradually replaced the numbness. The doctor hadn't offered much encouragement. Fumbling in her purse for tissues, Macy realized that she had never felt so alone and dejected. Suddenly, she heard a voice calling her name. Turning toward the door of the waiting room, her eyes fell on Zoe, her best friend.

Mary Magdalene was also weighed down by sorrow when she went to Jesus' tomb. Confusion and anxiety added to her grief as she discovered that someone had stolen his body. After reporting the news to two disciples, Mary stood alone outside the tomb, crying. The nightmare of the past two days washed over her anew as she realized that she would be denied the privilege of helping to prepare Jesus' body for burial. Asking the man she thought was the gardener for information, she was startled when a familiar voice called her name: "Mary!"

When trouble suddenly interrupts our lives, grief and confusion can overwhelm us to the point that we feel crushed by the weight of our situation. Since God loves us more than anyone else, he can comfort us like no one else. Sometimes he consoles us through other people. Sometimes his Spirit breathes words of reassurance or makes his presence known. Often, he comforts us through his written Word. Sorrow in life is a given, but we have the choice of accepting the comfort that God offers. In any difficult situation, if we pay attention, we will hear a familiar voice calling our name. It's the voice of our Best Friend and Master.

> The LORD comforts his people and will have compassion on his afflicted ones.
> Isaiah 49:13 (NIV)

April 13

Money Well Spent
WOMEN WHO SUPPORTED JESUS' MINISTRY

Luke 8:1-3

I put the newspaper down and shook my head. I had occasionally read similar stories, but I still had a hard time believing that someone would live that way. A woman had died alone in a modest, barely furnished home. Although she had lived like a pauper, authorities later discovered that she had a fortune in the bank. How sad that the woman had hoarded her wealth instead of putting it to good use.

The women in today's Bible passage put their money to the best possible use. When Jesus began traveling through towns and villages to preach, he took his twelve disciples and a group of women along with him. Jesus had healed these women of diseases and demon possession; now, they showed their gratitude by ministering to him and to the disciples. They also helped to support Jesus and his disciples financially out of their own wealth. The arrangement was highly unusual in that culture, but Jesus accepted the women's service and financial support. Mary Magdalene, Joanna, Susanna, and the others considered it a blessing and a privilege to contribute to the ministry of the One who had given them new life.

In an uncertain world, it's tempting to concentrate on storing up as much wealth as possible. God wants us to plan wisely for our future; he also expects us to contribute to his work. We can never repay the debt we owe our Savior, but giving back to God demonstrates our gratitude. Our contributions to our local church, outreach ministries, and missions can make a difference in others' lives and bring new souls into God's Kingdom. We will be rewarded for our faithfulness in this area. Using our finances for eternal purposes is always money well spent.

> *Provide purses for yourselves that will not wear out, a treasure in heaven that will not be exhausted, where no thief comes near and no moth destroys.*
> *Luke 12:33 (NIV)*

April 14

Some Things Can't Be Measured
PAUL'S LETTER

Ephesians 3:14-19

"After I get off the interstate, how many miles do I go before turning onto county road 1900N?" It was the type of question I dread. It's hard for me to give directions because I have no sense of distance, unlike my husband, who has an innate ability to estimate measurements in his mind. Richard doesn't understand why I can't immediately answer questions such as, "How high do you want this curtain rod?" "How long is their driveway?" "How wide is your entertainment center?" (Sigh.) It's not easy being measurement-challenged.

Maybe some of the women who lived in New Testament times also had this problem. Could they have told a traveler how many leagues to go down the road before reaching a certain village? One measurement they all struggled with was expressed in Paul's letter to the believers at Ephesus. I imagine that those women's hearts warmed as they heard Paul's prayer that they would be able to grasp the immensity of God's love for them.

However analytical our minds are, none of us is able to fully understand God's infinite love. We can count the blessings God has given us and recite verses such as "God is love" (1 John 4:8), but we've only scratched the surface. God gave us an idea of his love when he became human to suffer and die in our place so that we could be set free from the penalty for sin. We more easily comprehend God's love when we look at Jesus Christ: how high the Cross stood, how wide he stretched out his arms, how deep the sword pierced his side, how long his body lay in the tomb before his resurrection. Still, some things just can't be measured.

May you have the power to understand, as all God's people should, how wide, how long, how high, and how deep his love is.
Ephesians 3:18

April 15

A Severe Penalty
PRIESTS' DAUGHTERS

Leviticus 21:9

A teenage girl walked out of the clinic, hoping that she wouldn't meet any-one she knew. *This is so unfair,* she told herself. *This shouldn't be happening to me.* He had been her first boyfriend, and she had believed him when he claimed that she was his first girlfriend. When she learned that he was telling that to another girl, too, she broke it off, but he had left her with a reminder of their relationship: She had joined the twenty million other Americans with human papillomavirus. She had never even heard of HPV before, and now she had the high-risk kind. She also hadn't known that a sixteen-year-old could get cervical cancer.

Because sexual immorality is so damaging, God imposed severe penal-ties for disobedience when he set the nation of Israel apart as his own peo-ple. Women found guilty of breaking the law of purity were condemned to death, but daughters of priests were burned alive because their sin detracted from their fathers' holiness. We might imagine that such brutal punishment would keep women from engaging in immoral sex, but as humans, we ratio-nalize our behavior and convince ourselves that we won't get caught.

We are horrified at the strict penalties for sexual immorality laid down in the Old Testament. Unfortunately, we are not as shocked as we should be at the casual attitude toward sex today. God designed sexual intimacy as part of the marital relationship; any other sexual expression is sin. We don't live under Mosaic law, but there are still consequences for disobeying spiritual laws. Sexual sin damages our character, destroys relationships, hurts other people, and exposes us to diseases that can have permanent effects or even kill us. Our society portrays extramarital sex as harmless, but the Bible reminds us that it is a behavior that can carry severe penalties.

> *Run from sexual sin! No other sin so clearly affects the body as this one does. For sexual immorality is a sin against your own body.*
> *1 Corinthians 6:18*

April 16

Feeling Threatened
SAMSON'S BRIDE

Judges 14:1-17

We all stood around smiling as my friends' little boy stroked the Labrador puppies and squealed with delight. He was having the time of his life! Suddenly, the mother of the puppies came into the room and started barking, which made all of us jump. At the sight of the big dog, the toddler ran behind his dad. As he clasped his father's legs with both hands, he peeked around at the dog. With the security of having his daddy between him and danger, the little boy looked more curious than scared.

When Samson's bride was threatened, she didn't turn to the one person who could have protected her. Samson posed a riddle to the wedding guests, along with a wager. When the guests couldn't solve the puzzle after a few days, they demanded that the new bride get the answer or they would kill her and her family. The threat terrified the young Philistine woman, who knew that her fellow countrymen would do what they said. A silly wager had suddenly thrust her family's fate into her hands. Sadly, the woman failed to share the problem with her new husband. If only she had understood the strength that would have been at her disposal.

God wants us to run straight to him when we feel threatened, whether we're endangered by physical or emotional harm or attacked in the spiritual realm. His responsibilities as our Father include defending us. When someone threatens us, they are threatening him. Our responsibilities include being honest with God, taking our burdens to him, and trusting him to handle them in the best way possible. We can make a terrible mess of things when we try to solve serious problems on our own, without God's help. If only we understood the strength and power that is at our disposal.

Give all your worries and cares to God, for he cares about you.
1 Peter 5:7

April 17

Loose Lips
SAMSON'S BRIDE

Judges 14:17-19

Catherine ducked behind the greeting card rack, almost turning it over. *I have to get out of here without her seeing me,* she thought in a panic. It was hard to believe that only a year ago, she and Brianna had been good friends. That changed one evening when Catherine had dinner with a few girlfriends and did a little too much talking. She hadn't meant to, but the words just slipped out. Before she knew it, she had shared something that Brianna had told her in strictest confidence. Today, for the umpteenth time, Catherine wished that she could learn to control her mouth.

Samson's new bride also betrayed a confidence, with much more serious consequences than Catherine experienced. After a few days of pleading and crying, she finally got Samson to explain the riddle he had posed during their wedding feast. She shared the information with the men who had threatened her, and Samson became enraged when the men knew the answer. He had told only one person, so he knew who had betrayed him. Although his bride acted to save the lives of her family, Samson's explosive temper led him to kill and rob thirty of her countrymen in order to pay the wager.

Many people have a hard time keeping secrets. In the heat of a conversation, it's all too easy to share personal information about others that they would prefer to keep private. Careless words can have consequences ranging from feelings of discomfort to ruined reputations and broken relationships. True friendship revolves around the trust that we are safe with another person and don't have to worry about how much they know about us. Our mouths can cause great damage, whether we're accidentally betraying a confidence or sharing our own secrets with someone who can't be trusted.

> *A gossip goes around telling secrets, but those who are trustworthy can keep a confidence.*
> *Proverbs 11:13*

April 18

Given to Another
SAMSON'S BRIDE

Judges 14:20–15:6

Of all the dramatic scenes in the 2000 movie *Castaway,* one stands out in my mind. Tom Hanks plays Chuck, a workaholic who survives a plane crash and finds himself stranded on a remote island. After four years, Chuck strikes out on a makeshift raft, is spotted, and returns to family and friends who assumed that he was dead. His girlfriend, Kelly, opens her door to see the "love of her life" alive and well—but now she is married to another man with whom she has children.

Samson's bride knew something of what Helen Hunt's character felt. Her marriage to Samson may have been of the type where the bride lived with her parents and the husband periodically visited her, but when Samson learned that his bride had revealed the riddle's answer, he left before the marriage was consummated on the seventh night. The woman's father considered this an annulment and gave her to another man.

She probably assumed that she would never see Samson again, but one day, he shocked her by showing up as if nothing had happened. When her former groom discovered that his bride now belonged to another, his explosive temper ignited a chain of retaliations that resulted in her and her father being killed by their countrymen.

The New Testament often calls believers the bride of Christ and urges us to keep ourselves pure until he comes for us. Meanwhile, we live in a world that desperately tries to lure our hearts away from our first love. If we don't stay on guard and nurture our relationship with Jesus, we can give our affections away without realizing it. Samson's bride had no choice in her situation; her father made the decision to give her to another man. We choose whether or not we will be found faithful to our Groom when he comes for us.

May you be completely faithful to the LORD our God.
1 Kings 8:61

April 19

For Love of Money
DELILAH

Judges 16:4-5

I wonder what Kent is doing these days. . . . Marie shook her head. These fleeting thoughts of her high-school sweetheart had become a common occurrence lately. Marie had cared for Kent deeply and had dated him for three years. The problem was his lack of ambition. He was satisfied working in his dad's hometown business, but Marie had big goals. She planned to enjoy plenty of money—something she had done without while growing up. Now she had achieved her dreams. She was married to a CEO and had a career of her own, but lately, her big house seemed so empty in the evenings. It just didn't seem like enough anymore.

Delilah also seemed to be motivated by money when her fellow Philistines asked her to betray Samson. She might also have been motivated by the fact that Samson was an Israelite and therefore hated by her people. Maybe she felt flattered that rich, powerful men came seeking her help. But Delilah would have needed stronger morals than she possessed to resist the extraordinary amount of money the Philistine rulers offered her in return for the secret of Samson's superhuman strength. Looking forward to becoming an incredibly wealthy woman, Delilah sank to a new low as she coolly devised a plan to betray the man who was infatuated with her.

A love of money can entice us into all sorts of evil situations, although we're not a Philistine woman with low morals. There's nothing wrong with wanting enough money so that we can live comfortably, and God often blesses believers with wealth. But the Bible warns against the desire to get rich instead of being content with what we have. Chasing after riches instead of godly virtue opens us to temptations in all areas of our lives. Despite our society's beliefs, money can't buy happiness. No amount of wealth is worth betraying our principles and integrity.

> *The love of money is the root of all kinds of evil.*
> *1 Timothy 6:10*

April 20

Misusing Our Power
DELILAH

Judges 16:6-21

She finished brushing her hair and glanced at her watch. He would be here any minute. Of course, he'd bring flowers or candy, and maybe a box with something sparkling in it. She really should break if off—after all, it wasn't fair to him. She felt no real attraction to him, although he seemed serious right from the start. But not yet—it was nice to be worshiped and to call all the shots. All she had to do was to name a restaurant or play, mention a home repair that needed to be done, or talk about some financial worry. She knew she had a good thing going, and she wanted to enjoy it awhile longer.

Delilah was in a similar situation. When Samson fell in love with her, she could have insisted on a proper relationship as husband and wife. She could have influenced him to rise above his tendency to pull spiteful pranks and encouraged him to take his role as Israel's judge seriously. Delilah could have helped Samson to become a man whom others could respect and admire for more than his occasional displays of physical strength. Instead, she used her power to betray him to his enemies in return for riches.

We often don't realize the power we have in relationships with boy-friends, husbands, children, relatives, and friends. The closer the relation-ship, the more vulnerable the other person is. Whether we realize it or not, we use that influence in ways that either help or harm our loved ones. We can use the relationship for our own gain without considering the other person's needs, or we can bring out the best in them by encouraging them to develop into the person God intends them to be. Being the object of some-one's love brings great responsibility. We are ultimately accountable to God for how we handle it.

> *I have thought deeply about all that goes on here under the sun, where*
> *people have the power to hurt each other.*
> *Ecclesiastes 8:9*

April 21

Hard-Hearted Woman
DELILAH

Judges 16:21-27

It was one of those stories that made me sorry I had turned on the evening news. Police had discovered a half-starved, teenage girl confined to a cage in the basement of her adoptive mother's house. The girl weighed only forty-five pounds, lived in filth, and had no contact with outsiders. As I looked at the woman's face, I wondered how she could be so cruel to a child. Did she feel anything at all when the girl looked up at her with eyes filled with misery and hunger?

How did Delilah feel when the Philistines rushed into the room and gouged out the eyes that had gazed at her in adoration? Was her heart filled with remorse when she saw Samson humiliated and grinding grain in prison? Was she overwhelmed with sorrow when the man who had once amazed people with his strength now amused them like a pitiful circus performer? It's hard to imagine Delilah not struggling with guilt, when her actions had reduced the man who loved her to a life of degradation. Yet the Bible makes no mention of repentance on her part. She must have been a cold, hard-hearted woman interested only in cold, hard cash.

Delilah is the type of person described in Ephesians 4:18-19. The hearts of people who refuse to believe in God can become so petrified by sin that they lose the ability to feel shame when they do something evil. Jesus warned that when our hearts become hardened, it is difficult for us to see and hear the truth (see Matthew 13:15). Even believers need to watch constantly for signs in themselves of the gradual process of hardening toward wrongdoing. We need God's help to remain sensitive to the effects of our behavior. Otherwise, we may experience hardened hearts, as Delilah did.

> *Their minds are full of darkness; they wander far from the life God gives because they have closed their minds and hardened their hearts against him.*
> *Ephesians 4:18*

April 22

The Best-Laid Plans
DELILAH

Judges 16:28-30
Delilah laid a cunning plan to learn the secret of Samson's strength. When she was finally convinced that he had been honest with her, Delilah lulled him to sleep and had a man shave off his hair. Since he was a Nazirite, Samson's hair had never been cut. His hair was not the source of his power, but it was a visible sign of his special status. Samson's behavior had been selfish, sensual, and disobedient to God's calling. God saw his foolish indiscretion with Delilah as the last straw and withdrew the incredible strength he had given Samson.

Delilah's plan was successful. With one blow, she freed her nation from their most-hated enemy and got enough money to make her rich for the rest of her life. She could now enjoy all the pleasures and comforts of life. But God had another plan. As the Philistines partied, God granted the repentant Samson the strength to pull down the temple pillars, killing thousands of Philistines and beginning the deliverance of Israel from their brutal oppressors. Did Delilah meet her death that day? Perhaps she had attended the festival as an honored guest. Even if she escaped with her life, any surviving Philistine rulers probably wanted more than their money back, considering the way things turned out.

Most of us like to plan our day, or season, or year. Even if we don't make specific goals and detailed lists, we have some idea of how we want events in our lives to turn out. No matter how much thought we put into our plans, we will run into problems if we leave God out. Our best-laid plans can blow up in our faces or backfire. God has his own purposes for our lives. The safest and wisest plans are seeking his will and making sure that our plans line up with his.

You can make many plans, but the LORD's purpose will prevail.
Proverbs 19:21

April 23

Manipulative Women
SAMSON'S BRIDE AND DELILAH

Judges 14:16-17; 16:15-16

"Did you ask Travis about our girls-only road trip to Florida?" asked Joanie.

"He said we can't afford it this year," Sandy responded.

"Oh, I'm so sorry you won't be with us."

"Don't worry," Sandy laughed. "I'll be stretched out on the beach with the rest of you. After a few days of my pouting and sulking, he'll cave in. If worse comes to worst, I'll turn on the waterworks—that gets him every time."

Sandy sounds like two of the women in Samson's life. When his bride wanted to learn the answer to his riddle in order to save her life, she cried steadily for three days until he gave in. When Delilah wanted to learn the secret to his strength in order to betray him, she also pouted and pestered him. Each woman accused Samson of not really loving her and tormented him with her nagging until she finally got what she wanted.

Some women are experts at manipulating others to get what they want. They respond to frustration and disappointment with nagging, arguing, the silent treatment (which Samson probably would have preferred), or overly emotional reactions. These can even become ingrained habits that some of us revert to unconsciously, but if we substitute manipulative techniques for honest communication, we risk fostering resentment and anger in our relationships. We also make it difficult for others to respect us.

It is tempting to adopt similar attitudes toward God. We may openly or subconsciously accuse him of not really loving us when we face troubles and trials. Our praying may become more like pouting. God wants us to be open with him about our emotions and desires. He also wants us to trust him instead of trying to manipulate him. He doesn't want us to act like Sandy or one of Samson's women.

A continual dripping on a very rainy day and a contentious woman are alike.
Proverbs 27:15 (NKJV)

April 24

A Powerful Influence
EUNICE AND LOIS

2 Timothy 1:5; 3:14-17

Marla switched off the television and tried to ignore the familiar restlessness that was already seeping in. She loved to watch programs about outstanding women who influenced the world in politics, science, medicine, or philanthropy. But these shows made her dissatisfied with her own life. How could she do something important with no formal education, wealth, special talents, or extra time? Tomorrow was her turn to carpool and her day to volunteer in Andrea's classroom. After school, she would take Jeremy to his art lesson, and in the evening she would lead the board meeting for Helping Hands. *I guess homemakers can't be expected to make a difference in the world,* she sighed.

Paul's second letter to Timothy mentions two women who probably longed to make a difference in their world. Eunice and her daughter Lois were Jewish women who became Christians, perhaps through Paul's preaching. They probably did not have any public ministry or position of power, but they did have the opportunity to train Lois's son and teach him the Scriptures. Through the influence of his mother and grandmother, Timothy became a leading evangelist who influenced countless lives for Christ.

We may not feel that we're in a position to have an impact on the world, but each of us has the opportunity to influence someone. Mothers can train their children to grow up as followers of Christ, and in turn, their children will influence others. We may have a neighbor, friend, or coworker who needs the touch of God's love and truth. The only requirement for becoming a powerful influence is a willingness to be used wherever God has placed us. The examples of Eunice and Lois show that if we are faithful, we can make a lasting difference in the world from exactly where we are.

[Those who are righteous] will have influence and honor.
Psalm 112:9

April 25

Eyewitness to a Miracle
HEALING BLIND EYES

Matthew 20:29-34

I once attended a church where the pastor's wife had lost her sight a number of years before due to permanent tissue damage. The woman's family adapted to her new condition but continued to ask God to restore her sight. One day during the woman's usual prayer time, her sight suddenly returned. After examining her eyes, the doctors were baffled. The damage had not been corrected. Medically speaking, the woman should not be able to see.

We can picture a woman in the crowd following Jesus witnessing a similar miracle. She heard the two blind men desperately crying out for Jesus to have mercy on them. Her heart went out to the men, but the crowd yelled for them to be quiet. Blind beggars sitting by the road were a common sight, and the people wanted to hear this new Rabbi.

When the two men continued to shout louder, Jesus stopped. The woman couldn't believe her ears when Jesus asked the men what they wanted him to do for them. Wasn't that obvious? When the men told Jesus that they wanted to see, he touched their eyes. The woman gasped as the two men instantly jumped up and joined the crowd. One minute they were blind; the next, they could see.

In a sense, all of us are born blind, unable to see the spiritual world around us. When God opens our eyes to our sinful condition, we see the truth of Jesus' death on our behalf. With the Holy Spirit living in us, spiritual truths and Bible passages that once were blurred become crystal clear. And there is always something new to see. God wants us to cry out for him to open our eyes, just as the two blind men did. We will never fully understand everything in God's Word, but with his help we will always see wonderful things there.

> *Open my eyes, that I may see wondrous things from Your law.*
> *Psalm 119:18 (NKJV)*

April 26

Revenge Is Not Sweet
DINAH

Genesis 34:1-26

She slammed the front door, flipped the deadbolt, and peeked through the blinds. *It must have been my imagination,* she assured herself. Seven months had passed, and she still couldn't shake the feeling that someone was following her. Seven months, and the police still had no leads in the case. Feeling paranoid was bad enough, but the flashbacks were harder to deal with. Even worse were the thoughts that occasionally invaded her mind—fantasies of what she'd like to do if she could get her hands on the guy who had assaulted her as she left work that night.

Today's Bible passage relates the story of another woman who was raped, although with a totally different outcome. When Dinah's family moved to a new area and she went out to visit the women, a local prince raped her. Dinah's brothers killed her rapist, his family, and all the males who lived in the area. Although the Bible focuses on how Dinah's family responded to the crime, we can try to imagine how devastated she must have been personally. Not only did she suffer from the heinous crime committed against her, but her brothers' bloody vengeance did damage to her own family as well.

When people hurt us deeply, it's only natural to want to pay them back. We should do all we can to see that justice is done and that the perpetrators are held responsible for their actions according to the law. But there's a difference between wanting justice and desiring revenge. God alone claims the right to avenge wrongdoing. Nurturing our hunger for revenge allows people to hurt us over and over again. God wants us to release that desire. He also wants us to remember that even if those who hurt others escape justice here on earth, they will eventually have to face his righteous anger and judgment.

> Don't say, "I will get even for this wrong." Wait for the LORD to handle the matter.
> Proverbs 20:22

April 27

Putting God First
WIDOW FROM ZAREPHATH

1 Kings 17:7-14

My first book contract came at a time when my husband had been unemployed for two years. Our adult son, who lived at home, had also been laid off, and our daughter had just finished high school. Even working temporary jobs, we had to cash in retirement funds, which were now almost gone. The generous advance would help with the bills, including our property taxes. Then I remembered a long-ago prayer from when I fantasized about being a writer—I would give God all the money from my first sale in each different type of writing. Uh-oh. But with our situation, did he expect me to follow through?

The woman in this Bible passage also faced a difficult decision. How shocked the poor widow must have been when Elijah asked her for bread. Everyone knew that the area suffered from a severe famine caused by drought. Surely he could tell from one glance at her emaciated body that she was the last person to have extra food. Yet even after she explained that she had only enough flour and oil for a last meal for herself and her son, the man instructed her to serve him first. How could he ask such a thing?

Sometimes God asks us to demonstrate our faith in him by doing something that doesn't make sense from a human standpoint. He may ask us to give something up that we treasure or to put someone else's needs before our own. When God's call conflicts with human logic, we have tough decisions to make. Will we put our own reasoning aside and depend on his wisdom? Can we trust him to take care of us? Does he have the right to ask us to share our last morsel of food when we have a hungry child? Could he expect us to give him money based on an old promise rather than use it to pay necessary bills?

> *Seek the Kingdom of God above all else, and live righteously, and he will give you everything you need.*
> *Matthew 6:33*

April 28

Putting God First, Part 2
WIDOW OF ZAREPHATH

1 Kings 17:13-14

When faced with a tough decision, I prayerfully sought God's will—but first I did a lot of questioning and waffling. *Okay, God, what exactly did I say? Did I mean the first check? Was I referring to just the advance?* What I had said was *all* the money. *But it looks as if you're providing this money for our bills. Does that mean that my promise doesn't count?* Psalm 50:14 advises us to keep the vows we make to God. Finally, I determined to keep my rash promise and began asking God to help me to do so with joy. Several weeks later, my husband began a new job.

The widow in Zarephath didn't do any waffling. Elijah promised that she and her son would not run out of food if she used her last handful of flour to feed him first. Although the woman was not a Jew, she believed in the God of Israel so she immediately obeyed Elijah's instructions. Instead of starving to death as she had probably expected, the widow and her son had enough food during the rest of the famine. How she must have praised God as she saw her supply of flour and oil miraculously replenished each day, month after month.

God has promised to meet our needs if we put him first. Sometimes that means doing something that looks foolish according to human logic, until we remember that he controls all the wealth and resources in the world. God delights in showing his faithfulness in impossible circumstances so that we can respond with joy and praise. We can rest assured that when we concentrate on loving and obeying God, even during times of unemployment or famine, he will somehow keep our flour and oil replenished.

My God will supply all your needs according to his riches in glory in Christ Jesus.
Philippians 4:19 (NASB)

April 29

Search Mode
WOMAN SEARCHING FOR A LOST COIN

Luke 15:8-10

I took a deep breath and tried to stay calm. What a frustrating morning! Ever since breakfast I had been looking for my checkbook. My time hadn't been a total waste, though. So far I had found the missing DVD remote, one of my granddaughter's socks, my extra set of car keys, and a few other items I hadn't seen in a while. Finally, I found the checkbook—it had fallen out of my purse onto the shoes in my closet. Now I could pay those bills. There was only one problem: *Where in the world did I put my glasses?*

Jesus told a parable about a woman who was searching for a piece of silver. Some people think that the silver was from the row of coins on the headdress that married women wore. Others point out that the coin was probably equal to a day's wages at that time. Either way, the woman had lost something of great value and was desperate to find it. She lit a lamp, grabbed a broom, and swept every nook and cranny of her house. When she found the missing coin, the woman was overjoyed and invited her friends to celebrate with her.

The parable illustrates God's rejoicing when people turn to him and repent of their sin. We can also take a cue from this story concerning our approach to God. Some people search for God in wrong places, such as the occult, man-made philosophies, or false religions. But God is not hiding from us. He has revealed himself through his creation; his Word; and his Son, Jesus. Once we become God's children, we find guidance through his Spirit living in us and in the Bible. If we believe that God is worth searching for, he promises that we will find him.

[The Lord declares,] "You will seek Me and find Me when you search for Me with all your heart."
Jeremiah 29:13 (NASB)

April 30

Unwelcome Intruders
WOMEN SUFFERING FROM INVADERS

2 Kings 17:5-6; 2 Chronicles 24:23-24

I wasn't prepared for this aspect of living among the cornfields: As farmers harvested the field behind our house, unwelcome intruders invaded our home. I found mouse droppings here and there, and even with mousetraps, I occasionally saw a mouse dart across a room. But the topper came when my husband and I sat watching television one night. Glancing over at the brick hearth beside the entertainment center, I saw that we had been joined by a mouse who also liked old movies.

The women in today's Old Testament passages suffered from much more serious invasions. Each time the Hebrew people chose idols over God or chose a sinful lifestyle over obedience to his commands, God disciplined them by allowing their enemies to invade their land. An enemy invasion disrupted the women's lives as their city came under siege or was plundered. Their hearts broke when the oppressors carried them or their loved ones away as captives. God allowed each conquering nation to control his people until their hearts returned to him and they once again acknowledged his control over their lives.

We are all subject to enemy invasions on the battleground of our minds. If we concentrate only on avoiding sinful behavior to the neglect of our thought life, we leave ourselves open to Satan's intrusion. If we don't notice when Satan subtly introduces thoughts and daydreams into our minds, he can gradually begin to control our attitudes and behavior. What we put into our minds also affects our thought life. Are we allowing unwholesome movies, television shows, or reading material to influence how we think? Or are we concentrating on worthwhile things and taking in God's Word each day? With God's help, we can learn to focus our minds in a way that locks out unwelcome intruders.

> *Fix your thoughts on what is true, and honorable, and right, and pure, and lovely, and admirable. Think about things that are excellent and worthy of praise.*
> *Philippians 4:8*

May 1

Serving Up Gratitude
PETER'S MOTHER-IN-LAW

Matthew 8:14-15

I tried to stand up but quickly sank back on the couch. They weren't kidding about the seriousness of this Asian flu. For three days, I had been so weak that I could barely move. It had taken all my strength to make my boys cheese sandwiches at lunch. I felt bad when I saw that my two-year-old had pressed his slice of cheese onto the window. Now I felt even worse to see that it was gone. I only hoped that the sun hadn't spoiled the mayonnaise. More than anything, I longed to be able to take good care of my sons again, to cook a meal, even to scrub the bathrooms.

When Jesus came to Peter's house for a visit, his mother-in-law lay sick in bed with a fever. Jesus touched her hand and the fever immediately left her body. The woman wasn't just on the road to recovery; she experienced an instant healing. Instead of lying in bed recuperating and waiting to regain her strength, she jumped up and prepared a meal for Jesus and his followers. She was happy to be able to serve Jesus out of love and gratitude for his healing touch.

Right after I've recovered from the flu or other illness, I relish being able to do household chores, even my least favorite ones. Unfortunately, that attitude wears off rather quickly. My willingness to serve Jesus should never fade when I remember that he healed me from sin. God doesn't want us to serve him grudgingly or because we think we can earn bonus points. True service is an expression of love and gratitude for God's mercy and grace. We may not always feel like it, but when we think about what he has done for us, we'll follow the example of Peter's mother-in-law and jump at the chance to serve God or fellow believers.

Serve the LORD with gladness.
Psalm 100:2 (NKJV)

May 2

Mentors
OLDER WOMEN

Titus 2:3-5

Peggy finished cleaning up the kitchen and hurried out the door. Twice a month, Thursday was the highlight of her week. Last fall, she felt that she didn't have much to look forward to, as her last child had graduated and taken a job halfway across the country. Then Peggy volunteered to be a mentor with the MOPS (Mothers of Preschoolers) group that met at her church. She didn't have all the answers, but she willingly gave a listening ear and encouraged the young mothers as they shared their concerns and challenges.

The second chapter of Titus encourages older, more spiritually mature women in the church to train the younger women, helping them to grow in their relationships with God and in their family roles. Such an arrangement was beneficial to everyone involved. These relationships gave the older women honored positions in the group of believers, made them feel valued, and enriched their lives as they reached out to others. In turn, the younger women with growing families received the benefit of their mentors' practical wisdom and experience.

In our transient, urban-centered society, many young women live far away from their extended families. They miss having mothers, aunts, and grandmothers nearby to offer advice and encouragement for the demands they face. In many settings, different age groups are segregated. Groups such as MOPS make it possible to have relationships in the pattern that Titus suggests.

Whether or not we are in a formal mentoring relationship, someone is watching and learning from our example—whether good or bad. Regardless of our age, we all have some wisdom or insight that we can share with others, and there is always something we can learn from them. As long as we remain willing for God to teach us, we will have something to share with others.

> *Encourage each other and build each other up, just as you are already doing.*
> *1 Thessalonians 5:11*

May 3

The Best Role Model
ATHALIAH

2 Kings 11:3-16

As we waited after a wedding for the bride and groom to come to the reception, I walked toward a friend's college-age daughter to say hello. I hadn't seen her in several years. When she turned around, I almost gasped at how much she looked like her mom. She had the same brown eyes, the same bright smile, and a similar hairstyle. As we chatted, I noticed that she even sounded like her mother and used some of the same mannerisms. I had never seen such a strong mother-daughter resemblance.

Athaliah resembled her mother in life and in death. Like Jezebel, Athaliah ruled as a cruel, powerful queen who promoted idol worship. Just as her mother had done, Athaliah committed murder without hesitation. After seeing Jezebel's miserable end (see 2 Kings 9:30-33), did Athaliah ever question whether following in her mother's footsteps was a good idea? She had exposure to God's truth, yet she chose to pattern her life after Jezebel's wickedness. Athaliah ruled Judah for six years until a legitimate heir to David's throne was proclaimed king. Soldiers killed Athaliah at the horses' gate by the palace, and perhaps her body was trampled by chariots just as her mother's had been.

Hopefully, none of us have parents who set such evil examples as Jezebel and Ahab did (see 1 Kings 16:29-31). But even if we had good parents, we sometimes repeat their faults and mistakes in spite of having seen the consequences. Even worse, some people pattern their lives after famous stars whose lifestyles leave much to be desired.

God wants us to have the best possible lives. That's why he advises us to imitate him above everyone else. As God in human flesh, Jesus exhibited our heavenly Father's traits of love, forgiveness, mercy, justice, and compassion. He also demonstrated a life of loving service and obedience. We can't find a better role model to pattern our lives after than Jesus.

Imitate God . . . in everything you do, because you are his dear children.
Ephesians 5:1

May 4

Being a Safe Place
JEHOSHEBA

2 Kings 11:1-3

A young woman sat in the room staring at the sunlight on the floor. Her body still ached from the kicks her husband had given her after he knocked her down. She had a tooth missing from the last time he came home drunk. After two years of enduring his drunken rages, the woman had begun to fear for her life. She had hesitated when the social worker recommended the women's shelter, worrying about his retaliation if she left him. But now, for the first time in a long while, she felt a ray of hope. Had she found a safe place at last?

When Athaliah tried to kill all her grandsons so she could rule as queen of Judah, one of them found a safe place, thanks to his aunt. Jehosheba hid her infant nephew Joash in a bedroom so he wouldn't be murdered and then took him to the Temple where her husband served as high priest. How her heart must have ached that she couldn't save the lives of all her nephews, but during the next several years she rejoiced that Joash was growing up secretly in the Temple. One day, he would reign over Judah in his rightful place, and David's line would be restored.

Chances are that we won't ever rescue someone from being murdered as Jehosheba did, but we can all be safe places for those that God puts in our lives. We can offer our family, friends, and neighbors the security that comes from knowing that they are loved and valued. They need to know that their secrets are safe with us and that they can trust us to speak the truth to them. Then they will think of us when they need a place to run to in times of trouble or sorrow. We can't save the whole world, but we can experience the joy that comes from knowing that we are someone's safe place.

You have been my refuge, a place of safety when I am in distress.
Psalm 59:16

May 5

Grandmothers
MAACAH AND LOIS

2 Chronicles 15:16; 2 Timothy 1:5

I stood beside my grandmother's casket, hardly recognizing the woman with the teased hair and makeup. I remembered a woman in a simple cotton dress who worked hard and laughed easily. How I loved my summer visits as a little girl, going to vacation Bible school at Grandma's country church. At the beginning of the week, Grandma would pick a yellow squash that had grown too big for eating, draw a face on it, and fit it with a bonnet that she had sewed. It wasn't exactly the latest Barbie, but it made me feel special because it was made especially for me. Almost fifty years later, I still remember my squash dolls.

The verses in today's reading contrast two grandmothers and their influence. When King Asa decided to rid Judah of idol worship, he deposed his grandmother from her position as queen mother because Maacah had made an Asherah pole, a Canaanite fertility symbol. On the other end of the spectrum, Timothy's grandmother passed on her love of God's Word to her grandson, and he became an influential leader in the early church. Maacah exercised her power in a way that brought her dishonor, while the Bible commends Lois for her influence in her grandson's life.

Grandmothers are in a position to affect the next generation in a powerful way. According to a September 2005 report from the AARP, 4.5 million children live in grandparent-headed households, and many more have grandparents as primary babysitters. If our grandchildren live far away, it takes more effort and creativity to be involved in their lives, but with e-mails, phone calls, and photos, it is possible. Even if we don't have grandchildren of our own, we probably live close to a young family that would love a surrogate grandma or nana. It doesn't take much to make a difference in a child's life—just love, time, and perhaps a large vegetable.

You share the faith that first filled your grandmother Lois.
2 Timothy 1:5

May 6

Extreme Devotion
RIZPAH

2 Samuel 21:1-14

Camille looked at the clock. She couldn't believe that it was already time for Seth's therapy again. Although it was hard to tell if the exercises actually helped his muscles, she thought she had seen some improvement. With Seth's severe birth defects, their first doctor had advised institutionalized care. She and her husband had immediately found a new doctor who was willing to work with them. Camille hadn't realized how exhausting Seth's special care would be, but she vowed to keep doing the best she could for him, taking it one day at a time.

Rizpah was devoted to her sons in life and in death. Because of Saul's sins, his two sons by Rizpah and five of his grandsons were executed on a mountain. Rizpah stood by, helpless to save her sons' lives, but she determined that they would receive no further dishonor after death. For five long months, Rizpah watched over the men's bodies. Day and night, in heat and cold, she protected them from birds and wild animals. It's hard to imagine what filled the mind of this grief-stricken mother as she fought fatigue, discomfort, and weather to keep her guard.

Although we may not fully understand all of Rizpah's motives, we have to admire her dedication to her sons, which lasted long after their lives ended. She is a model for the kind of devotion that God desires to see in us. It's tempting to let our commitment to follow him wane when life gets hard, when we face a hopeless situation, or when it seems that our dreams have died. During those times, the best thing we can do is to stubbornly hold on to our trust that God rules over our lives. Rizpah's devotion touched King David, and he gave her sons and the others a proper burial. God will reward our devotion to him in far greater ways than that.

> *We should live in this evil world with wisdom, righteousness, and devotion to God.*
> *Titus 2:12*

May 7

Appreciating Discipline
MICAH'S MOTHER

Judges 17:1-6

Sally surveyed her family room, which looked as if a tornado had passed through it. She loved her sister and wished she could invite her over more often, but she couldn't stand her niece and nephews for very long. Deana had never been very strict, and now she seemed to give in to whatever her kids wanted. It wasn't enjoyable being around children who had no consideration for other people's feelings and no concept of consequences for their actions.

Micah's mother is an extreme example of a mother who spoiled her son. When someone stole eleven hundred pieces of silver she had saved, she pronounced a curse on the thief. After Micah admitted taking the money, she tried to replace the curse with a blessing from God. Instead of disciplining her son for doing wrong, she congratulated Micah on his honesty in confessing his crime. She even used part of the money to have an idol made to honor him. Micah and his mother lived during a period when Israel had abandoned God's standards, but common sense should have motivated Micah's mother to correct him when he stole money from her.

Sometimes we may wish that God would spoil us. Wouldn't it be nice if he would overlook our lapses in judgment or bless our actions even when we choose to ignore his instructions and do things our own way? The Bible teaches that when God disciplines us, it's a sign that we belong to him. Since we serve a holy God who wants us to become more like him, he has to deal with sin in our lives. Reaping the consequences of our sins may be painful, but in the long run it is beneficial. However much we want our own way, our heavenly Father loves us too much to let us get away with something that isn't good for us.

> *Just as a parent disciplines a child, the LORD your God disciplines you for your own good.*
> *Deuteronomy 8:5*

May 8

Seeing Past the Pain
THE MOTHER OF JABEZ

1 Chronicles 4:9-10

The woman in today's passage named her son Jabez because his birth was so painful. Many women can identify with the agony of a long, painful labor and delivery, but after the baby finally arrives, women usually forget their suffering. They don't choose a name for their child that permanently reminds them of the ordeal. Jabez's mother must have been so consumed by her suffering that she couldn't think of anything else when he arrived.

If this woman could only have foreseen the future at the moment of delivery. The Bible gives us little information about her son, but it does tell us that he grew up to be "more honorable than any of his brothers." As a further testimony to his godly character, Scripture records one of his prayers. Jabez asked God to bless him, expand his territory, be with him, and keep him from trouble and pain.

Jabez's mother must have been proud and joyful as she watched her son grow to love and obey God. The suffering she endured at his birth was worth it all as she witnessed God's granting her son's request. She didn't know that centuries later, her son's prayer would become the basis for a number-one *New York Times* best seller (*The Prayer of Jabez*) and appear on everything from mugs to t-shirts and key chains.

When we're enduring a painful ordeal, all we can see is our suffering. We may be tempted to turn from God and become bitter toward life. But God sees the future, and only he knows the purpose of our pain. Our worst trials sometimes turn out to be our greatest blessings. If we trust God's leadership, the memory of our suffering will eventually be eclipsed by deep, lasting joy—as the mother of Jabez learned.

I have refined you in the furnace of suffering.
Isaiah 48:10

May 9

Choices
ELISHEBA

Exodus 6:23; Leviticus 10:1-2

Marta looked at the pictures of her teenage sons and shook her head. They were both tall and had the same brown eyes, but the resemblance stopped there. Their temperaments couldn't have been more opposite. Ryan always worked hard in school, got along well with everyone, and came in earlier than curfew. Kenny had seemed determined to break every rule since birth, and he put more dedication into landing in detention than anything else. *How could two boys raised in the same home be so different from each other?* she wondered.

Elisheba also had children who were different from each other. She must have known both extreme joy and extreme disappointment in her role as a mother. Elisheba was married to Aaron, the head of the Hebrew priesthood, and she gave birth to four sons. God killed her two older sons, Nadab and Abihu, with fire after they disobeyed his clear instructions regarding the offering of incense in the Tabernacle. Elisheba's heart must have ached over her sons' tragic deaths, brought about by their rebellion against God's commands. In contrast, her younger sons, Eleazar and Ithamar, remained a source of pride as they faithfully carried out their priestly duties alongside their father.

People tend to credit parents when children turn out well. When children are disappointments, mothers tend to blame themselves even if others don't. The feeling that we're responsible for how our children end up can become a burden too heavy for us to bear. It is true that we influence others. However, individuals make their own personal choices, and those choices carry inevitable consequences. Understanding this helps to take the pressure off of us in any relationship, especially when we're trying to influence others for God. We can do our best to share truth with them, but they must choose whether to follow God's ways or rebel against him.

> *If you refuse to serve the LORD, then choose today whom you will serve.*
> Joshua 24:15

129

May 10

Asking for the Wrong Things
SALOME, MOTHER OF JAMES AND JOHN

Matthew 20:20-28

Marie watched out the window as her son got in his car and drove away. She hadn't meant to argue with him like that. She wanted only what was best for him. After he agreed to go into law, she sent him to the best schools and even used her connections to snag his internship with the most prestigious firm in the city. Just as she had hoped, the firm had offered him a position. Now he planned to pass up this unbelievable opportunity, and for what—to work in a nonprofit agency dealing with inner-city juvenile delinquents? He seemed disappointed that she wasn't thrilled with his decision. What was wrong with having great ambitions for her son?

Salome had great ambitions for her sons, James and John. Although she had served Jesus faithfully during his ministry, Salome viewed his coming Kingdom from a human perspective. Anxiety for her sons' futures prompted her to request the two places of honor beside Jesus when he began to rule. Salome's selfish and insensitive request came from her love for her sons and a sincere belief that they deserved the best. Jesus used the opportunity to teach his followers that God defines greatness by humility and service, often accompanied by great suffering.

It's human nature to want great things for our loved ones and for ourselves. Unfortunately, we often base our ambitions on worldly standards of success. In God's eyes, true greatness has nothing to do with reputation, prestige, or power. Not many of us have the goal of becoming servants, and we don't usually think of suffering as an honor. But if we desire to become like Christ, God will renew our thinking and align it with his eternal perspective. Eventually, we will be praying less to get a promotion or win an award than simply praying to serve him by serving others.

> *Even when you ask, you don't get it because your motives are all wrong—you want only what will give you pleasure.*
> *James 4:3*

May 11

God's Timing
ELIZABETH

Luke 1:5-25

"I love you, Mommy!" Valerie bent down to let her son's little arms wrap around her neck, then watched Sammy dart back to the playground. She remembered how shocked she had been to learn that she was pregnant in her early forties, just when her two daughters were in college. At first, it wasn't just morning sickness that had nauseated her, but things had worked out. True, she didn't have the freedom that her friends enjoyed, and some days she ran out of steam by dinnertime. And so what if she was the oldest mom at the park today? She waved back at Sammy on top of the jungle gym and smiled. *I wouldn't have missed this for the world.*

Today's passage tells the story of another woman who received the shocking news of a pregnancy. Although Elizabeth and her husband were both "very old," an angel announced that she would give birth to a son. Elizabeth rejoiced at the news, but in spite of her deep faith, perhaps she had momentary doubts as her aging body experienced the changes of pregnancy. Did she wonder if she would have what it took to be a good mother at her age? Any anxiety would have been dispelled if Elizabeth could have known that Jesus would later say of her son, "Of all who have ever lived, none is greater than John the Baptist" (Matthew 11:11).

Sometimes we wonder about God's timing. He can bring events and people into our lives at what looks like the most inconvenient times. But God's timing is perfect, even when it makes no sense to us. Rather than jumping to conclusions and worrying about the future, we would be better off learning to trust him with every aspect of our lives. Then when something seems to happen at the wrong time, we will eventually look back and say, "I wouldn't have missed this for the world."

> At the right time, I, the LORD, will make it happen.
> Isaiah 60:22

May 12

Nothing to Go On
EVE

Genesis 4:1

Eve, the first woman in the world to have a baby, had no one to turn to for help. She had no mother or female relative to offer advice, no friends to lend a hand, no child-care book to answer her questions. Eve didn't even have the memory of being a child herself. She had never experienced growing up or enjoying a relationship with a mother. Eve faced a lonely and terrifying experience as she dealt with childbirth and parenthood.

Eve must have struggled with anxiety and fear, as we all do, but today's passage gives a clue as to how she managed this strange new situation. After Cain's birth, she acknowledged that it had happened "with the Lord's help." Before being expelled from the Garden of Eden, Eve had enjoyed a unique relationship with her Creator, but sin had marred that intimacy. This new experience of motherhood pulled her into deeper dependence on God for wisdom, strength, and guidance. As the first mother, she had no one to turn to except her heavenly Father.

It can be terrifying to face a new situation and feel as if we have nothing to go on. Where do we turn when we lack the resources to deal with something for the first time, whether it's a job, a relationship, or a tough decision? Other people can offer helpful information or encouragement, but God should be our primary source of guidance. Even in circumstances where we feel confident, God's wisdom will be more trustworthy than our own. When we study God's Word and ask for his help, he promises to guide us through any new experience, no matter how terrifying it seems.

> *Trust in the Lord with all your heart; do not depend on your own understanding.*
> *Proverbs 3:5*

May 13

Our Heart's Desire
HANNAH

1 Samuel 1:2-20

Many women know firsthand the anguish of yearning for a child while being unable to conceive. For years, Tina's heart ached as she attended her friends' baby showers, struggling to share their joy while her arms remained empty. Mother's Day renewed her sadness each year, as she wondered why God didn't answer her prayers. Tina's family and church friends continued to pray, and today Tina and her husband are the proud parents of two sons and two daughters.

Hannah lived in a society that regarded barrenness as a curse from God. Although her husband Elkanah tried to comfort her by suggesting that having him was better than having ten sons, Hannah took her heartache to the Lord. As she prayed at the Tabernacle, her anguish was so great that Eli the priest thought she was drunk. Hannah explained that she felt very discouraged and had been pouring out her heart to the Lord. Eli then blessed her and prayed that her request be granted.

We may not struggle with infertility, but like Hannah, we all have some deep, unfulfilled longing. It may be disappointment with our marriage or with our singleness. We may ache over a wayward child or a troubled relationship with a friend or relative. We may long for a change in our job, environment, home situation, or personality.

God wants us to pour out our hearts to him as Hannah did. Like Elkanah, God also wants us to be satisfied with him alone. When we learn to give God first place in our lives, our hearts will long to know him and please him above all else. Then we can rest assured that he will either grant our desires or change them so that they are in alignment with his will for us.

Take delight in the Lord, and he will give you your heart's desires.
Psalm 37:4

May 14

Letting Go
HANNAH

1 Samuel 1:21-28

May and June are months when many mothers experience a bittersweet happiness. Watching our children graduate from high school or college fills us with pride and joy. At the same time, it forces us to acknowledge that our adult children are ready to make their own lives. Even though we knew this day would come, it is hard to let go of our children after years of loving, protecting, and nurturing them. Suddenly, eighteen or twenty-one years doesn't seem like enough time for childhood.

That day of letting go came much sooner for Hannah. When God allowed her to give birth to a son, she must have been wild with joy. At last, she had what she had desired for so many years. Still, Hannah's happiness in motherhood was mixed with pain. She had vowed to dedicate her son for full-time service to God, so Hannah had only a few years to devote herself to Samuel's care and training. She probably weaned Samuel at around age three, and then took him to the Tabernacle to live there permanently. Hannah rejoiced in the opportunity to give her son back to the One who had given him to her, but her mother's heart must have broken a little as she returned home without him.

Hannah's faith and devotion to God enabled her to give up what she wanted most. This painful lesson comes to all of us sooner or later. Whenever we hold on to something too tightly, it can become an idol in our lives. God may ask us to give up material possessions, a relationship, or a job. We can be sure that he always has a reason, just as Hannah knew when her son became one of Israel's great leaders. If we hold on to things loosely in this earthly life, it won't be so painful when we have to let go.

Everything we have has come from you, and we give you only what you first gave us!
1 Chronicles 29:14

May 15

Corrupt Environment
HANNAH

1 Samuel 2:12-19

Melanie waved and watched the school bus until it turned the corner. *He seems so young to be in school all day,* she thought for the hundredth time that week. She and her husband had done all they could to give Christopher the best possible start in life. They had made sure that he had a safe place to play and explore and plenty of opportunities for intellectual stimulation. But how could she protect him from the influences at school—bad language, fighting, or worse? She worried about sending him into an unknown environment.

Hannah had good reason to be concerned about the environment she was sending her son into at the Tabernacle. Although Eli was the high priest, his sons showed a total lack of respect for God. Hophni and Phinehas forced people who were making offerings to give them more than their lawfully prescribed share. They even seduced young women who served in the Tabernacle. Hannah must have worried about putting her three-year-old son under Eli's training and about his living around Eli's sons. Yet her steadfast faith in God gave her strength to trust in the power of prayer to overcome the evil influences that Samuel would be exposed to.

The Bible advises us to run from evil influences whenever possible. Since "the world around us is under the control of the evil one" (1 John 5:19), we all live in a corrupt environment. We will never be able to protect our loved ones or ourselves from the temptations and pressures exerted by ungodly people. In spite of Samuel's growing up around such evil influences, he grew into a godly man who influenced his nation for good. Hannah's visits with her son were few and brief, but she must have prayed for him continually. Her example shows the power of prayer for protection from a corrupt environment.

> *[Jesus said,] "My prayer is not that you take them out of the world but that you protect them from the evil one."*
> *John 17:15 (NIV)*

May 16

Blessing After Sacrifice
HANNAH

1 Samuel 2:20-21

The woman walked from the doctor's office in stunned silence. She sat in her car, staring at the ultrasound picture and letting it sink in. Just five years ago, she and her husband had been praying for a sibling for their three-year-old daughter. When the doctors gave them no hope of conceiving, they felt God directing them to adopt a baby from China. After working through all the red tape, they finally arrived at the orphanage to find that God had twin boys waiting for them. Now, three years later, a checkup showed that she was pregnant—with twins.

After Hannah fulfilled her promise to dedicate Samuel to God's service, God blessed her with more children. She had begged God to give her one son; he gave her three more sons and two daughters. The years of yearning for a child while enduring the taunts of Elkanah's other wife faded from her memory as more children were born. With visits to the Tabernacle to tend to Samuel's needs and caring for five children at home, Hannah enjoyed a full life. The pain she had suffered in relinquishing her firstborn after only a few years with him eased as she enjoyed the blessings that God sent to reward her faithfulness to him.

God delights in rewarding his faithful children. Jesus promised that whoever gives up anything for God will enjoy eternal life and be richly blessed in this life. Although we may not be compensated by the same thing we've given up, God blesses any sacrifice motivated by love and a desire to be obedient to his will. His rewards are often far beyond anything we would have thought to ask for. Like Hannah, we will discover that the more we relinquish for God, the more room there is in our lives for him to fill with blessings.

> *Everyone who has given up houses or brothers or sisters or father or mother or children or property, for my sake, will receive a hundred times as much in return and will inherit eternal life.*
> *Matthew 19:29*

May 17

Never Anonymous
NAMELESS WOMEN

Isaiah 49:14-16

I was five years old and chomping at the bit. Since children in rural areas didn't go to kindergarten, I would be going straight into first grade. I dragged my mother down the hallway, and we stopped at the list of names posted by the first classroom. No Dianne there. On the second list, there was a Diane Jones. On the third and last list, we found Dianne Stevens. My little heart sank to the bottom of my new saddle oxfords. Here I stood, ready for my first day of school, and my name wasn't on the class lists.

The Bible includes many women whose names were left out of the Scriptures. God didn't give us the name of the woman who saved the city of Thebez by dropping a millstone on the attacker's head. Scripture doesn't identify the woman who touched Jesus' robe for healing, the widow he praised for her sacrificial giving, or the Samaritan woman whose life changed after a conversation with Jesus at a well. We don't know the names of Peter's mother-in-law, Noah's wife, or Jairus's daughter. Their stories are significant enough to be included in God's Word, but for some reason, he chose to leave out their names.

It's easy to feel nameless in our society. While movie stars' names roll easily off everyone's tongue, it may seem that no one remembers ours. In the end, it won't matter how well-known we were, but how well we lived our lives. Once we become God's children through believing in Jesus, he writes our names in the Lamb's Book of Life. God compares this to having our names written on the palms of his hands as a constant reminder that we belong to him. No matter how anonymous we sometimes feel, God will never forget us or erase our names. That's a lot more important than any earthly list, even on the first day of school.

See, I have written your name on the palms of my hands.
Isaiah 49:16

May 18

The Comparison Game
IMPERFECT WOMEN

I settled in for my first day of school. At last came the moment I had waited for: the time to use our new writing tablets and chunky pencils. Mrs. Thompson instructed us to fill half a page with vertical lines and the other half with circles. I worked carefully and then leaned back to survey my work with pride—until I glanced across the aisle. The girl beside me had completed a page of evenly spaced straight lines and perfectly shaped circles. Suddenly, my own page looked like a sloppy mess. Disappointment replaced the feeling of satisfaction. Years later, I learned that the girl had already gone through first grade once.

It's hard not to compare our performances with those of others. If we compare ourselves with the Proverbs 31 woman, we will probably be discouraged, and if we look at Jezebel, all of us ought to look pretty good. The Bible never sugarcoats the imperfections of the women who fill its pages. In spite of failures and poor choices, God used some imperfect women in powerful ways. The list of faith heroes in Hebrews 11 includes Sarah, in spite of her mistakes and momentary lapses of trust in God's promises.

When we play the comparison game, we can always find someone who will make us seem superior, but in this earthly life, none of us can meet the standard of God's perfect holiness. Thankfully, Christ's death and resurrection have made it possible for those who believe in him to be perfect in God's eyes. While our status remains "perfect" in spite of momentary lapses and wavering faith, becoming holy is a process. To become more like Christ, we need to practice every day, just like filling a page with lines and circles.

> By that one offering he forever made perfect those who are being made holy.
> Hebrews 10:14

May 19

The Ultimate Security System
WOMEN WATCHING THE WALL BEING REBUILT

Nehemiah 2:11-18; 6:15-16

Rhonda looked over the brochure for the security system just installed in her home. It had all the latest technology, with detectors for carbon monoxide, smoke, water leaks, dangerously low temperatures, and oh yes— burglars. With this company watching her home twenty-four hours a day from the monitoring center, she was bound to sleep better tonight. The top-of-the-line model had put a huge dent in her savings, but it seemed well worth the price.

The women in Jerusalem probably slept better after the wall around the city was rebuilt. The Jews who returned from Babylonian captivity had found a city in disarray, filled with rubble, the wall broken down, and the gates burned. The city stood defenseless. As some of the people joined to rebuild the solid stone wall, the women must have breathed a sigh of relief. They watched the progress as each day passed and looked forward to the day when the project would be completed. Once an unbroken wall enclosed Jerusalem again, the city would be able to defend itself if enemies attacked.

Sometimes we need to rebuild the walls around our lives. Disobeying God's commands can cause our relationship with our Father and Protector to crumble. Ignoring him and pursuing our own desires leaves gaps in our protection that make us vulnerable to attacks from Satan, our number-one enemy. When this happens, we need to reconstruct our defenses by coming back under God's authority and turning away from rebellion. Through consistent prayer, we can restore the walls around our lives that help us guard against temptation and guide us to make wise choices. A close relationship with God is the ultimate security system. It takes time and effort, but it's well worth it.

> They replied at once, "Yes, let's rebuild the wall!" So they began the good work.
> Nehemiah 2:18

May 20

A Fresh Start
THE WOMAN CAUGHT IN ADULTERY

John 8:1-11

In a million years, she would never have dreamed that she would find herself in this predicament. After all, she was a loving wife, devoted mother, and committed follower of Christ. How could she have let her relationship with a coworker lead to an affair? For a while she'd ignored her nagging conscience and convinced herself that the relationship filled some deep need within her. Now, the pressure of living a double life had become more than she could stand. She had to come clean with her husband.

Haven't we all felt the burden of having a shameful secret to hide? The woman in John 8 had her guilt exposed in a cruel way when the religious leaders dragged her before Jesus and asked if she should be stoned, as the law of Moses stated. They planned that Jesus would either lose favor with the people or get in trouble with the Romans. All the woman knew was that she had been set up.

She stood alone, helpless and humiliated before the leering crowd. Her fate seemed to rest with the Man who stooped to write in the dust. The woman's shame and fear dissolved as Jesus spoke and her accusers slipped away, one by one. Fully aware of her guilt, the terrified woman was amazed to find mercy and forgiveness.

All of us have been adulterous in some way. The Bible teaches that adultery happens in thought as well as physically. It also teaches that loving something or someone more than God is adultery. Sooner or later, God will bring us face-to-face with our sin. There may be permanent consequences for our actions, but if we confess and turn away from our wrongdoing, we will find what the woman brought before Jesus and what the woman in the first paragraph found—a fresh start. That's something we all need every day.

There is no condemnation for those who belong to Christ Jesus.
Romans 8:1

May 21

A Fresh Start, Part 2
THE WOMAN CAUGHT IN ADULTERY

John 8:11

As I finished stitching the sleeve into the armhole, I proudly held the dress up to admire it. Then I threw it down in disgust. I couldn't believe that I had made the same mistake twice. After ripping out the stitches and pinning the sleeve in again, I had sewed it in backward for the second time. As I picked up the seam ripper once again, I thought, *Now I remember why I usually let my mother do most of my sewing.*

Sometimes making the same mistake again has more serious consequences. Jesus' words to the woman caught in adultery didn't end with his assurance that he did not condemn her. He also added "Go and sin no more." In a matter of minutes, this woman's emotions ran the gamut of shock, terror, and humiliation. These were followed by immense relief at the unexpected turn of events when her accusers left. As the woman struggled to grasp what had just happened, Jesus' face and words left an indelible impression on her mind. In the years ahead, the memory of the man who had saved her from the angry crowd must have empowered her to resist returning to her old habits.

God's forgiveness sets us free from our burden of guilt and shame when we've done something wrong. But if we're not careful, we may develop a flippant attitude toward his mercy. Some people fall into the habit of doing whatever they want, figuring that they can count on God's forgiveness later. Being a recipient of God's grace carries great responsibility. He doesn't forgive us just so that we can escape judgment, but so that we can have a new and better life. By staying close to God and doing our best to live in a way that pleases him, our fresh start will become a fresh lifestyle.

> *Jesus said, . . . "Go and sin no more."*
> *John 8:11*

May 22

Serving Refreshments
THE WOMAN FROM SHUNEM

2 Kings 4:8-10

I stretched my arms over my head and looked at the clock. I had been working at the computer for hours, and I needed some kind of pick-me-up. I scanned the refrigerator and cabinets—no pop, no ice cream, no cookies, no chips. I seemed to be out of the four basic food groups. I didn't even have fruit. Walking to the mailbox, I pulled out a decorated envelope with familiar handwriting. My friend Alice had custom designed a card on her computer to tell me that she was praying for me. I returned to my work unbelievably refreshed.

The woman from Shunem knew how to refresh a weary traveler. She noticed that the prophet Elisha often looked fatigued as he passed by her house on his frequent trips. She knew his reputation as a man of God. So she prepared a guest room for him on the roof of her spacious home. As she furnished and decorated the room, her thoughts focused on the comfort, rest, and privacy the room would provide the elderly prophet. What a joy to be able to express her faith in God by offering refreshment for another person's body and spirit.

We all need refreshment from time to time. God instituted a Sabbath day of rest so his people could be refreshed in body, mind, and spirit. Taking a break from our usual activities for even a brief quiet time of prayer and meditation on God's Word recharges and strengthens us. We can also refresh one another with expressions of love and appreciation, encouragement, kindness, or practical help. Refreshing another person's heart and spirit demonstrates our love for God. And as the woman in Shunem found out, any refreshment we offer to others renews our own spirits as well.

The generous will prosper; those who refresh others will themselves be refreshed.
Proverbs 11:25

May 23

Beyond Our Imagination
THE WOMAN FROM SHUNEM

2 Kings 4:11-17

Dena's hand trembled as she picked up the envelope from the community college. Her GED scores had finally come. After working a series of dead-end jobs, she wouldn't underestimate the value of education again. Dena figured that with some serious penny-pinching, she could manage one or two college classes a semester—assuming that she had passed the high-school equivalency test. As she ripped the envelope open, a note fell in her lap before she even saw her scores. Picking it up, she read, *As the recipient of one of the ten highest GED scores for the year, we are pleased to offer you a full one-year scholarship at our school.*

The woman in the Bible passage also received far more than she hoped for. When Elisha offered to do a favor for her in return for her hospitality, she assured the prophet that she had no special needs. But Elisha shocked her by saying that she would have a son within the year. The woman begged Elisha not to deceive her. Years had passed since she'd given up the dream of motherhood. Her emotions rose and fell over the following weeks as she wondered, *Do I dare to hope that it could happen?* Then came the day when she learned that she was pregnant.

We think that we have big dreams and plans for our lives, but they are tiny compared to what God has in mind for us. He does what seems impossible, and he wants to do things that we have never even dared to hope for. When we are seeking God's will and living in obedience to him, his power works through us to accomplish more than we would ever think of asking him for. God wants us to trust him enough to dream big, but even then we can't imagine what he has in store for us.

> *[He] is able to do immeasurably more than all we ask or imagine,*
> *according to his power that is at work within us.*
> *Ephesians 3:20 (NIV)*

May 24

Defining Moment
THE WOMAN FROM SHUNEM

2 Kings 4:18-20

Although the woman from Shunem had given up expectations of having a child, Elisha's prophecy came true and she gave birth to a son. The woman had been happy before; now she embraced the joys of motherhood and thanked God every day for his miraculous gift. Several years passed, and one day her son followed his father into the fields during harvest time. Suddenly, the boy got a severe headache. The distraught mother held him on her lap until noon, when he died.

The unexpected death of her son struck the woman like a lightning bolt. God had sent this precious child after she had become resigned to never being a mother. The boy had brought more light and happiness into her life than she ever dreamed possible. Now, God had allowed her son to die. This tragedy brought a defining moment into the life of this woman. The way she reacted would be a major factor in her relationship with God and in her ability to be a witness for him. Would she lose her faith in the God she had served so faithfully? Would her pain and despair change her view of God so that she saw him as cruel rather than loving and merciful?

It's easy to have a good attitude toward God when our lives are going smoothly. We enjoy God's blessings and thank him for being a loving and merciful God. Then God takes away something that we treasure, maybe even what we love the most. A job is lost that we've held for twenty years. A spouse leaves after thirty years of marriage. A sudden illness claims a child's life. Those dark days are the ones that reveal our faith. Will our change in circumstances change our view of God? Or will we stubbornly cling to the truth that God's character never alters no matter how badly we're hurting?

How will you respond if God takes away something that you treasure?

May 25

Telling Him First
THE WOMAN FROM SHUNEM

2 Kings 4:21-28

All afternoon, I rehearsed the conversation. That morning at church, a woman had criticized the way I chaired the fellowship committee and had declined to serve with me another year. Her stinging comments had hurt, and I longed to tell my closest friend. I knew that Lisa would reassure me that I was doing a good job and denounce the woman's remarks as unfair. But Lisa was out of town for the day. As I watched the clock, waiting for her return, I sensed God speaking to me: *Why don't you talk to me about it?*

The Shunemite woman talked to the right person about her trouble. When her son died suddenly, she immediately went to see the prophet Elisha. When Elisha's servant ran ahead to see if anything was wrong, she told him that everything was fine. The woman must have been in shock and anguish over losing her only child. She didn't bother to stop and explain her sorrow to the servant; she rode straight to Elisha. Then she poured out her grief to the prophet, who had predicted her son's miraculous birth. She had faith in Elisha's ability as a man of God to restore her son's life.

Whenever we're hurt or troubled, our first instinct is to run to a close friend. We want someone to reassure us and make us feel better. The Bible teaches that we should share our joys and sorrows with one another and encourage one another. Too often, though, we talk to everyone except God about what concerns us. He should be the first one we go to, not the last. If we have confidence in God's ability to comfort us and work out our problems, we'll immediately think of him when we need someone to talk to. And he is never out of town.

> *O my people, trust in him at all times. Pour out your heart to him,*
> *for God is our refuge.*
> *Psalm 62:8*

May 26

Walking with a Companion
THE WOMAN FROM SHUNEM

2 Kings 4:29-37

As she walked through the cavernous parking garage, Alana's eyes strained to see her familiar blue Taurus. She never relished having to drive downtown for nighttime company meetings, especially now, when the news had been reporting recent attacks on women. Alana looked at the security guard walking beside her. She'd been embarrassed about his offer to walk her to her car, but now she was glad that he had insisted. Sure was nice to have company at a time like this.

The woman from Shunem had company as she returned to her home, where her son lay dead. She had gone to find Elisha, and when she reached him, she fell to the ground and grabbed his feet. When he learned that something was wrong with her son, Elisha sent his servant to lay his staff on the boy. That didn't satisfy the grief-stricken mother. She vowed that she would not go home unless the prophet came with her. As the two made their way back to Shunem, the woman had no idea what would happen, but she had the comfort of having a person who could help her by her side.

When a crisis hits, our first instinct should be to run to God as the Shunemite woman ran to Elisha. We don't need to grab his feet and beg for him to come with us. He's already here, and he has promised to walk through every situation in our lives with us. After the Shunemite woman got home, Elisha prayed, and God restored her son to life. Although God doesn't always change our circumstances the way we desire, something miraculous will happen. He will give us the strength and courage to face whatever comes our way, and he will change *us* in the process. Whether we're dealing with a dark, scary night or the tragedy of death, Someone walks beside us every step of the way.

Yea, though I walk through the valley of the shadow of death, I will fear no evil; for You are with me.
Psalm 23:4 (NKJV)

May 27

Restoration
THE WOMAN FROM SHUNEM

2 Kings 8:1-6

The mother looked at her blooming garden and thought of all the years
of work she and her husband had put into their home and yard. They had
looked forward to raising their three young children here. Now, they were in
danger of losing their home. The city had threatened to seize their property
along with others in the area so that a developer could build upscale condo-
miniums. At first the woman couldn't believe what was happening; she had
later learned that it was not only legal but such actions were becoming more
common.

The woman from Shunem also had her property seized. When Elisha
warned her about a coming famine, she took his advice and moved her family away from Israel. Seven years passed, and she returned with her son to
find that her house and land had been taken over by other people. When
the woman went to plead her case with the king, she and her son walked
in just as Elisha's servant was recounting the story of how the prophet had
brought her boy back to life. The king ordered that her property be restored
to her and that she even be compensated for any crops harvested during her
absence. The woman's disappointment turned to joy.

While the Shunemite woman left Israel in obedience to Elisha, sometimes we move away from God out of rebellion. When we choose to live
the way we want to instead of obeying his instructions, we remove ourselves
from his abundant provision and blessings. We may end up in a place where
we don't want to be, longing to return to the closeness we once felt with
God. Although we often have to live with the consequences of our disobedience, God promises to renew our joy and peace when we repent and return
to his ways. When we call on our King with the right attitude, we can
always expect restoration.

> *Restore us, O LORD, and bring us back to you again! Give us back the joys*
> *we once had!*
> *Lamentations 5:21*

147

May 28

Grateful Mothers
JESUS BLESSES THE CHILDREN

Matthew 19:13-15

The young mother stood in line, holding her son's hand. Robbie had been ecstatic to learn that a star from his favorite children's show would pass out autographed pictures at the county fair. Although they had come early, they found a long line already snaking around the booths. The mother didn't mind waiting in the hot sun as the afternoon wore on. What bothered her was a fear that the star wouldn't stay long enough to greet all the children. If he left on time, there would be a lot of disappointed kids.

A mother in today's Bible passage probably walked across dusty roads and stood patiently at the edge of the crowd holding her child's hand. She was surprised to see how many mothers had come, but she was willing to wait her turn to have her child blessed by the new Rabbi. Suddenly, several men stood in front of the crowd, frowning and commanding the parents to go away. The mother's heart filled with disappointment as she turned around. Then she heard another voice reproaching the disgruntled disciples. Jesus spoke with authority and compassion, "Let the children come to me. Don't stop them!"

The hearts of the mothers present that afternoon must have swelled with gratitude and joy as Jesus took the time to bless every child present before he left the area. He wants to do the same thing today for all of us. We don't have annoyed disciples urging us not to bother the Master, so what keeps us from getting a blessing from Jesus every day? Too often, our busy agendas don't include a time of quietness with God. We let the things of the world keep us from receiving spiritual nourishment. God longs to bless us with encouragement, comfort, and a sense of his loving presence. All we have to do is take time to go to the Rabbi. We won't even have to stand in line.

He placed his hands on their heads and blessed them before he left.
Matthew 19:15

May 29

Childlike Faith
JESUS BLESSES THE CHILDREN

Luke 18:15-17

Glancing up, I quickly rose from my chair as I saw a toddler walking straight toward the deep end of the pool. Then I noticed her eyes locked on the face of her father, who was in the water, and on his uplifted arms. When the little girl hesitated at the edge, her father smiled and murmured words of encouragement. I watched, mesmerized, as the seconds ticked by . . . and then the girl suddenly relaxed and plunged straight into her daddy's arms.

Jesus made an important statement about childlike trust when he laid his hands on the children and blessed them. The disciples thought that young children weren't worth their Master's time, but Jesus welcomed them. He also used the opportunity to teach the importance of approaching God with the right attitude. After the mothers went home, they must have contemplated Jesus' statement that a person could enter the Kingdom of God only by becoming like a child. This contrasted sharply with the attitude of their religious leaders and teachers, who gloried in their positions and emphasized strict adherence to rules. Over and over, these mothers may have asked themselves, "Can a relationship with God really be that simple?"

However complicated we make things, a relationship with God is simple. Jesus used the picture of a child to illustrate the attitude required for a person to become a child of God. Like children, we come in humility and total dependence on him, not in pride and self-sufficiency. We approach him with no agendas of our own and implicitly trust him to save us. Even after we become God's children, it's important to keep our faith and trust childlike. When responsibilities, burdens, and problems weigh us down, what could be more comforting than jumping into our Daddy's arms, knowing that he will take care of things?

> *[Jesus said,] "I tell you the truth, anyone who doesn't receive the Kingdom of God like a child will never enter it."*
> *Luke 18:17*

May 30

Nonconformists
HEBREW WOMEN

Exodus 20:1-17; Deuteronomy 14:2

As I saw heads around me turning, I wished that I could have shielded the woman from the curious stares. Her serene face revealed no signs of embarrassment, however. *Is she used to this?* I wondered. Her plain blue dress was closed with straight pins instead of buttons, and her hair, pulled into a bun under a white cap, shouted that she belonged to the nearby Amish community. As she walked into the clinic, she couldn't help drawing attention.

Hebrews who observed God's laws didn't blend in with the crowd, either. Their worship practices, circumcision of males, special diet, and observance of a day of rest on the Sabbath all set them apart from the nations around them. How did the women feel about being different from other groups of people? A few probably wished that they could just forget God's laws and live like those around them. Others surely must have felt humbled and privileged to belong to a race that God had chosen for a unique role in history.

God didn't choose the Hebrew nation as his special people in order to exclude others; he set the Israelites apart to reveal his holiness to the world and draw everyone to him. Today, Christians have the privilege and responsibility of making God known to the world. The way we live and how we treat others should set us apart, demonstrating that we have a different set of values and goals from the rest of the world. We may wish that we could blend in with the crowd, but following God means being different. When the Hebrews started living like the nations around them, they suffered personally and lost their opportunity to witness for God. We don't want to repeat those mistakes.

> *You must be holy because I, the LORD, am holy. I have set you apart from*
> *all other people to be my very own.*
> *Leviticus 20:26*

May 31

Holding Grudges
EUODIA AND SYNTYCHE

Philippians 2:1-2; 4:2

"It's a beautiful day, Laura has her living room decorated in pink, and Katie is bringing one of her gorgeous cakes. Only one thing can ruin your baby shower now."

"What's that?"

"If Doris and Jill both show up."

"Ah, yes, the 'odd couple.' Have they always hated each other?"

"Believe it or not, they used to be close friends. Then they had a falling-out; now they create tension whenever they're in the same room. The only real solution is to seat them with their backs to each other. That way, they can't give each other dirty looks."

In Paul's letter to the church at Philippi, he addressed a disagreement between two women. Euodia and Syntyche were both committed followers of Jesus Christ. They had worked hard together to share the good news of God's love and forgiveness with others. Then they had a falling-out and refused to share that forgiveness with each other. Their strained relationship caused dissension in their group of believers, so Paul urged them to settle their disagreement because they both belonged to the Lord.

Sometimes it's possible to nurse a grudge against someone in secret while pretending that everything is okay in the relationship. More often, our resentment affects those around us and creates a spirit of discord. Holding a grudge hurts us physically, emotionally, and spiritually. It strains our relationships with others and hinders our relationship with God.

God enacted the most important reconciliation when Jesus' death made it possible for us to become his children. He also desires for us to be reconciled with one another. With his help, we can mend any broken relationship. Then we won't have to worry about being exposed in a letter to a church—or ruining a baby shower.

> *Make me truly happy by agreeing wholeheartedly with each other, loving one another, and working together with one mind and purpose.*
> *Philippians 2:2*

June 1

Home Alone
NEW WIVES

Deuteronomy 24:5

Arriving home from work, Karen picked up a note from the kitchen counter. David would be working a little late tonight. She shrugged her shoulders and grabbed a soda from the fridge. *Should I feel guilty about not minding?* she wondered. After all, they'd been married for only seven months. Her husband was loving, dependable, and hard working. So where had the spark gone? Why did Karen feel that she would be just as happy living alone? *I didn't think marriage would make my life perfect,* she thought, *but I did expect more than this.*

According to the laws established for Israel in Deuteronomy, a newly married man could not be drafted for military service or given business that would take him away from home. For the first year, his responsibility was to concentrate on making his wife happy. Having this time together free from other distractions allowed the relationship to mature and united the couple, who probably hadn't spent time together before their parents arranged the marriage. The wife must have enjoyed being the focus of her husband's attention for a whole year.

Even when we have great marriages, we can't expect our husbands to meet all our needs. Often we think that the right relationship, a better job, or a different lifestyle will make us happy. If we just had more money, or perfect looks, or lived somewhere else, we would be perfectly content. But God is the only source of true joy. He created us to enjoy a close relationship with him. Nothing on earth will satisfy us if we don't have that in place first. When we concentrate on loving, worshiping, and obeying God, then happiness will find us—and it will last a lot longer than one year.

> *Make me walk along the path of your commands, for that is where my happiness is found.*
> Psalm 119:35

June 2

Trophy Wife
QUEEN VASHTI

Esther 1:10-19

When Lady Diana and Prince Charles married in 1981, hundreds of thousands of spectators waited along the streets for a glimpse of the couple. After the ceremony, people around the world couldn't get enough details about Princess Diana—what she wore, how she styled her hair, how she spent her time. Reporters and photographers dogged her every step. Diana later admitted to being unhappy with the pressure of constantly being in the public eye. She died in a car crash as she and her companion fled from photographers.

Queen Vashti also knew about being on public display. The king capped off a six-month celebration with a banquet that featured heavy drinking. Xerxes had displayed his wealth and majesty, and now in his drunkenness, he decided to show off his wife. He ordered her to come to the banquet so that all the men in attendance could admire her beauty. Many commentators think that this request went against Persian etiquette. The queen was typically shielded from the public eye, and separation of the sexes was customarily observed at the time. Vashti must have been horrified at the king's request, because she refused to obey the order, probably hoping that he would come to his senses when he sobered up.

We may not be princesses or queens, but we can still identify with the feeling of being viewed as an object. We may sense that someone is interested only in our physical appearance. Perhaps we feel that we're just a means to getting a job done or of meeting someone's needs. We all long to be known and valued for who we are on the inside. That's just the kind of intimate relationship that Jesus wants to have with us. This King of kings calls us to come to him in quietness and solitude where we can simply be ourselves—and be loved for it.

> *Yes, what joy for those whose record the LORD has cleared of guilt, whose lives are lived in complete honesty!*
> *Psalm 32:2*

June 3

Never Good Enough
YOUNG WOMEN IN PERSIA

Esther 2:1-14

Brynn put the magazine down and went to the bathroom to find her magnifying mirror. Looking at some before-and-after pictures had started her thinking about ways that she could improve her appearance. While she didn't have a big nose, Brynn had always thought that a slightly different shape would suit her face better. And even though people told her she had great skin, maybe laser treatments would get rid of those few freckles. If Brynn had studied her attitude instead of her face, she would have realized that even though she had won beauty pageants in high school, she had never felt quite good enough.

The young women in today's passage were treated the same way that Brynn treated herself. The king appointed agents in each of his 127 provinces to hunt for the most beautiful young virgins and herd them into the palace like prize livestock. Even the most gorgeous girls in the land weren't good enough for the king until they had spent an entire year receiving special beauty treatments. It's hard to imagine the self-image of these women, who were involved in a twelve-month improvement program and still had to wait to see if the king would accept them.

Many women go through life feeling that they're never good enough. We tend to dwell on the flaws in our appearance and on the abilities and gifts that we don't have. Some women approach God with the same mindset, thinking that they have to "clean up" before they can have a relationship with him. We don't have to make ourselves good enough to become God's children—he accepts us in our natural state and then begins to shape us into his image. After that, any self-improvement should be done to honor the One who loves us unconditionally.

> *He saved us, not because of the righteous things we had done, but because of his mercy.*
> *Titus 3:5*

June 4

A Lose-Lose Situation
ESTHER

Esther 2:13-14

Esther seemed to be caught in a situation with no way out, facing two bad possibilities. After spending a night with the king, she might be taken to the harem where all the king's wives and concubines lived. Unless King Xerxes requested her by name, Esther would just live in the harem, separated from her relatives, friends, and the people who shared her faith.

The other scenario was no less depressing. If by chance Xerxes chose Esther as the next queen, she would be married to a pagan ruler known for his drunkenness, capricious moods, and explosive temper. Following her guardian's advice, Esther had not revealed her nationality. Since Xerxes would be breaking Persian law by marrying a Jewish girl, Esther's secret would be a heavy burden, along with the memory of what had happened to the former queen when she angered the king.

References to God are absent from the book of Esther, and on the surface, it looked as if he were absent from Esther's predicament. As a Jewish girl raised by a devout family that honored God's laws, she must have been horrified at the prospect of either possibility. Yet Esther clung to her confidence in God's character and sovereignty, while God quietly worked behind the scenes to accomplish his purposes. He used Esther's situation to protect the Jews from an enemy who would soon threaten their very existence.

We can all relate to the anxiety Esther must have felt when there seemed to be no positive options. Instead of hoping for the best, we sometimes find ourselves trying to identify the lesser of two evils. At such times, it may seem that God is absent from our lives. If we could see past the surface, we would understand that he is there, working to accomplish his purposes.

The LORD will work out his plans for my life.
Psalm 138:8

June 5

The Right Place at the Right Time
QUEEN ESTHER

Esther 3:12-15; 4:1-14

I listened with amazement as my friend Alice told about an incident from her childhood. Alice's sister had been on a new medication that affected her balance. One afternoon, she opened the door to the family's basement and tumbled down the stairs. Their dad had been in his basement workshop, and a sudden impulse made him walk toward the stairs. He arrived at the bottom step at precisely the right moment to catch his daughter in his arms and keep her from landing on the concrete floor.

Queen Esther saved many lives by being in the right place at the right time. Her guardian understood that it was no accident that the former queen had been deposed by a whim of the king or that Esther had been chosen out of the most beautiful girls in the empire to replace her. God had placed Esther in just the right position at just the right time to save her people from annihilation. Mordecai urged Queen Esther to use her God-given opportunity to approach the king and plead for mercy for the Jews.

God has placed each of us in a unique position. The people, needs, and opportunities around us are arranged by God so that we can make a difference in our corner of the world. Our hands may be the only ones to reach out to a neighbor. Our words of encouragement may be the only ones a friend hears. Our smile may be the only one a stranger sees. If we know God, we are daughters of the King, and like Queen Esther, we have been placed where we are for "just such a time as this."

Who knows if perhaps you were made queen for just such a time as this?
Esther 4:14

June 6

Defining Moment
QUEEN ESTHER

Esther 4:10-11

After becoming queen, Esther lived in two worlds. Nothing could be further from her Jewish upbringing than life in the palace of a powerful Persian monarch. Although Esther lived in luxury, with numerous servants to carry out her slightest whim, her role required her to live among people who did not know God. Esther conducted herself in a way that won the favor of those around her, yet she remained true to her heritage. She stayed in constant contact with her guardian, Mordecai, and followed his advice just as she had before she became queen.

A sudden crisis disrupted this settled arrangement and brought Esther to a defining moment in her life. When Haman scheduled a day for the Jewish people's annihilation, Mordecai urged Esther to intervene. Esther knew the dangers this entailed—approaching the king without an invitation meant death unless he chose to extend his scepter. Esther also didn't know how Xerxes would react when he found out that she was Jewish. Would she reveal her race or continue to conceal it? Would she speak up for her people or stay quiet and hope to avoid trouble? Esther's decision would change her world and that of her people, one way or another.

Many Christian women try to live in two separate worlds. We may work hard to fit in on the job, around the neighborhood, or in social settings while keeping our faith a private matter. Although we try to justify our silence as a desire not to force our beliefs on others, God will eventually require us to choose which world we represent. How will we react when speaking up for Christ brings us ridicule or poses a danger, such as losing a job? Whether we choose to conceal or reveal our faith, it will affect our lives and the lives of those around us.

Is there a setting in which God is asking you to reveal your faith?

June 7

Drawing Near
QUEEN ESTHER

Esther 5:1-3

Patricia blinked her eyes and looked across the restaurant again. "Is that who I think it is?" she asked Lisa.

Turning around, Lisa nearly jumped out of her seat. "Yes, it's him! Didn't you read in the paper about the movie being filmed here? Let's go get an autograph!"

Patricia started to grab a pen from her purse, then hesitated. "I don't know. . . . He has a reputation for being unpredictable and cranky. What if he made a scene in front of all these people? I'd just die!"

Queen Esther had much more than embarrassment at stake when she decided to approach the king. The law mandated death for anyone who entered the inner court without being summoned. If Xerxes was in a good mood, he would hold out his scepter and spare her life. It had been thirty days since Xerxes had called for Esther. Did he still care for her more than the many other women available to him? Would he be angered by her audacity, or feel like showing mercy? Esther stood in the court dressed in her royal robes, watching to see how the king would react and waiting to find out if she would live or die.

Sometimes we hesitate to approach God, as if we fear how he will react to us. Some women experience God only through formal worship rituals, never dreaming of the personal relationship he desires to have with them. While it is important to recognize God's majesty and holiness, he doesn't want us to remain distant from him. Because of Jesus' death, we can approach God freely at any time and in any situation. When we draw near to God with the proper attitude, we don't have to wonder how he will react to us. He won't extend a gold scepter to us—he will hold out his nail-pierced hands.

> *Draw near to God and He will draw near to you.*
> *James 4:8 (NKJV)*

June 8

Timing Is Everything
QUEEN ESTHER

Esther 5:3-7

As her husband came in the back door, Judy resisted the urge to blurt out all the things weighing on her mind. The mechanic from the garage had called to say that her car needed new brakes, Derek's teacher had requested an appointment to discuss a behavior problem at recess, and she was thinking about taking night classes to finish her degree. *This is not the right time,* she reminded herself. *Not after a ten-hour workday and a long commute.* They would have their discussion after Ed had a chance to enjoy his dinner and read the paper. After ten years of marriage, she had learned the importance of timing.

When Xerxes admitted Esther into the inner court, Esther may have felt the urge to blurt out what weighed so heavily on her heart. The lives of all the Jewish people, including her relatives and friends, were at stake. But since Esther had prepared herself with prayer, she sensed that this was not the right time to make her request. Even in such a perilous situation, she controlled her emotions and waited for God to guide her. Instead of pleading for the lives of her people, she invited the king to a banquet and promised to explain her request the next day.

I admire Queen Esther's discernment and restraint. Too often, I succumb to the temptation to speak before thinking. When we say the wrong thing, or the right thing at the wrong time, it can trigger unpleasant or even disastrous consequences. The Bible teaches that we are accountable not only for what we say but also for when and how we say it. If we pray before dealing with a problem, God's Holy Spirit will guide our words and our timing. With his help, we can learn to say the right thing at just the right time.

> *The heart of the godly thinks carefully before speaking; the mouth of the wicked overflows with evil words.*
> *Proverbs 15:28*

June 9

Time for Action
QUEEN ESTHER

Esther 6; 7

Vanessa stood at the edge of the set and peered up at the bright overhead lights. Trying out for a commercial had seemed like an exciting adventure, but now she wasn't so sure. She had her few lines of dialogue memorized, and she understood exactly how they wanted her to deliver them, but she hadn't envisioned this throng of people hovering around during the filming. As she blotted the perspiration from her forehead with the back of her hand, Vanessa heard the director call out, "Lights, camera, action!" Vanessa froze.

Sometimes it's hard to restrain ourselves from acting impulsively; at other times it's difficult to act at all. Queen Esther avoided pleading the Jews' case with Xerxes the first two times he asked for her request. The next night, the king learned that Mordecai had saved his life but had never been rewarded. This made the banquet the next day the perfect time to tell Xerxes about Haman's plot to exterminate the Jews. It took courage for Esther to accuse the king's most trusted advisor of treachery, but she knew that God had set the stage and given her the cue to play her assigned role.

Instead of acting in haste, Esther depended on God to show her the right time to move. By the time she told Xerxes that she was among the people scheduled for annihilation, God had arranged events in such a way that the king saw Haman and his plan in a different light than before. When we face a problem, God may want us to wait for him to order events. But we also need to ask for the wisdom and courage to be ready to do our part. By depending on prayer and God's guidance, we won't freeze when he directs us to act.

> *Don't act thoughtlessly, but understand what the Lord wants you to do.*
> *Ephesians 5:17*

June 10

Asking for the Impossible
QUEEN ESTHER

Esther 8:1-12

"I'll be sure to pray for you," Ann promised. after Betty had finished listing her problems.

"A lot of good that will do," snorted Betty as she walked away. She didn't put much stock in prayer these days. *Prayer didn't keep my husband from losing his job, or my son from leaving his wife. It didn't cure my mom's cancer. It didn't even get us the asking price for our house. I guess the things I asked God for were just too hard for him.*

Queen Esther made a seemingly impossible request of King Xerxes. Haman had issued a decree in the king's name calling for the total destruction of the Jewish people in the empire. Filled with horror at the prospect of death for herself and her people, Esther begged the king to reverse the order. But according to the law of the Medes and Persians, a royal decree could never be revoked. King Xerxes could, however, sign another decree to offset the first one. The second decree allowed the Jews to come together and destroy their enemies, which protected them from the harmful effects of the first decree without canceling it.

Nothing is impossible for God. Sometimes we don't get what we ask for because it goes against his purposes or would require him to violate someone's free will. Before God created the world, he decreed that the penalty for sin would be death. When Adam and Eve disobeyed, God couldn't revoke that law. But he had a second decree ready. He would become a man and die for the sins of the entire human race. For those who choose to believe, Jesus' sacrifice offsets the harmful effects of the law of sin and death without revoking it.

> *The law of the Spirit of life in Christ Jesus has made me free from the law of sin and death.*
> *Romans 8:2 (NKJV)*

June 11

God's Instrument
QUEEN ESTHER

Esther 4:13-14

When Mordecai urged Esther to intervene for the Jewish people, he told her that even if she refused to act, the Jews would still be saved somehow. Mordecai trusted in God's promises to his people and realized that God would not allow their destruction. After the crisis had passed, Mordecai's words must have lingered in the queen's mind. No one could deny that Esther acted courageously and wisely, but she knew that God had orchestrated every detail of the Jews' rescue.

God had placed Esther in a unique position to intervene with the king. He had guided Esther to wait until the perfect time for revealing her request. In the meantime, he arranged for Xerxes to learn of the debt he owed Mordecai for saving his life. When Esther finally revealed Haman's plot that endangered her life, Xerxes walked into the garden in a rage. At the moment that he returned to the room, he saw Haman falling on the queen's couch and assumed that he was assaulting her (7:6-8). This final detail sealed the doom of the Jews' bitter enemy.

When we accomplish some important task for God, it may be easy to get puffed up with our success. Any sense of self-importance disappears when we remember that God is the One in control over everyone and everything in his world. He doesn't need our help, but he allows us the blessing of participating in his work. If we refuse to fulfill our assigned role, God will find another person or another way to work it out. Queen Esther knew that she was God's instrument, and she gave the credit for the Jews' deliverance to God. Like Esther, we need to remember that although God never needs our help, we always need his.

He is not served by human hands, as if he needed anything, because he himself gives all men life and breath and everything else.
Acts 17:25 (NIV)

June 12

Sound Advice
HAMAN'S WIFE

Esther 6:13; 7:10

Holding her daughter's hand, Phyllis listened as Tori sobbed out the story of the breakup with her boyfriend. *I could see this day coming,* Phyllis thought. She had seen the obvious warning signs. From the beginning, she had urged Tori not to get involved with the guy. But her strong-willed daughter had ignored her advice and angrily accused her of being narrow-minded. At one time, Phyllis had imagined herself saying, "I told you so." But now, all she could think about was how much pain and heartache her daughter could have avoided if only she'd listened.

Haman's wife gave him good advice, and his refusal to listen to her led to his death and her deep suffering. She saw that God had protected and honored Mordecai, so she urged Haman to quit opposing him. Haman continued with his plot against Mordecai, with the result that the king executed him and his sons and seized his property. Because of her husband's stubbornness, Haman's wife lost her family and her home. For the rest of her life, she must have imagined how her life would have been if Haman had only followed her advice.

It's hard to watch those we love headed for trouble, but all we can do is give them our opinion that what they are doing is a mistake. We can't force others to follow our advice even if it's in their best interest. God never forces us to follow his counsel even though he always knows what is best for us. His Word gives us the instructions we need to enjoy the best possible life, but we often ignore his guidance and go our own way. When we reap the consequences of our rebellion, God stands ready to comfort us. All the while, he longs for us to see how much pain and heartache we can avoid by following his advice.

> *Your laws please me; they give me wise advice.*
> *Psalm 119:24*

June 13

Adopted Daughter
ESTHER

Esther 2:5-11

As Moira pulled the faded certificate from the box, tears stung her eyes. She remembered when Roy had placed this paper in her hands as they sat in a restaurant far too fancy for a four-year-old. "I'm not just marrying your mommy," he had said. "I'm also choosing you to be my daughter. This paper says that we belong to each other for all time." Moira looked in the box again and saw the little gold ring her new father had put on her finger at the wedding ceremony the following week. He'd kept his promise. She couldn't have asked for a more loving father or a better grandpa for her children.

The heroine in the book of Esther was also an adopted daughter. After Esther's parents died, her older cousin Mordecai adopted her and raised her as his own child. When Esther was taken into King Xerxes' palace, Mordecai walked near the harem every day, trying to gather information about Esther's well-being. After Xerxes crowned her queen, Mordecai still kept watch over her. For her part, Esther honored and obeyed him even after she became a powerful queen. Esther refused to let the dramatic change in her life disrupt the bond that united her with her adoptive father.

All believers are adopted children in a spiritual sense. *To be adopted* means "to be chosen," and the Bible teaches that God chose us before he created the world. Jesus died so that a holy God could adopt us as his daughters. The Holy Spirit is our adoption certificate, proving that we have become a part of God's family. God promises us his full protection, provision, and guidance. Our part is to honor and obey him to the best of our ability, regardless of the circumstances of our lives. We could never ask for a more loving Father.

> *God decided in advance to adopt us into his own family by bringing us to himself through Jesus Christ. This is what he wanted to do, and it gave him great pleasure.*
> *Ephesians 1:5*

June 14

Less-Than-Perfect Father
LOT'S DAUGHTERS

Genesis 19:6-8, 30-38

"You were always there for me, Dad!" Sierra shoved that card back in the rack. "How can I thank you for all the things you taught me as a child?" *Not quite right, either.* She grimaced. *Where's a card that won't make me feel like a hypocrite? Something like "You were always too busy with your career to come to my recitals and school plays so I don't really have childhood memories of fun times with you and now we feel so distant from each other that conversation is mostly about the weather or the news, but Happy Father's Day, anyway."*

No father is perfect. The Bible describes Lot as a righteous man (see 2 Peter 2:7-8), but he failed his daughters in a way that caused much misery and degradation. When men from Sodom demanded sex with the two men who were Lot's guests, he offered them his virgin daughters instead. Lot placed greater importance on his role as host than on his role as father and protector.

It's hard to imagine how the girls felt about being offered to a mob for sexual pleasure, and by their own father. We do know that they had no respect for themselves or for Lot. The girls later tricked their drunken father into having sex with them. They placed greater importance on continuing the family line than on basic laws of morality. Their sons became the ancestors of two of Israel's bitterest enemies.

We have all felt let down in some way by our parents, whether by minor disappointments or the deep wounds of neglect or abuse. It helps to remember that while our earthly fathers are human and prone to mistakes, our heavenly Father is perfect, and his love will never let us down. He is also ready to help us forgive all the hurts that have been done to us. In cases like Sierra's, he can help us rebuild that father-daughter relationship so that buying a Father's Day card is easier.

> *See how very much our Father loves us, for he calls us his children, and that is what we are!*
> *1 John 3:1*

June 15

A Remarkable Inheritance
JOB'S DAUGHTERS

Job 42:12-15

My jaw dropped lower and lower as I stared at the document in my hands. The fact that my great-uncle had included me in his will didn't really surprise me; after all, he was childless and had always been close to my family. What totally shocked me was the amount of my inheritance! We had no idea that the man was so rich! My mind raced with plans—my husband quitting his job, buying a new house, helping the kids out, traveling with my family. This money was going to change the way we lived. . . . Suddenly the phone rang—and I woke up.

Today's Bible passage mentions another surprising inheritance, but this one wasn't just a dream. After Job endured the devastating loss of his children and all that he owned, God blessed him in his later life. Ten more children were born to him, including three daughters, described as the fairest in the land. At a time when women didn't normally receive an inheritance, Job included Jemimah, Keziah, and Keren-happuch in his will along with his sons. These women must have felt cherished, knowing that their father loved them enough to go against the social norm to provide generously for their future.

God's daughters also have a remarkable inheritance. That a perfect God would someday share his home and riches with imperfect women is amazing, but when we become God's adopted children through believing in Jesus, he promises us a future that is wonderful beyond anything we could ever dream of. The knowledge that we have a Father who loves us so much that he sent his Son to die to secure our future should make us feel special and cherished. And it should change the way we live right now.

We live with great expectation, and we have a priceless inheritance—an inheritance that is kept in heaven for you, pure and undefiled, beyond the reach of change and decay.
1 Peter 1:3-4

June 16

Safe in the Father's Hands
JEPHTHAH'S DAUGHTER

Judges 11:29-40

Bible scholars disagree as to what actually happened to Jephthah's daughter. Because the Spirit of God was with him and had helped him in battle, he had made a vow to the Lord to sacrifice the first thing that came out of his house when he returned home. Some believe that because of superstitious, pagan influences, Jephthah literally offered his child as a burnt sacrifice in thanksgiving. Others argue that since God had clearly forbidden human sacrifice, Jephthah dedicated his daughter to lifelong service to the Lord instead of allowing her to marry and have children as all Israelite women desired to do. Either way, what most stands out to me in the passage is the daughter's response.

As Jephthah returned from battle, his daughter met him, playing a tambourine and dancing for joy at his victory over the nation's enemies. As soon as he saw her, Jephthah cried out in anguish over his rash vow. His daughter, however, calmly and courageously submitted to the fulfillment of her father's promise to God. In her innocence, did she grasp the meaning of her father's initial comment? Was it only later that she understood exactly what he had promised? Scripture records no words of blame toward her impulsive father, and no exclamations of her horror—only a profound sense of sorrow that she would never bear children.

As God's daughters, we have a heavenly Father who is always wise and good. We don't have to worry about his doing something rash that endangers our lives. He promises to work out everything in our lives for good when we give him control. It's not easy to trust him when bad things happen to us, but even in the midst of our disappointments, God asks for total submission to his will. If Jephthah's daughter displayed such an attitude toward her flawed earthly father, we can surely submit to our perfect heavenly Father, knowing without a doubt that we are always safe in his hands.

Our lives are in his hands, and he keeps our feet from stumbling.
Psalm 66:9

June 17

A Father's Longing
JAIRUS'S DAUGHTER

Mark 5:21-24

As she felt the anesthesia begin to relax her body, Tonya's thoughts focused on her father rather than on worries about the success of the surgery. Her dad had been one of her best encouragers over the past few years, driving her to doctors' appointments and later to dialysis treatments. When her doctor stressed the urgent need for a kidney transplant, he immediately volunteered. Tonya questioned the wisdom of his giving up a kidney at his age, but he was adamant. Although her cousin was also a good match for the donation, Tonya's dad insisted that his kidney be used. He wanted to be the one involved in his daughter's healing.

Today's Bible passage tells of a twelve-year-old girl whose father longed for her healing. Jairus was a local synagogue leader whose only daughter had become deathly ill. Falling at Jesus' feet, the distraught father earnestly begged Jesus to come and lay his hands on her so she wouldn't die. The little girl lay at home on her sickbed, unaware of the depths of her father's grief or his desperate efforts to find a way to save her life. She had no idea that her father's faith would soon lead to her receiving a touch from the very hands of God.

Each one of us has a Father who earnestly longs for our healing. Jesus willingly died so that we could be healed of the fatal disease of sin that leads to eternal separation from God. God further desires to heal us from anything that keeps us from fully enjoying the life he intended for us: wounds from our past, harmful habits, and sinful tendencies that prevent us from being spiritually healthy. If only we knew the depths of our Father's grief over the things that hurt us, we would reach out for his healing touch.

> O LORD, if you heal me, I will be truly healed.
> Jeremiah 17:14

June 18

Hearing His Voice
JAIRUS'S DAUGHTER

Mark 5:35-41

"Time for dinner!" Jackie yelled again from the kitchen. Minutes ticked by, and there was still no response. Irritated, she stalked down the hall and knocked on her son's door. "Didn't you hear me calling you?" Jackie demanded. Not a sound came from the room. Pushing open the door, she saw her teenager sitting on his bed, earphones planted on his head and his new MP3 player in his hands, totally oblivious to her calls.

The girl in Mark 5 heard a voice calling her, and not just from outside her door. When Jairus begged Jesus to come heal his daughter, the twelve-year-old girl died before they got to the house. Going into her bedroom, Jesus took her cold, lifeless hand and called out to her: "Little girl, get up!" In that instant, the girl was restored to life and health.

How did the girl feel to hear the powerful voice that even death obeyed? Perhaps Jesus' voice was familiar to her if she had heard his teaching or had been among the crowds that followed him. Maybe she only sensed that her spirit was being irresistibly drawn to a voice of love and authority.

Jesus' voice is calling each of us today. If we are spiritually dead, he is calling us to new life through faith in him. If we have already accepted the gift of eternal life, he calls us daily to follow his leading and to live in a way that pleases God. When we're surrounded by constant noise, we can miss out on Jesus' still, small voice. We have to plan some quiet time away from television, radios, cell phones, and MP3 players. We don't want to block out Jesus' calling to us—a lot more than dinner is at stake.

> *[Jesus said,] "Look! I stand at the door and knock. If you hear my voice and open the door, I will come in, and we will share a meal together as friends."*
> *Revelation 3:20*

June 19

A Powerful Story
JAIRUS'S DAUGHTER

Mark 5:42-43

We all sat mesmerized as the guest speaker at the banquet shared her amazing life story. Everyone in the audience was touched. In 1977, Gianna Jensen survived an abortion by saline injection when her mother was seven and a half months pregnant. Gianna weighed two pounds and was later diagnosed with cerebral palsy due to lack of oxygen to her brain during the failed abortion. Doctors predicted that the little girl would never be able to lift her head. Today, Gianna travels the country speaking and singing, and she also runs marathons. Everywhere she goes, those who hear her are touched by her amazing life story.

Jairus's daughter also had an amazing story to share with others. As this little girl grew up, she probably never tired of hearing about the miracle of her life—how she had died while her loving father was begging Jesus to heal her, and how Jesus had come to their home and called her back to life and health. Everyone in the neighborhood soon learned her story and pointed her out as the girl who had been brought back from death. As a woman, she knew that her life had purpose and meaning because her father's love and Jesus' touch had given her a second chance.

Some women have dramatic stories to tell about how God delivered them from abusive situations, freed them from addictions, healed them of terminal diseases, or rescued them from danger. We may not feel that our story can have an impact on others, but if we're believers, we have a compelling testimony to share. Our Father's love and Jesus' touch not only healed us of the fatal disease of sin but also gave us new life that will never end. Any life transformed by God's love has a powerful story, and one worth sharing with others.

> *Give yourselves completely to God, for you were dead, but now you have new life.*
> *Romans 6:13*

June 20

The Great Robbery
LABAN'S DAUGHTERS

Genesis 31:1-16

I knew I shouldn't have given in! Lily felt like pounding the walls with her fists. At first, she'd balked at the idea of letting her drug-addicted brother move in, but he'd needed a place to stay for only a few days, just long enough to get into rehab. A week later, Lily had come home from work to find him and her television set gone. As she rushed into the bedroom, her worst fears were confirmed. Her jewelry and her emergency cash had also disappeared.

Leah and Rachel knew how it felt to be robbed by a relative. When Jacob wanted to leave his father-in-law and return to his homeland, the two sisters readily agreed, since they believed that Laban had exploited them. Leah and Rachel had received no benefits from the dowry that Jacob had paid to marry them, which was fourteen years of labor. Since Laban had denied them their customary rights, Leah and Rachel felt that their father had treated them like foreign slaves instead of highly valued daughters. They felt no qualms about slipping secretly away with their husband and the wealth he had accumulated—along with their father's valued idols.

Whether we know it or not, all of us have been robbed. Satan is the great thief who stole something precious when he introduced sin into God's perfect world. In contrast, Jesus came to earth to give his life so that we could regain our rightful relationship with our Father. Even after we become believers, Satan still tries to rob us. When we compromise our standards, play around with sin, or give something other than God first place in our lives, we may find that our joy, our peace, and our contentment have been snatched away. If we notice something missing, it's time to run to our Father, who wants to help us regain what is rightfully ours.

> *[Jesus said,] "The thief's purpose is to steal and kill and destroy. My purpose is to give them a rich and satisfying life."*
> *John 10:10*

June 21

The Original Convenience Food
WOMEN AND MANNA

Exodus 16:11-15; Numbers 11:7-9

Homemade Dinners in Twenty Minutes. The title caught my eye, but as I flipped through the book, I saw that the meals were based on ready-to-serve convenience foods. *This is home cooking?* I thought. *Opening packages and cans?* I remembered the pie from last night's dinner, made with cherries I had picked from our tree, then pitted and baked in a homemade crust. Our breakfast had included muffins made with applesauce that I had made after a trip to the orchard, as well as raspberry jam made from berries I had picked at a farm. *Maybe I go too far to the other extreme.*

The women in today's Bible passage knew something about convenience food. During the forty-year period that the Israelites wandered in the wilderness, God provided for them by raining down food from heaven each morning. Exodus 16:31 describes the white manna as tasting like honey wafers. All the women had to do was walk out of their tents and pick up as much as their families needed. True, they still had to prepare it, but at least they didn't have to kill it, skin it, and cut it up. Each day, the women knew what was on the menu. They just had to decide whether to boil it or bake it.

Many people think that spiritual growth should be quick and easy, like cooking with convenience foods. But we can't open up a package of godliness. We don't just flip open our Bibles and understand God. Becoming like Christ takes hard work. Although our salvation is a gift, many Scriptures urge us to work and study to become who God intends us to be. While I don't always have time these days to cook from scratch, I do need to find some time each day to prepare my heart for God. I'll find the ingredients listed in his Book.

> *Work at living a holy life.*
> *Hebrews 12:14*

June 22

Daily Bread
WOMEN AND MANNA

Exodus 16:4-5, 16-20

My hands trembled as I measured the Cream of Wheat cereal into the boiling water. Behind me, my toddler sat in his high chair, crying at the top of his lungs. Morning after morning, we went through the same routine. How long would it be before he figured out that I didn't plan to let him starve—that I had fed him the day before, so I would feed him again today?

When the Israelites' food ran out, they accused God of planning to let them starve. God wanted the people to trust him to supply their needs, so he instructed the Israelites to gather enough manna for only one day at a time. This would have been especially hard for the women who were used to preserving, preparing, and serving the food. They *were* in the middle of a wilderness, after all. What if the manna didn't come the next day? What if their children went hungry later because they had left food on the ground? Some people disobeyed God's instructions and tried to hoard the manna. The next morning, it was crawling with maggots and it smelled awful.

The Israelites had a hard time believing that God would provide for their basic needs, even after all the miracles he had performed on their behalf. We often doubt God's provision in a similar way. Even though we have trusted him to save us from eternal judgment for sin, it's sometimes hard to believe that he will take care of us in other ways. Whether we need material provision, help with emotional or relational problems, or guidance for difficult decisions, we can count on God to supply it. But he will give us only what we need for that particular situation. That way, we'll grow up and learn to trust him to keep feeding us on a daily basis.

> *Give us day by day our daily bread.*
> Luke 11:3 (NKJV)

June 23

Paul's Letter
CHERISHED WOMEN

Ephesians 5:25-33

At a time when many cultures regarded wives as property to be dealt with according to their husbands' wishes, Christianity elevated the role of wives to unheard-of heights. The passage in Ephesians 5 doesn't seem revolutionary to us, but it must have sounded radical to the women who first heard Paul's letter when it was read to early groups of believers. To show his love for his "bride," Jesus Christ had willingly given up his life for everyone who would follow him. Now, Paul's writings commanded husbands to love their wives with that same sacrificial heart.

Some of the original recipients of Paul's letters had probably endured harsh treatment. Perhaps some of them lived with indifferent or uncaring spouses. Even if they had learned to accept their situations, God's words must have made them feel valued in a way they had never known before. Whether or not the men obeyed the instructions, the women had the assurance that God intended for their husbands to love and care for them as much as for their own bodies. God desired for wives to experience the kind of love that always acted in their best interest.

What woman wouldn't want a man with deep, unselfish love that would lead him to lay down his life for her if necessary? Many wives today feel that they are in loveless marriages. Some experience a distorted version of the relationship that God intended, which makes them feel used. Regardless of the nature of our marriages or our marital status, we *have* experienced the love described in Ephesians 5. Jesus gave up his life for us before we even knew him. He suffered and paid the price for our sin so that we can have a worthwhile life on earth, and then live with God forever. Once we accept what Jesus offers, we are cherished women indeed.

He loved us and offered himself as a sacrifice for us.
Ephesians 5:2

June 24

RSVP Required
BERNICE

Acts 25:23; 26:1-30

The woman walked slowly away from the banquet hall in disbelief. How could the doorman refuse to let her into the reception? She was a well-known musician, and everyone there already recognized her even before she had sung at the wedding an hour earlier. But because her name wasn't on the guest list, she had been turned away. Now she would miss the dinner and dance, and all because she had not sent in her RSVP.

The woman in today's Bible passages also neglected to respond to an invitation. When Bernice and her husband visited the Roman governor Felix, they were very curious about his controversial prisoner. They listened as Paul shared his testimony in detail and proclaimed Jesus' resurrection. As a Jew, Bernice understood Paul's references to the promised Messiah, but apparently she refused to accept the gospel message. The Bible never mentions her again. Perhaps her heart was so hardened from a life of deliberate rebellion against God's laws that she couldn't recognize the truth when it was offered to her so clearly.

God has sent each of us a very precious invitation. He offers us the chance to be set free from the penalty for our sinful nature and receive the promise of eternal life with him. God's offer requires an RSVP from us. We must believe and trust in Jesus' sacrificial death and resurrection and must turn away from our old lives of sin. Many people listen to the gospel, but they don't want to be bothered with changing their lifestyles. Since we don't know how much time we have left, it's dangerous to delay in responding to God's invitation. That's one reception we definitely don't want to miss.

> *If only you would listen to his voice today!*
> *Psalm 95:7*

June 25

I Want My Rights
DAUGHTERS OF ZELOPHEHAD

Numbers 27:1-4

Each year, more than one hundred million lawsuits are filed in U.S. federal courts, and the number continues to mushroom. The Bible records one of the earliest lawsuits in history, an unusual one involving five women. Since only sons inherited property under Hebrew law, Zelophehad's family would not be allotted a portion of the Promised Land. His five daughters approached Moses and requested an inheritance in their father's name. The request was unusual, but the women's motives could not be questioned. They didn't seek personal gain, but desired only to preserve their family line, a concept which God clearly valued.

It's human nature to demand our rights. Advertising feeds this tendency and tries to convince us that we deserve whatever we desire. Even if our goal in life is to follow God, we can fall into the trap of thinking that we have a right to good health, well-behaved children, a secure job, and a nice home. But God never promised us perfect lives. Doing his will often requires us to subordinate our personal liberties and place others' interests above our own. As his children, he asks us to yield our rights to him and fully trust his control over the events of our lives.

On the other hand, we often don't exercise the rights we have been given. As God's children, we have the incredible privilege of approaching him at any time to request his help. He gives us the right to exercise authority over our sinful nature and over Satan's attempts to lure us away from God. Any rights that we demand pale in comparison to the right to be called God's daughters.

> *To all who believed him and accepted him, he gave the right to become children of God.*
> *John 1:12*

June 26

Coheirs with Christ
DAUGHTERS OF ZELOPHEHAD

Numbers 27:5-11

When Zelophehad's daughters presented their petition to be granted land, Moses didn't know how to handle the situation, so he took their case before the Lord. God affirmed that the women had a legitimate claim to the Canaanite land that would have been assigned to their father or his sons. God also made it a permanent law in Israel that when a father died with no sons, his inheritance belonged to his daughters.

Mahlah, Noah, Hoglah, Milcah, and Tirzah must have been remarkable women to boldly ask for something that went against the written law. Instead of rebuking them, God rewarded their courage. These sisters enjoyed the rare privilege of being the only females with assigned property in the Promised Land. For the rest of their lives, they must have felt thankful that they hadn't let the laws and customs favoring males intimidate them and keep them from speaking up. Their case set a precedent for all Israelite women who would come after them.

It's hard for our modern sensibilities to grasp how remarkable this decision was. It's also difficult for us to grasp how remarkable our position is in Christ. Once God accepts us as his adopted children, we become his heirs. Our inheritance begins immediately, with everything we need to live a godly life and the spiritual blessings that come from being in a loving relationship with our Father. It extends to our future as co-heirs with Jesus Christ, entitled to share the riches of God's Kingdom for eternity.

Our inheritance also includes the price of following Jesus in a world opposed to him. We are all called to endure suffering to some degree, just as he endured persecution, humiliation, and death on a cross. Even when our positions as God's heirs cause us to suffer, we can be thankful that his inheritance goes equally to daughters and sons.

> *If we are children, then we are heirs—heirs of God and co-heirs with Christ, if indeed we share in his sufferings in order that we may also share in his glory.*
> *Romans 8:17 (NIV)*

June 27

Empty Promises
TAMAR

Genesis 38:1-11

"I promise I'll send you a check by the end of the month." Colin's words echoed in Bonnie's mind as she surveyed the pile of bills on her desk. It certainly wasn't the first time she had heard them—her ex-husband had a ready supply of excuses for why he couldn't make his child support payments. Bonnie had sympathized with Colin's problems at first, but now she was fed up with his rationalizations. After all, empty promises wouldn't pay the bills.

Tamar knew how it felt to wait for a promise to be fulfilled. When her husband died, the law required that the next son in the family marry her and raise up offspring to preserve his brother's name. The levirate law (see Deuteronomy 25:5-10) sounds strange to us, but it protected childless widows by providing sons to receive their late husband's inheritance and continue the family line. After Tamar's second husband died, her father-in-law promised to marry his youngest son, Shelah, to her when he reached the appropriate age. Tamar lived in her father's house in a state of limbo, watching the years pass by without any sign that Judah would keep his promise.

We live in a world where promises are easily made but frequently broken. Many people give their word about something and then don't follow through. The effect on our lives can range from inconvenience to deep hurt and disappointment. Thankfully, we never have to wonder whether God will keep his promises. It's not in his character to go back on his Word. To those who believe in his Son, God promises forgiveness of sin, strength and comfort in hard times, guidance in confusing times, and glorious eternal life with him after death. God's Word is full of his promises, and they are never empty.

> All the LORD's promises prove true.
> 2 Samuel 22:31

June 28

Double Standards
TAMAR

Genesis 38:12-24

Regardless of what the letter said, Carla knew the real reason for her dismissal. She had been expecting it since her last birthday. It was the old double standard—Carla was now too "mature" for her position of news anchor, while the male announcer's graying hair and lines made him "distinguished" and "more believable."

The woman in today's passage experienced a double standard in a life-or-death situation. Tamar eventually realized that Judah had no intentions of arranging for his youngest son to marry her, so she came up with a plan of her own to get a child. When her widowed father-in-law came to her village, Tamar covered herself with a veil and sat by the road. Judah mistook her for a prostitute and had sex with her. A few months later, when someone told Judah about Tamar's being pregnant, he ordered that she be burned to death.

Tamar must have felt indignant, knowing that Judah had condemned her when he had sinned too. Since his guilt remained secret, he didn't hesitate to call for the most severe punishment on her. Still, Tamar had a measure of security because she had some of Judah's personal articles in her possession that proved his involvement.

People tend to impose a harsher judgment on someone else's behavior than on their own. Jesus said this hypocritical attitude was like worrying about a speck in a friend's eye while having a log in our own (see Matthew 7:3). God never imposes double standards; his requirement of perfection is the same for everyone. Since none of us can claim to be perfect, we are all in the same boat. Thankfully, God provided a way for us to be freed from condemnation for our sin. The opportunity to believe in the sacrifice of Jesus Christ is also the same for everyone. We may impose double standards, but God believes in equal opportunity for all.

Everyone has sinned; we all fall short of God's glorious standard.
Romans 3:23

June 29

Redeeming a Bad Situation
TAMAR

Genesis 38:25-30

Maya thought about the trouble she was in as she waited for the church service to begin. After getting her nursing degree, she had moved near a large city to take a hospital position. Unfortunately, budget problems had eliminated her job before she even started. The woman next to her interrupted her thoughts as she introduced herself. She turned out to be the wife of a doctor at the local clinic. Two weeks later, Maya began a new job a few miles from her apartment, with better benefits and hours than her original one.

It's hard for us to imagine what motivated Tamar to lure Judah into such an immoral act. Was she tired of living as a widow in her father's house, unable to marry again because Judah withheld the man who should have been her husband? Since society considered motherhood a woman's primary role, was Tamar determined to have a child at any cost? Did Tamar share the Hebrews' sense of the importance of continuing the family line?

Whatever her reasoning, God could not condone Tamar's use of deception, her incestuous union with her father-in-law, or Judah's use of a prostitute. Yet God allowed Tamar to conceive twin sons, and through one of them, he continued Judah's family line that led to Jesus' birth. In spite of Tamar's Canaanite background and the morally reprehensible way that she attained motherhood, God included her and one of her sons in the genealogy of the Savior of the world.

The Bible records many instances of God's redeeming a situation from someone's poor judgment. He does the same thing in our lives, though we often don't realize it. In spite of our mistakes, failures, and wrong choices, God continues to work out his plan. Jesus died to redeem us from our sin, and God redeems each negative circumstance of our lives and uses it for good.

Redeem me and show me mercy.
Psalm 26:11

June 30

Sacrificial Giving
THE WOMAN WHO GAVE TWO SMALL COINS

Mark 12:41-44

Darlene fought back tears as she watched the images of the hurricane-ravaged town. Then she thought of the check she'd written earlier that evening. A coworker was collecting money to fill a truck with basic supplies that he planned to drive down. As a single mom, Darlene was barely making ends meet, but she was determined to help. With input from her three children, she listed ways that the family could cut back on expenses. Now, as Darlene watched the news, she felt doubtful. The needs were so great—would her small contribution make any difference?

The widow in Mark 12 made what seemed like a negligible contribution. Her two pieces of copper were the smallest Jewish coins, each worth about an eighth of a cent in our money. She knew the amount wouldn't go very far in the upkeep of the Temple, but she found joy in the act of giving. While many of the rich people made sure that others saw their large gifts, this poverty-stricken widow tried to slip her coins in unnoticed, trusting that God would accept her offering even if others would not appreciate it. Jesus saw her sacrifice and said that her gift was worth more than any of the others. This woman gave all she had, while the rich gave only a small portion of their surplus.

God is more interested in our attitude toward giving than in the amount. He's not impressed if we give a tiny percentage of our wealth while keeping most of it for our own pleasure. It also doesn't mean much if we give solely out of a sense of obligation. When we give of our resources out of love and gratitude, he can multiply any amount to accomplish his purposes—even if it's worth less than a penny in the world's eyes.

> *You must each decide in your heart how much to give. And don't give reluctantly or in response to pressure. "For God loves a person who gives cheerfully."*
> *2 Corinthians 9:7*

July 1

A Godly Heritage
EUNICE AND LOIS

2 Timothy 1:5; 3:14-15

Elise rolled the letter up tightly and pushed it into the base of her bouquet. Her mom couldn't be at the wedding, but Elise would carry her words close to her heart. Later, the letter would go into the pink satin box along with similar letters from other important milestones in her life—from her birthdays, first day of school, entering high school, first date, college graduation. Elise's first year of life had been her mom's last, and her mother had spent it recording her hopes, dreams, and prayers for her daughter's future. With no memories of her mom, Elise clung all the more tightly to her heritage, expressed through those precious letters.

The Bible mentions Eunice and Lois by name only once, but these women also left a powerful legacy that lived on long after they died. This mother and grandmother dedicated themselves to teaching the Scriptures to their son and grandson, Timothy, from his early childhood. Their daily lives also demonstrated faith in action. As a result of his godly heritage, Timothy became a leading evangelist whose ministry led countless people to know Jesus as the Messiah. Eunice and Lois had no idea of the role their son and grandson would play in early Christianity, but their legacy lives on to this day.

Some kind of heritage has been passed down to each of us, whether godly or otherwise. We didn't choose it, but we do decide how we respond to that legacy. Just as many Americans choose to reject our nation's heritage of government based on godly principles, individuals choose whether or not to follow what they were taught. Each of us will also leave a legacy to those who come after us, shaped by the way we live our lives. The best kind of heritage to pass on is love for God and a commitment to follow him.

Your testimonies I have taken as a heritage forever, for they are the rejoicing of my heart.
Psalm 119:111 (NKJV)

July 2

Living by Rules
"SLAVE WOMAN"

Galatians 4:21-30

Nora tried to hide her surprise as her friend talked about her plans to play cards with her sisters after church. *She definitely comes from a different background than I do,* Nora observed. Nora's family had a long list of things they weren't allowed to do on Sundays. Movies were taboo all the time, and girls and women couldn't wear slacks. Although Nora loved her new church and the people's passion for God, she still struggled with her ingrained attitudes. Sometimes she felt confused and wanted to shout, "Just what *are* the rules, anyway?"

Nora resembles the "slave woman" of Paul's metaphor in Galatians 4. This passage illustrates new life in Christ by contrasting two women from the Old Testament, Hagar and Sarah. As a slave woman, Hagar represents the old covenant, under which people tried to please God by following rules and regulations. Her mistress, Sarah, represents the new covenant, a life of grace in which believers rely on God's Spirit instead of on laws to guide them in holy living.

Rules are often necessary, but in the spiritual life, no amount of adherence to laws and rituals can help us earn God's love. We become acceptable to God by believing in Jesus, being forgiven of our sin, and receiving the gift of new life. Jesus' sacrificial death accomplished what the old covenant could not: It empowers us for godly living through obedience to the Holy Spirit living in us. If we are legalistic in our approach to God, we miss out on the life of grace that he intended. God gives us a choice: Will we live like slave women or free women?

> *Now that you know God (or should I say, now that God knows you), why do you want to go back again and become slaves once more to the weak and useless spiritual principles of this world?*
> *Galatians 4:9*

July 3

True Liberty
"FREE WOMAN"

Galatians 4:31–5:16

Ducking around a corner, Jasmine waited until the coast was clear. She avoided those two coworkers from the third floor whenever possible. They had turned into weirdos since they went to that Christian rally last year. Now they dressed, talked, and acted differently, and it made Jasmine down-right uncomfortable to be around them. They could change if they wanted to, but she had no intention of giving up her party lifestyle. She wanted to enjoy life, not worry about a bunch of boring rules. *I can't help it if I'm a free spirit,* Jasmine assured herself.

What does a true "free spirit" look like? The passage in Galatians explains that faith in Jesus Christ sets us free in two ways: First, we are freed from trying to earn God's favor by following rules and regulations. Instead, we become bound to the law of loving God with all our hearts and loving other people as ourselves. Second, we are no longer slaves to sin. God's Spirit lives in us and gives us the power to resist our sinful desires. We still have a selfish nature, but we no longer have to be controlled by it.

Some people view the Christian life as following a set of strict rules that stifle our personalities and suppress our desire for fun. But faith in Christ actually sets us free to become the people that God created us to be. This allows us to enjoy life fully. As his Spirit transforms us on the inside, any changes that we make in our dress, our talk, our behavior, or our life-style should be expressions of our love for him. As we grow in our desire to become more like Christ, we discover that the life of grace truly sets our spirits free.

> *It is for freedom that Christ has set us free.*
> *Galatians 5:1 (NIV)*

July 4

Patriotic Women
SHALLUM'S DAUGHTERS

Nehemiah 3:1-12

In Nehemiah's time, the wall around Jerusalem was a disgrace that threatened the city's safety. Since Shallum didn't have any sons, his daughters worked with him to restore the section of the wall assigned to their family. As a half-district ruler over Jerusalem, Shallum could easily have gathered workers to assist him, so maybe his daughters insisted on taking part. As they worked alongside the men, their joy in contributing to their nation's security probably overshadowed their fatigue and discomfort from the hard physical labor. These young women knew that they were investing their time and energy in Israel's future.

The historical event of rebuilding Jerusalem's wall inspired the name of an organization called WallBuilders. Founded by former educator and school administrator David Barton, WallBuilders is dedicated to "presenting America's forgotten history and heroes, with an emphasis on the moral, religious, and constitutional foundation on which America was built—a foundation that in recent years has been seriously attacked and undermined." WallBuilders educates and encourages Americans to take a role in rebuilding the original foundations of our nation.

With our full lives, it's tempting to focus exclusively on our personal interests, but God also calls each of us to be responsible for our country's well-being. Some of us may be involved in politics on a local or national level. Some serve on town councils or school boards, while others represent Christ in their neighborhoods. All of us are called to intercede for our nation and its leaders through prayer. If we each labor on the section assigned to us, like Shallum's daughters did, we can rebuild our nation's walls and invest in its future.

> *If my people who are called by my name will humble themselves and pray and seek my face and turn from their wicked ways, I will hear from heaven and will forgive their sins and restore their land.*
> *2 Chronicles 7:14*

July 5

Living in a Hostile Society
HEBREW WOMEN IN EGYPT

Exodus 1:1-10

Christie instinctively leaned back from the edge of her balcony as she watched the parade pass through the street below her. Angry protesters spat out words that she hardly understood even though she'd studied the language for several years. Earlier, she had witnessed the burning of an American flag. When Christie had first arrived for her year-long, study-abroad program, the people had welcomed her with open arms, but lately Christie had noticed a shift in the political climate and in the attitudes toward her. Not everyone had changed, of course, but when she walked down the street, she got enough hostile stares to make her uneasy. *Maybe it's just as well that my time here is almost up,* she thought.

The women in today's passage knew how it felt to live as foreigners in a hostile country. When Jacob's family first arrived in Egypt, the pharaoh treated them with honor and respect. But after many years, the story of how Joseph had saved the country from starvation passed out of memory, and the Egyptians began to feel threatened by Jacob's descendants. Although the Israelites lived in a separate part of the country, they must have felt the pressure of being surrounded by people who viewed them with distrust, suspicion, and even contempt.

Today, devoted followers of Christ are the ones that most often experience social hostility. The world's standards and purposes directly oppose those expressed by God in his Word. When we take a stand for God's truth, we can expect those who don't know him to treat us with distrust, suspicion, and contempt. No one enjoys that kind of treatment, but if we want to be faithful to God, we will be enemies of the world. That is much better than the other way around.

> *Don't you realize that friendship with the world makes you an enemy of God?*
> James 4:4

July 6

Living in Slavery
HEBREW WOMEN IN EGYPT

Exodus 1:11-14

When the Egyptians grew alarmed over how numerous the Israelites had become, they forced the Israelites into slavery. The rulers appointed brutal slave drivers to wear them down by forcing them to make bricks, build cities, and work in the fields. How the hearts of the women ached as they were enslaved by ruthless masters that treated them and their loved ones cruelly. As they watched their children growing up, did they dare to hope in a future that held something better for them than this bitter life of slavery?

We tend to think of slavery as something from the distant past, but the abhorrent practice still thrives today. An article on the National Geographic Web site estimates that twenty-seven million men, women, and children around the world are enslaved today—"physically confined or restrained and forced to work, or controlled through violence, or in some way treated as property." Modern slavery takes several different forms and affects all ages and races. Often people become trapped in bonded labor after being tricked into a debt that they can never repay. These circumstances can be handed down from one generation to the next.

In a spiritual sense, every person is born into slavery. The Bible teaches that anyone who sins is a slave of sin. When Adam and Eve disobeyed God in the Garden of Eden, sin enslaved the world until Jesus was crucified. Now we have a choice either to live in slavery to sin or to walk away free. When we identify with Jesus' death and resurrection, we can be released from sin's hold on us. Sin is a brutal slave driver, but thanks to God's mercy, we can have a better life.

Jesus replied, "I tell you the truth, everyone who sins is a slave of sin."
John 8:34

July 7

Mocking
PENINNAH

1 Samuel 1:6

Liz sat on her mom's couch, fidgeting with her long gold earrings. It had been fun getting ready for her ten-year, high school reunion—shopping for a new dress, getting a new hairstyle and a manicure, and booking the flight to her hometown. It would be great to see the gang again . . . but what if *she* came? Liz flushed and glanced up at the ceiling. *How could I have been so mean back then?* Liz hadn't started it, but she had sure played along. "Captain Hook"—it had seemed so funny at the time. *I never even took the time to find out what was wrong with her hand.*

Peer pressure never justifies making fun of someone, and neither does jealousy. Although Peninnah was the wife who had several children, her husband treated his barren wife with great tenderness. Peninnah expressed her discontent by taunting Hannah about her barrenness. Hannah never retaliated, and this provoked Peninnah all the more. As she exalted herself over Hannah because she had children, Peninnah forgot that God had given them to her. Instead of empathizing with Hannah's disappointment, Peninnah used her own blessing to hurt Hannah.

Many teenagers cover up their insecurity by making fun of others. As we grow older, we hopefully learn to empathize with others' feelings and realize that we all have flaws that could be the object of ridicule. But much of the humor in popular television shows revolves around making fun of others. While we may avoid overt name-calling, a mocking attitude may creep into our thinking as we joke about someone's weight, accent, lack of ability, or any one of a thousand other things. It's worth the effort to keep our conversation free of mockery so that we never have to worry about meeting someone face-to-face as Liz did.

> *Oh, the joys of those who do not follow the advice of the wicked, or stand around with sinners, or join in with mockers.*
> *Psalm 1:1*

July 8

The Mocked
HANNAH

1 Samuel 1:7

As she fumbled with the buttons on her dress, Nancy asked herself for the hundredth time, *Do I really want to go to this?* The reunion meant a chance to see friends who had moved away after high school graduation, but it also brought the risk of meeting people she would rather avoid. Several kids had teased Nancy about her left hand, which was always tightly balled up because of a lack of oxygen to her brain during birth. None of them had been as cruel as Liz, the senior-class president. What if *she* came back to town for the reunion?

Besides dealing with her deep disappointment at not having children, Hannah had to endure Peninnah's cruel taunts. Living in the same house and sharing the same husband made it impossible to escape her tormentor. Peninnah's sarcasm about Hannah's barrenness cut her as sharply as any knife. Couldn't Peninnah see how hurt she already was? Why did she have to rub it in that she had given Elkanah several children? The taunts must have increased on holidays when the family celebrated together. Hannah was reduced to tears and had no desire to eat. How could she stand the pain any longer?

Many of us have memories of being mocked, and for some, the wounds have never healed. Maybe others made fun of our looks, our poverty, our lack of ability in academics or sports, or because we just didn't fit in. Many people still have differences that make them feel self-conscious. The only way to deal with such pain is to follow Hannah's example—to pour it out before God, who knows very well how it feels to be mocked. Jesus' own people jeered at him, many religious leaders treated him with sarcasm, and the Roman soldiers cruelly taunted him. When someone makes fun of us, we can talk to the One who endured much worse for our sake.

He will be handed over to the Romans, and he will be mocked, treated shamefully, and spit upon.
Luke 18:32

July 9

Acting without Thinking
RHODA

Acts 12:1-14

As I scrubbed the bathroom sink, I noticed dust on the lightbulb. I grabbed a cloth, wet it, and started to wipe off the lightbulb. The moment the wet cloth touched the hot bulb, I heard it crack. I had let my cleaning frenzy override my common sense. *What was I thinking?* I wondered as I dealt with the pieces of the burst lightbulb. It's lucky I wasn't shocked!

Today's passage tells of a young woman who acted without thinking. When God miraculously freed Peter from prison and certain death, he headed to the house where the persecuted Christians in Jerusalem were meeting. His knock on the door brought Rhoda, a servant girl. She recognized Peter's voice, But instead of flinging the door open, she rushed back to tell the news to the group that had been fervently praying for Peter's release. Rhoda's mind was filled with joy in knowing that their beloved spiritual leader had been set free. She didn't stop to think that she endangered his life again by leaving him standing outside on the street.

Many of us could tell stories of times when we've acted without thinking. During a pressing decision or crisis, it's hard to remember that the first thing that comes into our minds is not necessarily the best thing to do. When we react emotionally, the consequences can range from embarrassment to danger. God has given us his Spirit, his Word, and prayer to help us live wisely. Rhoda acted foolishly by failing to let Peter into the house; we would be foolish not to open God's Word and admit his guidance into our lives.

Wise people think before they act.
Proverbs 13:16

July 10

Called a Liar
RHODA

Acts 12:15

Eileen hung up the phone and rushed outside to look for her husband.
They hadn't expected Carl's sisters until the next day; instead, they were
already on the edge of town. Eileen found Carl in the garage covered with
grease. "Very funny," he laughed, "almost as good as the gag I pulled on you
yesterday." Eileen tried to convince Carl that it was true, but he just laughed
again and took off on the mower.

The woman in today's passage wasn't believed when she shared her
news, either. When Rhoda recognized Peter's voice outside the door, she
couldn't wait to tell the wonderful news that he had been freed from prison.
But the believers greeted her outburst with jeers, telling her that she must be
out of her mind. Rhoda knew that she was only a servant girl and that it was
her word against that of a large group of people, but she also knew whose
voice she had heard. Rhoda didn't let the others intimidate her. She stuck to
her story. When she kept insisting that Peter had knocked on the door, the
group decided that it must be an angel taking his form.

We never know how someone will respond when we talk about God,
whether we're sharing a verse or a principle from the Bible or our personal
testimony of what God has done. Depending on the condition of his or her
heart, a listener may react with interest, indifference, gratitude, hostility, or
sarcasm. It's hard to take a stand for our convictions when we don't know
how we'll be treated. Although we are responsible for sharing God's truth
in a spirit of love, we're not responsible for how people respond. We can't
afford to let fear of rejection silence us. If we do, we may miss the opportunity to share news that someone has been waiting to hear.

> [Jesus said,] "Since I am telling you the truth, why don't you believe me?"
> John 8:46

July 11

Too Good to Be True?
SURPRISED SAINTS

Acts 12:16-19

Greta walked out of her boss's office in shock. Had she really been given the promotion? Although she had applied for every senior management position that came up, Greta couldn't believe that she had finally been accepted for one of them. It seemed too good to be true.

The believers in today's passage couldn't believe it when they got what they had been hoping for. At the time of Peter's arrest, Herod had been persecuting the Christians in Jerusalem. He had already executed James, and Peter seemed to be next in line. Knowing that their leader was in grave danger, the believers had gathered to pray throughout the night for Peter's safety, yet when God answered their prayers, they couldn't believe it. How could a heavily guarded man in Herod's prison possibly have escaped? In their shock and disbelief, the group left poor Peter standing outside.

In a world full of trickery, deception, and scam artists, it pays to be skeptical at times. Over the years, I've learned to doubt all those announcements that I've won a Florida vacation or "one of the following valuable prizes." My husband likes to remind me that "if it seems too good to be true, it probably is!"

We shouldn't go by that rule in our spiritual lives, however. Since we know that nothing is impossible for God, why are we surprised when he performs miracles? Why should we be shocked when the doctor says that the tumor has disappeared, a hopeless marriage is restored, or a life is changed? Although we don't always get what we want, the Bible urges us to believe in God's power and expect him to act when we pray. Then we won't be like the believers in Jerusalem who didn't even recognize it when God gave them exactly what they had been asking for.

I do believe, but help me overcome my unbelief!
Mark 9:24

July 12

Building a Sanctuary
MARY, MARK'S MOTHER

Acts 12:12

As with many other women in the Bible, only one verse mentions this Mary by name, but these few words give us a glimpse into her life. We know that her son Mark wrote the second Gospel. We also know that Mary had a servant and a home spacious enough to provide a gathering place for the early Christians in Jerusalem. Mary lived out her devotion to God by offering up her home for his purposes. When an angel released Peter from prison, he immediately went to Mary's house.

Americans are building bigger and bigger homes and spending more money on furnishing them. With the growing popularity of home decorating shows and magazines, dissatisfaction with our own homes may prevent us from inviting friends over. What people remember most after being in our homes will be the atmosphere, not the furniture or the paint on the walls. If our goal is to reach out lovingly to others as Jesus did, we won't obsess over our decorating schemes. We'll concentrate on making our homes a sanctuary where people can be refreshed and sense God's love.

The attitudes of our hearts determine the atmosphere in our homes. Just as God's presence can hopefully be sensed in our church buildings and in our homes, his Holy Spirit lives in each believer. Peter referred to believers as "living stones" that God uses to build his spiritual temple. As we allow God to conform us to Christ's image, he makes us part of this sanctuary. When the goal of our lives is worship and obedience, that's a "decorating scheme" people can't help but notice.

> *You are living stones that God is building into his spiritual temple.*
> *1 Peter 2:5*

July 13

Following Instructions
RAHAB, THE WOMEN AT THE FIRST PASSOVER

Joshua 2:17-20

The local news was unusually sad that night. Two fatal accidents had occurred within a few hours of each other. A teenage girl had lost her life when she ran a stop sign. In another part of town, a woman had collided with a truck as she drove the wrong way on the interstate. Both deaths had resulted from ignoring traffic signs.

As God had prepared to judge the Egyptians for their sin, he instructed each Israelite family to kill a lamb and smear its blood over their door. If they followed these instructions, the angel of death would pass over their home and their firstborn son would not be killed. When the Israelites were about to destroy Jericho, Rahab's life also depended on her following the instructions the Israelite spies had given her. In return for Rahab's help, they agreed to spare her family if she would leave a scarlet rope hanging from her window.

It's human nature to want to do things our own way, but in a life-and-death situation, we don't want to be stubborn. If we're standing by the emergency exit in a smoking building, it's not a good idea to go looking for another way out. Rahab and the Israelites in Egypt were protected only because they followed the instructions they were given.

Many people believe that there are a number of different paths to God, but the Bible doesn't teach that. Jesus claimed to be the only way to God the Father. Only trust in Jesus' death and resurrection will save us from the coming destruction of all who oppose God. There is only one way to guarantee our eternal safety, and the Bible gives us the clear instructions that we need. It's our choice whether to follow them or to ignore them.

> *Jesus told him, "I am the way, the truth, and the life. No one can come to the Father except through me."*
> *John 14:6*

July 14

Judging Right from Wrong
DEBORAH

Judges 4:1-5

A professor at a prestigious university advocates for the choice to kill severely disabled infants. One Internet article questions why our government does not develop "anti-fetal drugs" to remove what it considers organisms that invade women's bodies—unborn children. Some university students in an ethics class think it is incorrect to state unequivocally that the Nazis' slaughter of Jews was wrong. National polls show that most Americans believe that truth is relative and that morality is a matter of personal opinion.

Deborah's heart surely must have been broken because her nation, Israel, had for the most part abandoned God's absolute standards of right and wrong. She has a unique place in biblical history as the only woman to rule the nation during the period when Israel had no king. As Deborah sat under a palm tree near her home, Israelites asked for her counsel, and she settled their disputes. As a judge and prophet, she shared God's wisdom and instruction at a time when everyone did whatever seemed right to them. Deborah did not seek power or authority for her own gain; her burning desire was that her nation would turn back to God from their idolatry.

We live in a time similar to Deborah's. People define "right" as whatever seems to fit a situation, or even as whatever they desire. Anyone who takes a stand for objective principles of morality is labeled judgmental or intolerant. In reality, each of us is a judge. We decide how we will treat other people and how we will live. In order to judge correctly, we need to base our decisions on the standards of right and wrong that God has laid down in his Word. After all, someday he will judge us all.

> In those days Israel had no king; all the people did whatever seemed right in their own eyes.
> Judges 21:25

July 15

Warriors Wanted
DEBORAH

Judges 4:6-10

The young woman waved as she took a last look from the bus window. It would be a long time before she saw her family and friends again. Her stomach churned as the bus pulled out. Looking around, she wondered if the others felt the same way. She had no idea what basic training would be like—would she make it through? Suddenly, she remembered the package her parents had handed her. Tearing away the paper, she saw a beautiful book on the history of the Marine Corps. As she ran her fingers across the emblem with the eagle, globe, and anchor, her heart swelled with pride.

Deborah's unique position in Israel's history included a military aspect. When she summoned Barak to muster an army to fight against their oppressor, Deborah was speaking God's commands as his prophet. Was she appalled by the military general's response that he would go only if she went too? Regardless of her feelings, Deborah rode out with Barak. The reward for her willingness to accompany him was the sight of Israel's forces charging into battle. Her heart must have swelled with joy and gratitude, knowing that God had promised them victory over the larger and more powerful enemy.

Whether or not we know it, we are all involved in spiritual warfare. Satan and his forces of evil constantly battle against God, trying to keep people from knowing Christ. If we belong to God, Satan attacks us to weaken our faith and witness and to make our service ineffective. His weapons include fear, doubt, greed, materialism, and a whole arsenal of temptations; our weapons are prayer, God's Word, and the support of the Holy Spirit and other believers. God is looking for warrior women who are willing to take a stand against evil and oppression. No matter how powerful our enemy looks, we can confidently face the battle knowing that God has promised a victory.

Every child of God defeats this evil world, and we achieve this victory through our faith.
1 John 5:4

July 16

Spiritual Cheerleader
DEBORAH

Judges 4:12-16

I slumped over my computer, fighting the panic that welled up inside me. What was I thinking—*me* write a book? Where would I find enough ideas for a whole year's worth of devotionals? How would I finish in six months with all the other stuff going on? Who thought I could write well enough to—just then, the phone rang. I told my friend all about the project, including my doubts. "Dianne," Julie stated firmly, "I can't believe God would give you this tremendous blessing just to let you fail."

Everyone needs a little encouragement sometimes, and Barak was no exception. In spite of his doubts, Deborah wanted to see him successfully carry out the task that God had assigned to him. As Barak and his forces faced the enemy's nine hundred iron chariots, Deborah spurred him on to the attack: "This is the day the LORD will give you victory over Sisera, for the LORD is marching ahead of you." With her steady faith and encouraging words, Deborah ignited Barak's confidence and filled him with the courage to lead his army to victory.

We all need a spiritual cheerleader sometimes. When we face a formidable challenge, our faith can be shaky. In our own eyes, we seem small, weak, and powerless. At those times, we need someone to remind us of God's goodness and his promise to give us the power we need to accomplish whatever he assigns us. When the odds seem stacked against us, the right encouragement can make all the difference in our perspective. When I had panicked at the thought of writing a book, my friend's words immediately energized me and lingered in my mind over the next six months. Her encouragement helped me win a victory over my insecurity.

> *Encourage each other and build each other up, just as you are already doing.*
> *1 Thessalonians 5:11*

July 17

Good Advice
DEBORAH

Judges 5:31

Brooke wished that she had picked a different booth to sit in. She couldn't avoid overhearing the conversation going on next to her. A young woman barely out of her teens was telling a friend about her problems with her live-in boyfriend, who kept losing jobs because of his drug habit. He sometimes disappeared for days at a time with no explanation. The note of desperation in the woman's voice touched Brooke as she asked her friend, "What do you think I should do?"

Brooke had to bite her lip when the woman's friend replied, "Just follow whatever your heart tells you to do."

When Deborah was Israel's judge, she advised people to follow God rather than their hearts, which the Bible says are deceitful (see Jeremiah 17:9). Deborah took her role as the nation's spiritual leader seriously and dedicated herself to instructing the people in God's laws. As she sought God's help in fulfilling her role, God granted her wisdom and insight to share with those seeking her counsel. Because Deborah depended on God for understanding in all matters and because she shared his Word rather than her own opinions, the nation of Israel enjoyed forty years of peace under her leadership.

We have plenty of sources for advice these days, such as newspaper columns, radio call-in programs, and talk shows. Unfortunately, most of these sources do not give counsel that aligns with God's thinking. Whether we get advice from a friend or a professional counselor, we need to make sure that it doesn't conflict with God's Word. When friends come to us for counsel, we must tell them something more meaningful than "Just follow whatever your heart tells you to do." If we devote ourselves to prayerful study of the Bible, we'll be equipped to share wise advice—whether we're sitting under a palm tree like Deborah or in a restaurant booth.

The godly give good advice to their friends.
Proverbs 12:26

July 18

No Mercy
JAEL

Judges 4:17-24

Kara wanted to turn off the television, but she didn't. Her history professor had given his class an assignment to watch this movie about the Holocaust. Kara had expected some violence, but she had been unprepared for the disturbing images. Sometimes she had to cover her face during scenes of Jewish people being savagely tortured or murdered inside the concentration camps. Kara wondered how the guards could be so cold and merciless toward their prisoners.

It's also difficult to read about Jael's act of cruelty. Since she was not an Israelite, she had no trouble persuading Sisera to hide in her tent when he fled from the battle with the Israelites. After he fell asleep, Jael hammered a tent peg all the way through his head. In this act of murder, Jael used deceit and broke the ancient code of hospitality that put the life of a guest above one's own. The Bible passage gives no hint of any emotion on her part as she killed him, but we do know that Sisera was an army commander who had ruthlessly oppressed Israel for twenty years, so we can conclude that he was an enemy now being judged by God.

We may have a hard time relating to the way that Jael killed Sisera, but we are all called to be single-minded in opposing sin. Haven't we all been tempted to overlook minor lapses that seem hidden and harmless? But sin is evil, and compromise with evil is always dangerous. Little habits grow into ingrained attitudes that shape our behavior. What seems so harmless can explode in disastrous consequences. We can't afford to harbor thoughts or attitudes that go against God's principles. Sin is the one area in which God wants us to show no mercy.

> *If through the power of the Spirit you put to death the deeds of your sinful nature, you will live.*
> *Romans 8:13*

July 19

Humility
DEBORAH

Judges 5:1-27

As her coworkers filed into the conference room, Angie shifted in her chair. *I can't wait to hear Bev's presentation,* she thought. Although Angie had worked for the marketing company for almost two years, she had never been involved with such a large account before. Her boss had adopted many of her ideas and allowed her to do all the research. Now all those late nights and extra hours on the weekends would be worth it. As the folders passed around the table, Angie opened hers and turned white. There was only one name written at the top of the report—that of her boss.

When Deborah ruled Israel, her leadership style was opposite to that of Angie's boss. Deborah had played an instrumental role in the military victory against King Jabin. She had summoned the Israelite military commander, given him instructions, and accompanied him to the battlefield at his insistence. Yet in her victory song, Deborah didn't claim any credit. She gave the glory to God and mentioned everyone who had had a part in the day's success. She honored Israel's leaders and those who volunteered for war, listing each tribe by name. She praised Jael and detailed her killing of the enemy army commander. Deborah downplayed her own part and referred to herself simply as "a mother for Israel."

It's only natural to want the credit that's due to us, but when we concentrate on whether or not others are recognizing our efforts, we miss the opportunity to be used by God. When we let go of our desire for glory, we can encourage others and bring honor to him. Even if others don't acknowledge our contributions, God sees them and will reward us. He's looking for leaders *and* followers with humble spirits—and he will honor those who don't honor themselves.

> *Humble yourselves before the Lord, and he will lift you up in honor.*
> *James 4:10*

July 20

Sad for the Wrong Things
WOMEN WEEPING FOR TAMMUZ

Ezekiel 8:13-14

Lakisha reached for another tissue. She couldn't imagine how one woman could stand so much grief and pain. Her heart went out to Alana each afternoon during the hour between one and two. *Maybe I should just stop watching the soaps,* Lakisha thought. Her tears had always come easily, but lately they seemed to be getting out of hand. Last night she had trouble going to sleep after crying over *Steel Magnolias,* even though she had already seen it eight times.

The women in today's passage also sat crying for the wrong reason. When God wanted to show Ezekiel the extent of the people's idolatry and wickedness, he showed the prophet a series of scenes in a vision. At one point, Ezekiel saw a group of women at the north gate of the Temple crying for Tammuz. When vegetation died during the hot, dry summer months, worshipers of this pagan god believed that it was because he had died and descended to the underworld. His followers wept and mourned his death, then celebrated his return in the spring with fertility rites. Instead of crying over their nation's rejection of God, some Israelite women were shedding tears over a false god.

We shouldn't be ashamed of having a tender heart that moves us easily to tears. I remember hearing a pastor say, "When your eyes leak, your head can't swell." God wants us to be empathetic and cry when it's appropriate, even during sad movies. But he doesn't want us to waste our tears on trivial matters while remaining unmoved by significant causes for grief. If we allow our hearts to become hardened to the sin in our lives, we may cry over everything except our need for repentance and change. Anything that grieves God is worth shedding tears over.

> *Let there be tears for what you have done. Let there be sorrow and deep grief.*
> James 4:9

July 21

Innocent Bystanders
KING DAVID'S CONCUBINES

2 Samuel 15:13-16; 16:20-22

"I was taken away by the attackers; they were all in uniforms. They took dozens of other girls and made us walk for three hours. During the day, we were beaten. . . . At night, we were raped several times." This quote comes from one of hundreds of similar reports from Sudanese women collected by Amnesty International in 2004. No one can estimate the number of women who have suffered similar atrocities in war-torn countries when mass rape is used as a weapon of war.

The women in today's passage were also victimized because of war. When David fled from Jerusalem because of the conspiracy against him, he left behind ten concubines as palace housekeepers. One of Absalom's first acts upon entering Jerusalem was to rape his father's concubines as a sign that he now claimed the throne and all that belonged to David. The atrocious act took place in a tent on the palace roof so that everyone could see the women's humiliation. The women had stayed at the palace in obedience to the king, so they suffered unjustly when Absalom used them as a weapon against his father.

In everyday life, women sometimes suffer because of someone else's sin or because they are in the wrong place at the wrong time. Some people see the evil and injustice in the world as proof that God doesn't exist rather than as proof of the reality of the sin that infects the world. When God came to earth as a man, he suffered unjustly so that someday we can be free from the effects of sin. But Jesus wasn't victimized; he chose to put himself at the mercy of his attackers on our behalf. When we're hurt and treated unfairly, it's hard to see God's goodness, but it is greater than all the evil in the world.

He was beaten so we could be whole. He was whipped so we could be healed.
Isaiah 53:5

July 22

Needing Comfort
KING DAVID'S CONCUBINES

2 Samuel 20:3

"Five to six men raped us, one after the other, for hours over six days, every night. My husband could not forgive me after this; he disowned me." This young woman from Darfur in Sudan became an innocent victim when government-backed militiamen attacked her village in retaliation against insurgent groups in the area. Besides the usual devastating effects of sexual violence, she had to deal with her husband's rejection. She faces a grim future in a society in which women depend on men for survival.

Israelite society viewed the ten concubines raped by Absalom as defiled. When King David returned to Jerusalem and his throne, he placed the women in strict seclusion, where they remained until they died. He provided for their needs, but he no longer had physical relationships with them. In addition to the memory of the outrage committed against them, these women had to live with the shame of being treated like widows even though their husband was alive. Through no fault of their own, the women carried the consequences of someone else's sin for the rest of their lives.

In reality, each of us is defiled from birth because of our inherent sinful nature. Once we accept God's forgiveness through Christ's sacrifice, no one can do anything to defile us or make us worthless in God's sight. Despite what others think of us, he wants to help us rebuild our lives. Unfortunately, a deep sense of shame and guilt may cause us to shut everyone out, including God. He longs to console us and restore our joy, but we have to receive his comfort by spending time in his Word and in prayer. No matter what happens to us, God promises to give us the comfort that no one else can, if we will receive it.

> *I will turn their mourning into joy and will comfort them and give them joy for their sorrow.*
> *Jeremiah 31:13 (NASB)*

July 23

Standing Tall
A DISABLED WOMAN HEALED BY JESUS

Luke 13:10-17

Amy's new neighbor was telling her who lived in their subdivision.

"What about that older woman who goes out walking every day—the one who keeps her eyes on the ground? I try to say hello but she never looks up."

"Oh, that's Shirley—you won't get much out of her. She used to be really outgoing. Then her husband committed suicide after losing their business. One daughter was killed by a drunk driver; the other one moved away and never visits. Now, Shirley just keeps to herself."

"Wow—no wonder she looks like she's carrying the weight of the world on her shoulders."

The physician who wrote the book of Luke tells about a woman who was forced to keep her eyes on the ground. For eighteen long years, this woman suffered from a disability that kept her body bent double. Besides the physical pain and discomfort, she had to endure other people's pity or disgust in reaction to her handicap. Fortunately, this didn't keep her from going to the house of worship on the Sabbath. When Jesus touched her, the woman immediately stood up straight and praised God.

Sometimes life beats us up so badly that we can hardly stand up straight. Financial needs, relationship problems, sickness, disappointments, and losses can deal us crippling blows. When we're weighed down by troubles, it's hard to see anything more than our earthly situations. If we choose to worship God anyway, we can soon lift our eyes to heaven. Doctors may heal our bodies, but only Jesus can heal those bent over by life's hurts. The religious leaders reproached Jesus for healing the woman on the Sabbath, but any day is a good day for a touch from Jesus. After that, we will surely walk a little straighter.

He touched her, and instantly she could stand straight.
Luke 13:13

July 24

What's in a Name?
JEZEBEL

1 Kings 21:1-16
"Everyone brings joy to this office—some when they enter, and some when they leave." I smiled at the sign on the wall, but later, I did some serious thinking about which category I fit in. *How do people feel when they see me coming—delighted or deflated? I wondered. Do they associate me with fun and laughter? pleasant conversation and warm friendship? Or do they think of complaining, bitterness, or self-centeredness when they hear my name?*

Even people who haven't studied the Bible know that a "jezebel" is wicked, shameless, or scheming. Although the name originally meant "chaste," not even the dictionary contains enough adjectives to describe the evil that Jezebel perpetrated.

This woman committed treachery and murder on a whim. She dragged the country of Israel into degradation by installing her native cult of Baal worship with all its despicable practices, including self-mutilation, sexual immorality, and human sacrifice. Blessed with intellect and power, Queen Jezebel used all her resources to fight against the true God. Her evil infected her husband, her children, and an entire nation.

We may not be listed in the dictionary, but we all have a reputation of some sort based on the character we exhibit. When people hear our names, they automatically think of . . . something. The best way to make sure that our names have positive connotations is to live according to the wisdom found in God's Word. If we pattern our lives after Christ's example and treat others the way he did, we won't be known as jezebels but as Jesus followers. That's the best reputation anyone could hope for.

> *A good name is more desirable than great riches; to be esteemed is better than silver or gold.*
> *Proverbs 22:1* (NIV)

July 25

Defining Moment
JEZEBEL

1 Kings 21:17-29

Jezebel arranged for false witnesses to accuse Naboth of blasphemy so that he and his sons could legally be stoned to death, according to the Israelites' own laws. The queen then smugly told her husband that she had obtained the vineyard he had set his heart on. When Ahab strolled out to inspect his new property, however, he brought back the report of a chilling encounter. Perhaps Jezebel listened as Ahab told of Elijah's prophecy of horrible deaths for Ahab, his descendants, and Jezebel. She saw Ahab humble himself before God in repentance, and she heard how God softened his judgment. This brought Jezebel to a defining moment in her life. Would she also take the prophet's words seriously and turn away from her false gods? Would she seek mercy and forgiveness from the true God?

We are surrounded by warnings every day, displayed on practically every building we enter and every product we handle. When we are very familiar with certain words or phrases, we find it easy to ignore them. Some warnings are especially dangerous to ignore, such as a caution that a bridge may be icy or a weather alert that a tornado is passing through our neighborhood. Although a warning is designed to ensure our safety and well-being, we choose whether or not we will respond in an appropriate way.

It's extremely dangerous to become complacent about God's warnings to us. The Bible is filled with instructions on godly living. It tells us of the blessings that accompany obedience and warns about the consequences of rejecting God's ways. The lives of many people in the Old Testament illustrate the cost of disobedience. Each time we read a Scripture passage that warns us of God's judgment on sin, we have a choice to make. Will we take God's Word seriously and turn away from habits, attitudes, and behaviors that displease him? Or will we ignore his warnings and continue to live the way we please?

What warning from God have you been ignoring?

July 26

Time for Justice
JEZEBEL

2 Kings 9:30-37

As soon as Bobbie saw the patrol car, she jerked her foot off the accelerator. When she had passed the car, she breathed a sigh of relief. *Thank goodness I have sharp eyes and quick reflexes.* She smiled. *I always see them in time to—uh-oh!* She spotted flashing lights in her rearview mirror. As Bobbie pulled onto the shoulder, she knew that she couldn't plead ignorance of the flashing sign and all the orange barrels she had passed. She would pay dearly for speeding in a work zone.

Queen Jezebel could not escape payback either. The prophet Elijah predicted that God would put her family to death for their evil reign, with Jezebel suffering an especially appalling end. When her husband died exactly as prophesied, her heart was so hardened that instead of repenting, she continued her tyranny over Israel. Ten years later, as her end drew near, she still showed no remorse. Instead, she painted her face and hurled sarcasm at the person God had sent to judge her. In spite of her power and her domineering personality, Jezebel was eaten by dogs, as prophesied.

Sometimes we convince ourselves that we're getting away with something, when in reality, it's just a matter of time before we get what's coming to us. The longer we go without getting caught, the more flippant we become in our wrongdoing. In the same way, many of us ignore God. As time passes, our hearts become hardened, and we don't think about what is ahead. The Bible says that each of us will face judgment after death. Those who know Christ will receive eternal life and its rewards; those who have rejected him will receive eternal punishment. Now is the time for us to choose which type of payback we prefer.

Each person is destined to die once and after that comes judgment.
Hebrews 9:27

July 27

A Wasted Life
JEZEBEL

1 Kings 16:30-31

Coming home late in the evening, Casey fell onto the sofa, exhausted. She knew that it shouldn't have been this way—working a job she hated while taking night classes. Casey had grown up in a loving, supportive family. After high school, she started college on a full scholarship. Looking back, Casey thought she must have gone crazy that first semester. She dropped out of school, went through a series of worthless relationships, and even spent a year on the streets. Now she wished that she could regain half of the opportunities she had thrown away.

Jezebel also wasted her opportunities. As a Sidonian princess, she enjoyed wealth, power, education, and a sharp intellect. More important, Jezebel had the chance to rise above her pagan upbringing when she married the king of Israel. Although Ahab was not a godly man, Jezebel had access to the Israelite prophets so she heard about God's miracles—in fact, she witnessed at least one. Yet she chose to direct her energies and resources toward fighting against God. Jezebel had many prophets killed, and she pressured countless Israelites into adopting idol worship. In the end, she was betrayed by a servant; nothing remained of her except for a few bones scattered over a field and the continuing cycle of depravity that eventually wiped out her family line.

Each of us represents a unique combination of family background, natural abilities, education, and life experiences. We may feel resentful when we look at someone who seems to have been given more opportunities than we have, but what determines the direction of our lives is our response to the opportunity to know and follow God. Even if we pour our energies and resources into some noble cause, in the end nothing will remain of eternal value if we neglect our relationship with God. However successful we may appear in the world's eyes, our lives will have been wasted.

[Paul said,] "Yes, everything else is worthless when compared with the infinite value of knowing Christ Jesus my Lord."
Philippians 3:8

July 28

All That Matters
PHOEBE

Romans 16:1-2

The Bible doesn't give us any details about Phoebe, but the three sentences in these verses sum up her life as well-lived. Apparently she served her church in an official position. Paul gave Phoebe great responsibility and honor when he entrusted her with the task of carrying his letter to the believers at Rome. She must have been a woman of wealth and prominence, since she made this long journey at a time when few women traveled. What truly mattered about Phoebe's life was that she loved God and served his people. She had a reputation for always being ready to help believers who were in need.

Not many people know the details of Mother Teresa's background and early life, but we all know that her life was centered on serving God by helping other people. Mother Teresa expressed her love for God by ministering to the destitute, rejected, suffering, and dying people in society. When we hear Mother Teresa's name, we probably don't think of her family background, her education, or any honors she received. The one thing we remember is the passion for ministering to needy people, which was fueled by her love for God.

It's easy to get bogged down by the details of our lives. We think that we could enjoy a fuller life if we had a different family background, some great talent, a different career, or one of a thousand other "ifs." The world may judge the worth of a life by wealth, prestige, education, or earthly accomplishments, but those things have no eternal value. At the end of our days on earth, all that will matter will be our relationship with God and how we expressed that faith by loving others. That's the definition of a life well-lived.

What is important is faith expressing itself in love.
Galatians 5:6

July 29

Never Too Old
SARAH, MIRIAM, ELIZABETH, ANNA

As I listened to my younger friend moan about her approaching birthday, I didn't want to do the math. I had reached the point where each year brought some new surprise—appointments with a chiropractor for back pain, bifocals, and orthotics in my shoes for fallen arches. What was next— duct tape to hold my body together? I had finally admitted to a marked decrease in energy and a definite increase in weight, and sometimes I had trouble catching all the words in a conversation. *Guess I should count my blessings, such as blonde highlights instead of gray streaks,* I laughed to myself.

We don't look forward to aging, but God sometimes reserves very special events for a woman's later years. At the age of ninety, Sarah gave birth to Isaac, whose descendants were the Jewish people. Miriam was around ninety when she helped her younger brothers, Moses and Aaron, lead the vast throng of Israelites to the Promised Land. Elizabeth was advanced in age when she became pregnant with John the Baptist, who was destined to prepare people for Jesus' coming. Anna may have been a hundred or more when she was privileged to see the promised Messiah after his birth.

In our youth-obsessed culture, it's easy to forget that aging carries a positive connotation in the Bible. If we belong to God, then each year offers an opportunity to grow in wisdom and become more like Christ. What is it about aging that frightens us so much—loss of attractiveness? Potential health problems? The possibility of feeling lonely and useless? These may be valid concerns, but God's promises trump all our worries. He promises to take care of us throughout our lives and beyond, when we will go to be with him. Who knows what exciting events he has planned for our later years?

Even in old age they will still produce fruit; they will remain vital and green.
Psalm 92:14

July 30

Good Intentions
WOMEN PROMISING TO OBEY THE LAW

Exodus 19:7-8; 24:3, 7

Jenna reached in the freezer and grabbed the carton of butter-pecan ice cream. She probably shouldn't even have this stuff in the house. With her high cholesterol, elevated blood pressure, and family history of diabetes, her doctor had stressed the necessity of losing those extra fifty pounds. Jenna had promised him that she would make major changes in her diet. Oh well, she would just have a few bites while she read the paper. Fifteen minutes later, Jenna found the empty carton more depressing than the front page news. *And I had such good intentions!*

The Israelite women who promised to obey everything that God commanded also had good intentions. God had delivered them from slavery and displayed his power in miraculous ways. When God prepared to give his laws to Israel in written form, the people enthusiastically vowed to do whatever God commanded. The Israelites sincerely wanted to honor the One who had claimed them as his special people. On that promising day in the nation's history, these women fully believed that they could carry out their promise to God. They had no idea how soon they would fall away from him and do the very things he had warned them against.

Even the best of intentions aren't enough to help us avoid sin's pull. However hard we try, we will never have enough strength of our own for godly lives. Often we find ourselves repenting of a sin only to repeat the same mistake again and again. The Bible warns that if we think we are standing up to temptation, we're probably headed for a fall. When we understand our weaknesses, we can depend on God's power. God doesn't want us to make promises that we can't keep; he wants us to rely on the promises he has made to us.

> *Let him who thinks he stands take heed that he does not fall.*
> *1 Corinthians 10:12* (NASB)

July 31

One Last Look
LOT'S WIFE

Genesis 19:15-26

After the angels rushed Lot's family away from the city, they ordered them to run for their lives and not look back. As the family reached the village of Zoar, the Lord rained down fire and burning sulfur to wipe out the cities. Lot's wife disobeyed the angels' instruction and looked back.

Was she curious about what was happening, or did she not believe that God would do what he said? Was her heart attached to the city, so that she looked back with regret over what she had left behind? The Bible gives only one sentence about her action, including her punishment for disobeying: She turned into a pillar of salt.

When someone tells us not to look, our natural response is a burning desire to turn our heads. Sometimes it's hard to keep from looking back at what we left behind before we became believers. Old sinful habits that we once relished call us to return. As with the Israelites in the wilderness, our old lives of slavery might start to look more enjoyable than our present situation (see Exodus 16:3). But it's often guilt and regret over our past that pulls our eyes backward.

Jesus said, "Anyone who puts a hand to the plow and then looks back is not fit for the Kingdom of God" (Luke 9:62). God wants us to learn from our past, but he also wants us to keep our eyes fixed on where we're going. Dwelling on failed relationships, missed opportunities, or wrong choices paralyzes us and stunts our spiritual growth. When we accept God's grace, he forgives our past and promises us a wonderful future. Why would we gaze backward when we have so much to look forward to?

I focus on this one thing: Forgetting the past and looking forward to what lies ahead, I press on.
Philippians 3:13-14

August 1

Faithful Servant
DEBORAH

Genesis 35:1-8

I walked toward the church kitchen, dreading the next couple of hours. The previous night's banquet had been a success, but it had ended rather late. As chairman of the fellowship committee, I was responsible for finishing the cleanup chores. Pushing the door open, I was amazed to see a spotless room. The dishes were all washed and put away, including the large punch bowls. The counters sparkled, the floor had been swept, and the trash cans had been emptied. I knew instantly who had been there. Kayla didn't have an official title, but she was always working behind the scenes, quietly doing whatever needed to be done.

Today's passage refers to another woman who faithfully served behind the scenes. Although we aren't told when Rebekah died, Scripture does record the details of her childhood nursemaid's death. Deborah had accompanied Rebekah when she left home to become Isaac's bride. After she helped to care for Esau and Jacob, perhaps she became a part of Jacob's growing household. Deborah died soon after Jacob returned to Canaan. She was honored and greatly mourned by the family she had served for two generations. Jacob buried her beneath an oak tree that was afterward known as "the oak of weeping."

We know nothing about Deborah's life except how it ended and that she served faithfully. When our own lives come to an end, all that will truly matter is how well we served God. Any earthly titles, honors, or awards will be meaningless. When God rewards his servants, he will look at how devotedly they carried out the work he assigned them and whether they served him willingly out of love and gratitude. Although she was a servant, God honored Deborah by putting the details of her death in his Word. Someday, he will honor all his faithful servants, including the quiet ones like Kayla and Deborah.

Well done, my good and faithful servant.
Matthew 25:21

213

August 2

Twisted Thinking
MICAH'S MOTHER

Judges 17:1-6

One night as I read the newspaper's editorial section, one letter warmed my heart and another sent a chill down my spine. The first writer commended the paper on a recent article about breed rescue, featuring an "underground railroad" for rescuing unwanted dogs and finding them loving homes. She said that the article was timely since it came at the season when rescue groups were dealing with unwanted Christmas puppies. The second letter praised abortion rights, showing a total disregard for the lives of the thousands of unborn children killed each year. Seeing these letters side by side, I was struck by the confused and twisted morality of our country.

Micah's mother was affected by the confused thinking prevalent in Israel during the period of the judges. When her son returned the money he had stolen from her, she dedicated it to God. Then she gave two hundred silver coins to a silversmith who made an image and an idol for Micah's house. What was this woman thinking? She seemed to sincerely want to honor God, but her method for doing so broke his first commandment. Her motive may have been good, but her lack of understanding about true worship of God encouraged her family's idolatry, and that ended in disaster.

Some people claim that it doesn't matter what people believe as long as they are sincere about it. Some teach that there are many different ways to find God, and since he looks at our hearts, our lifestyles are not that important. Such ideas directly contradict what the Bible teaches. God does examine our motives as well as our actions, and good intentions and warm feelings are not enough. We are responsible for learning how to live in a way that pleases God. Without a solid foundation of biblical knowledge, our thinking can easily become as twisted as that of Micah's mother.

My people are destroyed from lack of knowledge.
Hosea 4:6 (NIV)

August 3

Never Good Enough
COMPLAINING WOMEN

Numbers 11:1-10

Joan stifled the urge to do cartwheels out of her supervisor's office at the thought of moving to a different department. For six years, she had worked in customer service—and for six years she had listened to people complain, whine, and grumble about big things, little things, and everything in between. It hadn't been a fairy-tale career, but some days she felt stuck in one—this porridge is too hot, too cold; this chair is too big, too small; this bed is too hard, too soft. Sometimes a customer could really be a bear.

Ever since Creation, God has been listening to the human race whine, complain, and grumble. After he miraculously delivered the Israelites from slavery, they grumbled that he was trying to starve them. When God sent them manna, they whined for meat. God displayed divine patience and met their needs, but later he responded to their continued grumbling by destroying some of them with fire from heaven and some by a severe plague. Surely, seeing God's harsh punishment must have helped some of the Israelites break the habit of grumbling when circumstances didn't suit them. Yet some of them continued to complain against Moses and God throughout their journey.

Complaining comes naturally to all of us. It's usually our first response whenever we're disappointed or don't get what we want. God arranges the details of our lives. When we are discontented with who we are or grumble about our circumstances, we're complaining about his provision. God wants us to trust that he knows what is best for us and will work things out for good. Complaining is contagious in a group, and it binds us to a negative mind-set. We are better off using our mouths for prayer and praise instead of grumbling. Then, like Goldilocks, we may finally come to the conclusion that our lives are "just right."

> *Do everything without complaining and arguing.*
> *Philippians 2:14*

August 4

Ready Answers
HULDAH

2 Chronicles 34:14-22

I listened as the young woman behind the counter explained how this latest skin-care product would lift, firm, tighten, smooth, brighten, and otherwise transform my complexion. When I asked her what active ingredients the lotion contained, she didn't know. I asked what made this product better than the miraculous discovery introduced by the same company several months before. She wasn't sure. As we talked, I found out that the woman in the lab coat didn't know much about basic skin care, much less about the products she sold.

Huldah had answers ready when she was asked about God's Word. When workers found a scroll hidden away in the Temple, King Josiah sent the high priest and other representatives to seek out Huldah, a woman known for spiritual discernment. Although Huldah's family members were keepers of the royal wardrobe, she gladly filled her prophetic role when the opportunity came. Huldah rejoiced in her heart that after many years Judah again had a king who desired to follow God. But she may have been surprised that the king inquired of her rather than one of the two male prophets, Jeremiah and Zephaniah. Undaunted, Huldah answered the men's questions.

When we stand for something, we need to be prepared to answer questions. If we claim to be following God, other people should notice something different about us and our lifestyles. Sooner or later, someone will ask us about our beliefs. We don't have to be theologians or Bible scholars for people to seek us out with faith questions. Even if our official job is keeper of the wardrobe, we should be able to answer questions about God in a way that sparks interest in him and in his Word.

Always be prepared to give an answer to everyone who asks you to give the reason for the hope that you have.
1 Peter 3:15 (NIV)

August 5

Our Two Cents' Worth
HULDAH

2 Chronicles 34:23-28

As Tamara picked up the phone, she reminded herself that she needed this job, even though she hated some things about it. Right now, for example, she had the unpleasant duty of calling a nice man and informing him that his request for a small-business loan had been refused. She felt sure that he would lose his diner as a result. Knowing that the decision had come from the board and that the man's problems stemmed from his own unwise business decisions didn't make it any easier to deliver the message.

Huldah also had a hard message to deliver, but she didn't hold back. First, she confirmed that the newly discovered scroll was indeed the lost Book of the Law. Then Huldah told the king's messengers that God planned to judge Israel for their idol worship and send the people into exile. Predicting her nation's downfall couldn't have been easy, but Huldah made it clear that she wasn't giving her own intellectual opinion. Four times she repeated, "This is what the Lord says," or a similar phrase. Huldah knew that speaking God's truth gave her words credibility regardless of her listeners' response.

It's only natural for us to dread being asked our personal opinions about controversial issues such as homosexuality, abortion, or gay marriage. Since our culture values tolerance more than truth, we risk being labeled as unloving, intolerant, or narrow-minded if we express biblical views. But what's important is God's opinion, not ours. He created the world and everything in it, and he is the ultimate authority whether people recognize it or not. Following him often requires us to take a stand that's unpopular with the rest of the world. If we know God's Word well, we can deal with a difficult issue by honestly saying, "This is what the LORD says. . . ."

The word of the Lord stands forever.
1 Peter 1:25 (NIV)

August 6

The Power of the Truth
HULDAH

2 Chronicles 34:29-33

Sitting across from Jason and Trista in the restaurant, Gail could hardly believe that they were really her brother and sister-in-law. Instead of two angry people fighting and cursing at each other, she saw a loving couple treating each other with respect. When Gail had referred them to a Christian counselor, she hadn't expected such an amazing transformation, but she rejoiced to see it. After only eight months, Jason and Trista had joined a church and Bible study, cleaned up their lifestyle, and revived their marriage.

Huldah also rejoiced to see people responding to God's truth. Her message about God's judgment on Israel's idol worship ignited a national revival. Led by King Josiah, the people abandoned their idols, renewed their covenant with God, and promised to obey him. Israel's judgment could not be avoided after so many years of rejecting God's calls for repentance, but God did postpone it because of King Josiah's obedience. How Huldah must have praised God to see the hearts of her fellow Israelites turn back to God.

It's amazing to see how God's truth can transform people. His Word has the ability to renew relationships, soften hearts, and revive our zest for living. As our attitudes and desires change, the internal transformation affects our behavior and lifestyles. But in order to be changed by the Word, we have to do more than carry a Bible to church on Sundays. God wants us to study the Scriptures so we can know him more intimately, discern his will, and apply it to the way we live. As we respond to what he shows us, we discover the amazing power of his truth to change our lives. And he rejoices at our transformation.

> *The word of God is living and powerful, and sharper than any two-edged sword, piercing even to the division of soul and spirit, and of joints and marrow, and is a discerner of the thoughts and intents of the heart.*
> *Hebrews 4:12 (NKJV)*

August 7

False Sense of Security
FALSE WOMEN PROPHETS

Ezekiel 13:17-23

God led Ezekiel to denounce the false prophets in Israel who had been leading God's people astray. These false women prophets sold magic charms that supposedly protected their wearers from illness and harm. Their gullible customers never suspected that these charms were luring them into idolatry. The women prophets also passed off their own opinions as revelations from God and predicted peace for the people of Jerusalem. God predicted judgment for the prophets who encouraged wicked people to continue in their sin by promising that everything would be fine.

Today, we seem to have a wider variety of false prophets than ever before. Many people imagine something and promote it as a revelation from God. Teachers and religions that focus on God's love and grace while denying his promised judgment of sin are especially growing in popularity. The idea that God would never allow someone to go to hell deceives many into thinking that their eternal destinies are secure, much like the gullible people referred to in Ezekiel. Some people claim that what they believe about God doesn't matter much as long as they acknowledge the existence of a "Higher Power."

Since our culture is obsessed with tolerance, many people think that one belief system is as good as any other. If we question what someone teaches, we may be accused of attacking that person's religious freedom. But God teaches that the *only* way to come to him is through faith in Jesus Christ as the Savior who died for our sins. We want to make sure that we are depending on God's truth, not on some man-made philosophy that gives a false sense of security. Then we never have to worry about hearing those awful words on Judgment Day: "I never knew you. Get away from me" (Matthew 7:23).

> *They offer superficial treatments for my people's mortal wound. They give assurances of peace when there is no peace.*
> *Jeremiah 6:14*

August 8

True Women Prophets
PHILIP'S DAUGHTERS

Acts 21:8-9

After enjoying huge success as a film star during her early childhood, Shirley Temple Black spent twenty-seven years working for the State Department. Her career included such assignments as U.S. ambassador to Ghana in 1974 and ambassador to Czechoslovakia in 1989 and 1992. As an ambassador for the United States, she represented the American government to these other countries and was responsible for safeguarding her country's honor.

In the Bible, true prophets were God's representatives on earth, sharing messages and revelations from him. The Old Testament names Miriam, Deborah, and Huldah as examples of authentic female prophets. They faithfully shared God's Word with their nation regardless of the popularity of the message or the political climate. The New Testament indicates that the gift of prophecy was also evident in the early church. An evangelist named Philip had four unmarried daughters who were prophets. It must have been highly unusual to have so many in one household with this calling.

Since we have been given the complete written Word of God and the Holy Spirit to guide each believer, there are differences of opinion about the gift of prophecy and its place in the modern church. Regardless of this debate, every believer is called to represent Jesus Christ on earth, even as Jesus represented the Father during his earthly life.

Our assignment is to speak for him regardless of the political climate, sharing the good news of reconciliation with God through Christ. Our duty includes safeguarding the honor of the One who sent us. Our words and actions help to shape what others think of him. There is no greater honor than being an ambassador who represents Christ to a lost world.

We are Christ's ambassadors; God is making his appeal through us.
2 Corinthians 5:20

August 9

Keeping On
THE PERSISTENT WIDOW

Luke 18:1-8

It's about time! I thought, as I read the letter. Four months earlier, I had noticed an error on our bill. I explained the situation to someone in the clinic's billing department, who assured me that it would be taken care of. I did the same thing the next month. The month after that, I spent an hour on the phone as our insurance company shuffled me from person to person. Eventually, I wrote a letter to the clinic and included copies of the bills and any related papers I could find. Finally, my persistence paid off.

Jesus told a parable about a persistent widow who refused to give up her pursuit of justice. Time after time, the woman came before a judge to ask for a settlement of her case against an enemy. Each time, the uncaring judge ignored her request. How often did the woman feel tempted to give up her hope for justice? Yet she kept taking her case to the judge in spite of her disappointment until she finally wore him down. Eventually, the judge resolved her case just so she would quit nagging him.

The widow's story encourages us to persevere in prayer even when we feel like giving up. In contrast to the uncaring judge, God loves us deeply. When it seems that he is ignoring our requests, he has a reason. God promises to answer our prayers in his own time and way, as long as we're in a right relationship with him, our requests line up with his will, and we believe that he will answer when we pray. Sometimes I persevere more in worldly problems, such as a billing error, than I do in prayer. The story of the persistent widow reminds me that God always welcomes prayers offered by his children in faith, and he delights in answering them in the best way possible.

> [Jesus said,] "Keep on asking, and you will receive what you ask for. Keep on seeking, and you will find. Keep on knocking, and the door will be opened to you."
> *Matthew 7:7*

August 10

A Divine Appointment
THE WOMAN AT THE WELL

John 4:1-6

The Samaritan woman licked her parched lips as her worn-out sandals pounded the hard, dusty road. She paused to shift the weight of her water jar. She hated making this long trip to the well every day, but it had to be done. *At least the other women in the village can draw their water in the cool of the day,* she thought bitterly. She hated waiting until noon, when it was so hot, but she knew how the other women would treat her if she showed up when they did. What the woman didn't know was that she was on her way to an appointment that had been scheduled by God.

When Jesus and his disciples left Judea to return to Galilee, he didn't choose the normal route. The Jews had long hated the mixed-race Samaritans and their attempts to combine Judaism with elements of a pagan religion. Jewish travelers made a long detour to avoid Samaria, but love compelled Jesus to go straight through it. As his disciples set off to buy food in the village and Jesus sat down to wait, he had something more in mind than taking a rest. He knew that a woman with a heavy heart would soon come to the well—a woman who needed to talk with him so that her life could change forever.

Every day, our heavenly Father waits for us to come and talk with him. He wants to comfort us when we hurt, encourage us when we're down, guide our decisions, and strengthen us for the trials and difficulties our day may bring. Unfortunately, with our busy lifestyles, it's too easy to rush into the day without spending time with him. What an unbelievable privilege we pass up when we skip our daily divine appointment.

> *My heart has heard you say, "Come and talk with me." And my heart responds, "LORD, I am coming."*
> Psalm 27:8

August 11

Shocked by Grace
THE WOMAN AT THE WELL

John 4:7-10

Shauntelle stood in stunned silence as he walked away. She could hardly believe that she had been talking with *him* for the past ten minutes. He had been so polite and interested, asking about her job, her family, her future plans. It wasn't that she never saw him—she occasionally caught a glimpse of him, but usually he stayed in his penthouse suite of offices. Shauntelle never expected the president of such a huge corporation to come down to the mail room, much less have a friendly conversation with her.

When the Samaritan woman approached the well and saw a man sitting there, she didn't expect a conversation. Jesus' request for a drink shocked her for several reasons. Men and women didn't talk to each other in public, especially strangers. Because of her bad reputation, the woman had become used to the silent treatment even from her own people. Besides, Jews and Samaritans did not associate with one another. Why in the world would this man ask her for a drink? Didn't he know that a Jewish man who drank from her water container would be considered unclean?

A female, a Samaritan, and a bad reputation—this woman had three strikes against her, but she was not out of God's reach. Jesus had come to Samaria specifically for the purpose of sharing God's love and forgiveness with this lonely woman whom society regarded as worthless.

In the same way, God goes out of his way to seek us out and draw us to himself. Jesus didn't die for us because we deserved it or because we had anything to offer him. He sacrificed himself so that we could be forgiven and accepted by God regardless of what we've done. No matter how many strikes we have against us, we're never out of reach of God's shocking grace.

> *God showed his great love for us by sending Christ to die for us while we were still sinners.*
> *Romans 5:8*

223

August 12

Thirsty for the Truth
THE WOMAN AT THE WELL

John 4:11-15

Every time I read an article on good health habits, I resolve to drink more water. Some days, my only fluid intake is a cup of coffee for breakfast and a couple of soft drinks later in the day. Medical experts stress that drinking plenty of water is essential for good physical and mental health. Even slight dehydration can cause headaches, fatigue, muscle weakness, impaired concentration, and other symptoms. Thirst is usually an accurate gauge of the need for fluids, but not always. In some cases, our bodies may be crying out for water without our realizing it.

When a Samaritan woman went to draw water from Jacob's well, Jesus made a mysterious comment about water and thirst to draw her into a spiritual discussion. She had to make daily trips to and from the well, lugging her heavy clay jar. Jesus told her that people who drank the water he had would never be thirsty again. The woman was confused, but intrigued. How much easier her life would be if she didn't have to draw water! But how could this man make such an incredible offer? The Samaritan woman began to understand that Jesus was talking about something deeper than physical thirst.

We may not realize it, but our souls thirst and hunger for the God who created us. We will never be satisfied until we fulfill that need by entering into a personal relationship with him. Even Christians can become spiritually dehydrated without realizing it. We can forget to take in God's presence and his Word on a daily basis, resulting in spiritual weakness and a lot of headaches in our lives. The Man who sat by a well in a Samaritan village is still the only Source of living water. If we know him, we don't ever need to be spiritually thirsty again.

My soul thirsts for you; my whole body longs for you in this parched and weary land where there is no water.
Psalm 63:1

August 13

No Secrets
THE WOMAN AT THE WELL

John 4:16-18

"I'm glad the guy at table 13 is ready for his check," Louanne told her coworker. He was beginning to creep her out. At first, she thought he was asking questions just to be friendly, and this was a small town, after all. But soon, she realized that he knew details of her life that a stranger shouldn't know, and she certainly didn't recognize him. Louanne headed for the table, and a few minutes later, she had a good laugh with her cousin, who had grown up on an air force base in Germany.

The woman at the well also found herself talking with a stranger who knew a lot about her. With her curiosity aroused, she asked the man to give her the water that keeps people from being thirsty. Surprisingly, he responded by telling her to go and get her husband. The woman probably stiffened. She didn't want this Jewish teacher to know the truth about her. "I don't have a husband," she answered. To her amazement, Jesus' response showed that he already knew the sordid details of her life—that she had had five husbands and currently lived with a man to whom she wasn't married.

We may be able to hide details about our lives from other people, but not from God. He knows each of us so intimately that he can tell the number of hairs on our heads. God can see our thoughts, feelings, and attitudes. It may seem frightening to be so exposed, until we understand that the One who knows us best loves us despite the sordid details of our lives. Once we accept his forgiveness, we find the freedom to be open and honest with him. We can come into his presence with no secrets and no fear.

[Jesus said,] "The very hairs on your head are all numbered."
Matthew 10:30

August 14

Defining Moment
THE WOMAN AT THE WELL

John 4:17-18

The woman at the well didn't like the direction this conversation had taken. She had been surprised that a Jewish man would talk with her and even ask for a drink. His talk about "living water" and the way he spoke with such authority had piqued her interest. But the fact that this stranger knew the intimate details of her personal life probably horrified her. How could he possibly know that she was in a sinful relationship? What business was it of his, anyway? How should she react to being confronted with her guilt by a total stranger? The Samaritan woman had come face-to-face with a defining moment. Her response would determine whether her life continued as usual or whether it would change dramatically.

When someone exposes our guilt, we have several choices as to how to react. If our boss discovers that we use work time for personal business, will we get indignant at his intrusion or apologize and stop doing it? When a friend confronts us about our failure to keep a promise, do we make excuses or make an effort to keep future commitments? Each time we're faced with a failure or wrongdoing, it's an opportunity to strengthen our character and make positive changes in our lives. Or we can blame others, rationalize our behavior, and get angry at the one who confronts us.

Although God knows when we're ready to face an area of sin in our lives, we choose how to react when he reveals it to us. Will we ignore the conviction of sin we feel through his Holy Spirit, or will we honestly confess it and resolve to make a change? When we face a defining moment as the Samaritan woman did, our response determines whether our lives will continue as usual or be dramatically changed to reflect God's presence.

How do you react when God convicts you of some sinful behavior?

August 15

Finding Answers
THE WOMAN AT THE WELL

John 4:17-26

When Jesus revealed that he knew the details of her sinful lifestyle, the Samaritan woman didn't deny the facts or storm off. In continuing the conversation, she admitted the truth of Jesus' words, although she steered the talk away from her personal life. This stranger knew all about her, yet he talked to her respectfully and offered her "living water." He must be a prophet. Perhaps he knew the answer to the debate between the Jews and the Samaritans over whether Jerusalem or Mount Gerizim was the appropriate place to worship God.

Jesus answered not only her spoken question but her unspoken ones as well. He bluntly told the woman that she had grown up with a false religion and didn't know as much about God as she thought she did. He explained that since God is Spirit, a worshiper's attitude matters more than a location. Then Jesus astounded the Samaritan woman. For the first time in his ministry, he overtly revealed his identity as the Messiah. The woman's mouth must have dropped open—she had received more than an answer to a theological argument; she had discovered the One who is the Answer to all of life's questions.

We all have questions, but sometimes we don't find the answers because we stubbornly refuse to admit our need. If we're driving around looking for a location, we won't get the directions we need until we admit that we're lost. When we have a health problem, we won't find the advice we need until we call the doctor and admit that we're sick. Similarly, we can't receive God's forgiveness until we admit that we are sinners. The Messiah still reveals himself to those who admit their need of the Savior. Then we settle something more important than any theological debate— we find the Answer to our deepest needs.

Jesus told her, "I AM the Messiah!"
John 4:26

August 16

Lightening the Load
THE WOMAN AT THE WELL

John 4:27-38

As Heidi stepped outside the door of the clinic, she realized that she would have to get used to walking normally again. Ever since the water-skiing accident, her right leg had been encased in a thick cast that reached from her ankle to her thigh. She had finally become used to the feeling of dragging around a concrete block. Now, with the cast removed, her leg seemed weak, but she felt as if she could fly to the car.

The Samaritan woman left more than her water jar behind at the well. When Jesus revealed himself as the Messiah, she understood that he offered her forgiveness instead of condemnation for her sinful past. She immediately ran to share the news with others, leaving behind her the burden of guilt, shame, and humiliation. She left behind her the old identity as an immoral woman viewed as an outcast by society, and she began the new life of a righteous woman accepted by God as a beloved daughter. The same woman whose heavy footsteps had plodded along the path toward the well now raced with light feet down a different road.

We all carry burdens—a troubled past, present problems, or worries about the future. Sometimes we feel that our spirits, if not our backs, will break. God never meant for his children to drag around such heavy loads. But how can we let go of our burdens when we have legitimate worries? It's a hard lesson to learn, but God wants to teach us. The more we get to know him through prayer and his Word, the more we learn that we can trust him to control the circumstances of our lives. When we honestly share our burdens with our heavenly Father, our loads are lightened, and we can go through life with lighter footsteps.

> *Give your burdens to the LORD, and he will take care of you.*
> *Psalm 55:22*

August 17

Sharing Our Pasts
THE WOMAN AT THE WELL

John 4:39-42

I tried not to look shocked as the woman spoke about her life. After going to church with her for a couple of years, I had decided that she must come from a perfect family background and enjoy a problem-free life. Otherwise, how could she always look so sweet and serene? Now, she told about the violence in her family as she grew up and how she still struggled with its aftereffects.

The Samaritan woman came to the well in the middle of the day to avoid other people, but after a conversation with Jesus, she ran into the village to tell everyone that she had found the Messiah. She no longer worried about what others thought about her or how they might treat her. She had one burning desire—to share what she had learned about God. The people knew her reputation, but they now saw something different about her.

As a result of her testimony, the people listened to Jesus' message, and many believed in him as the Savior of the world. Because of her shady past, the woman became a powerful witness for Jesus and his ability to change people's lives.

When we become Christians, we sometimes try to act as if our lives were perfect. But we all come with baggage from our past. God may instantly set us free from some of it, while allowing us to work through other parts of it our whole lifetime. When we share our struggles and problems with others, our lives become testimonies to God's grace and power. Since God loves and accepts us, we are free to be real with other people. We can admit that although our lives have changed, we may still have baggage, but now we have a different destination.

> *We are in this struggle together. You have seen my struggle in the past, and you know that I am still in the midst of it.*
> *Philippians 1:30*

August 18

Lifelong Learners
WOMEN TAUGHT BY JESUS

Luke 8:1-3

I counted out twenty double-pocket file folders, making sure that I had an assortment of colors. Participating in the Helping Hands school-supplies drive gives me an opportunity to shop the back-to-school sales. I love soaking up the atmosphere in the stores—it brings back memories of getting my own children ready to return to school. The scent of the vinyl binders even takes me back to my own school days—the excitement of picking out just the right notebook and the anticipation of a new school year with a new teacher and new things to learn.

In Bible times, only boys went to school, while girls stayed at home to prepare for their domestic roles as wives and mothers. Women were not allowed to be taught by rabbis, who considered women unable to understand their teachings. Jesus shattered this convention by teaching women as well as men. The women who traveled with Jesus and ministered to him and the twelve disciples must have eagerly absorbed his every word, keenly aware of the privilege. They understood that to him, they were as important as the men, and as capable of learning.

When people believe in our ability to learn, we're motivated to work hard and meet their expectations. God expects his children to be good students of his Word. Many passages in Scripture are difficult for us to understand, especially when Bible scholars disagree in their interpretations. But God has given us the "school supplies" we need. As we prayerfully study the Bible, rely on the Holy Spirit to show us its meaning, and obey what we've already learned, God will teach us everything we need to know to live a godly life. As lifelong students of God's Word, we can always anticipate learning something new.

I will study your commandments and reflect on your ways.
Psalm 119:15

August 19

Learning a New Language
WOMEN IN THE CITY OF BABEL

Genesis 11:1-9

When Eric, my oldest child, decided to learn a foreign language in high school, I encouraged him to try French and promised to help him with his homework. Since I had loved French classes in my high school and college days, I looked forward to working on the language again. It was fun at first, but soon my confidence eroded when the words and grammar rules were no longer familiar. I hadn't realized how much of the language I had lost by not practicing it.

The women in today's Bible passage learned a new language instantaneously and lost their native one at the same time. Instead of obeying God's command to spread out and fill the earth, the people had stayed together. And then in their pride, they decided to build a tower that would reach to heaven. Because the human race was rebelling against God, he gave them different languages to force them into separate groups. It's hard to imagine the confusion and panic that erupted. Suddenly, a woman's friends couldn't understand what she was saying, and they seemed to her to be speaking gibberish. What had happened to the world?

Once we become God's children, we have a new language to learn, but unlike at the tower of Babel, this does not happen instantaneously. The Bible is our textbook. Two of the Ten Commandments forbid taking God's name in vain and lying about other people. Many passages instruct us to guard against using our mouths for gossip, slander, useless arguing, obscenity, or too many words. God also gives us a clear picture of what our words *should* be like. We are to express praise and thanksgiving to God and encourage and build up other people. Although our culture admires obscene humor and clever put-downs, God calls us to a higher manner of speech. But we have to do our homework and practice using our new language.

> Let your conversation be gracious and attractive so that you will have the right response for everyone.
> Colossians 4:6

August 20

The One and Only
ADAH AND ZILLAH

Genesis 4:19-24

I couldn't believe the words on the screen. While researching polygamy for an article, I had stumbled upon a Web site touting the benefits of the practice and including articles purportedly showing it to be commonplace. The site's stated goal was "to provide a resource for people who wish to move beyond present day monogamy and to promote plural marriage by encouraging honorable individuals wishing to pursue polygamy as the marriage structure for their family and to support those individuals living plural marriage with integrity." I tried to imagine how I would feel if my husband decided to add another wife.

The first polygamous relationship recorded in the Bible came only six generations after Adam. Lamech went against God's original plan by marrying two women. How did Adah and Zillah feel about being the first women to share one husband? Perhaps they squabbled and suffered bouts of jealousy as they both tried to fulfill their roles as wives. Or maybe each one secretly longed to be in a monogamous marriage where she would have her husband's attention and affection all to herself. Adah and Zillah had no idea that their relationship would begin a trend that would lead a king of Israel to marry a thousand wives.

No clear-thinking woman wants to share her husband with anyone else. Neither does God want to share *us* with anyone else. He designed us for meaningful, loving relationships with family and friends, but no one else should take his rightful place in our hearts. It's not always obvious when a person is spiritually polygamous, but our lifestyles reveal whether or not God is at the center of our affections and allegiance. We won't enjoy true intimacy with our heavenly Father until we give him first priority in our hearts. Our Creator wants us all to himself, and he openly admits that he is jealous for our affection.

> *You must not bow down to them or worship them, for I, the LORD your God, am a jealous God who will not tolerate your affection for any other gods.*
> *Deuteronomy 5:9*

August 21

"Beloved"
LO-RUHAMAH

Hosea 1:2-6

This passage from Hosea is hard to interpret. God commanded the prophet Hosea to marry a promiscuous woman who would be unfaithful to him. Their marriage was to symbolize Israel's unfaithfulness to God when the Israelites turned away from him to worship false gods. When Gomer had a daughter, God chose her name—Lo-ruhamah, which meant "not loved" or "I will no longer show compassion." The girl's name represented the point in history when God would remove his mercy and allow the Israelites to be punished for their sins. In a society that placed great importance on a person's name, this little girl was burdened with a name that carried the message of God's coming judgment.

The book *Dorie: The Girl Nobody Loved* tells the true story of someone who lived out the meaning of Lo-ruhamah's name. Dorie was dropped off at an orphanage as a little girl after being shunned by her mother. She had never been hugged or held. At the orphanage, Dorie experienced further rejection and was beaten every night. Physical, emotional, and sexual abuse continued through a series of foster homes. Finally, Dorie found the home she'd always longed for when she married a godly man and had two children. Today, Dorie Van Stone travels worldwide, offering hope and sharing the message of God's love and grace.

No matter how the world feels about us, God sees each of us as someone who is worth dying for. Unlike Lo-ruhamah, we live in a period of grace, when Jesus' sacrifice makes a permanent relationship with God possible. If we accept the gift of salvation and become God's children, he makes an unbreakable covenant with us. There will be times when he disciplines us and occasions when we must live with the consequences of our sin. But God will never remove his love and compassion from us. Once we become his children, we take the name "Beloved."

"With everlasting love I will have compassion on you," says the LORD, your Redeemer.
Isaiah 54:8

August 22

Expensive Women
GOMER

Hosea 3:1-3

Gloria stared at the locket through the glass case. Yes, that was the one that had been custom designed for her mother and later passed down to her. *How dare he. . . .* Gloria had begun to think that she had lost the precious keepsake, until her husband tearfully admitted to pawning it. He knew how much the silver locket meant to her, but gambling apparently meant more to him. Now Gloria was about to buy back something that rightfully belonged to her.

Gomer's husband bought her back even though she was legally married to him. When Gomer deserted Hosea, she became someone else's legal property, perhaps as a prostitute. In spite of her unfaithfulness, Hosea still loved his wife. He bought her back with silver and goods equaling fifteen shekels, the typical price of a slave. Then Hosea told his wife that her old lifestyle of adultery had ended. Gomer must have felt a deep sense of gratitude toward Hosea for redeeming her in spite of the way she had hurt and wronged him.

God created us, but he had to buy us back because we were sinners. Since sin entered the world in the Garden of Eden, each of us has been born as a slave to sin. God redeemed us from sin's tyranny at a very high cost— the priceless blood of Jesus Christ. Once we accept the transaction made on our behalf, God tells us that our old lifestyle has ended. We no longer have to obey our sinful nature. How can we help but feel a deep sense of gratitude and love toward the One who gave his own blood to buy us out of slavery? We'll never take our salvation for granted when we remember how much he paid to redeem us.

> *You know that God paid a ransom to save you from the empty life you inherited from your ancestors. And the ransom he paid was not mere gold or silver. It was the precious blood of Christ, the sinless, spotless Lamb of God.*
> *1 Peter 1:18-19*

August 23

Covered by Love
THE WOMAN IN BAHURIM

2 Samuel 17:15-22

During World War II, Corrie ten Boom and her family used their home as a hiding place for Jews and other people targeted by the Nazi regime. The underground activities of the ten Boom family and their friends saved the lives of an estimated eight hundred Jews and many Dutch Resistance workers. When the Nazis arrested the family in 1944, they suspected that Jews were hiding in the house but were unable to find them. Forty-seven hours later, Resistance workers rescued six people who were hiding behind a false wall in Corrie's bedroom.

A woman in Bahurim saved King David's life by hiding two men who were taking him a crucial message. Jonathan and Ahimaaz had been sent to warn David that his son Absalom planned to attack. When a boy spotted them, the two messengers escaped to the village of Bahurim, where a man hid them in a well. The man's wife covered the top with a cloth and spread grain on it to dry in the sun so that it would be overlooked as a possible hiding place. Because of her quick thinking and willingness to help, David escaped into the wilderness.

Most of us would be willing to hide an innocent person from danger if it were in our power to do so. Yet we often find it difficult to do something as simple as overlooking another person's faults. The Bible urges believers to treat one another with respect and love, and thus to cover one another's sins. Although sin must sometimes be exposed and dealt with, many problems are caused by our simple lack of patience with one another. Rather than cling to petty annoyances, God wants us to love in such a way that we forgive others' mistakes. And covering another person's faults with our love is a true heroic act.

> *Most important of all, continue to show deep love for each other, for love covers a multitude of sins.*
> *1 Peter 4:8*

August 24

Signature Scent
MARY OF BETHANY

John 12:1-8

I walked from room to room, breathing in the fragrance and smiling. Before today, I'd always bought the cheap potpourri—the stuff that smells good in the package but doesn't give off much fragrance after it's been poured into a container. My friend was right—the more expensive brand was definitely worth the money. Just before dinner, I would light the matching scented candle so we could enjoy the full effect. Little did I realize how my husband and adult son would complain about the "stink" in the house.

Mary of Bethany also got mixed reactions to a scent. Mary longed to express her love and gratitude to Jesus, especially after he raised her brother, Lazarus, from the dead. During a dinner party, she slipped in with a jar containing twelve ounces of pure nard, oil from a rare plant in India. As Mary poured the perfume over Jesus' feet, the heavy scent filled the entire house and drew everyone's attention. Some disciples scolded her for wasting the equivalent of a laborer's yearly wages, but Jesus defended her act of worship and said that Mary had done a good thing.

If we are God's children, we have a signature scent that people react to in different ways. As our lives testify to God's love and forgiveness, he uses us to spread the knowledge of Christ everywhere we go, like an exquisite perfume (see 2 Corinthians 2:14). People will react in one of two ways: Those who reject the gospel will perceive the repulsive smell of death. Those who choose to believe and receive Christ will smell "a life-giving perfume" (2 Corinthians 2:16). Our most important work is to diffuse the sweet fragrance of Christ wherever we go, even though some people will think that our faith stinks.

> *Our lives are a Christ-like fragrance rising up to God. But this fragrance is perceived differently by those who are being saved and by those who are perishing.*
> *2 Corinthians 2:15*

August 25

Looking like a Fool
NOAH'S WIFE

Genesis 6:9-22

Pam smiled as she watched the sun disappear behind the apple trees. Friends thought she and Russell had lost their minds when they bought the acreage with a run-down farmhouse. Their friends had been sure of it when the couple quit their jobs to work on the property full-time. Sixteen years later, hard work and dreams had transformed the farmhouse into a comfortable home, and the ramshackle barn into an antique shop. U-Pick berry patches and orchards sprawled across fields where only briars once grew. Those same friends who had called them crazy now jumped at an invitation to spend a weekend in the country.

Noah's wife knew how it felt to be ridiculed while pursuing a project that seemed foolish to everyone else. It took Noah and his sons years to build the ark and then to stock it with everything needed for the animals. In the meantime, how often did friends tell Mrs. Noah that her husband was a lunatic for building a huge boat and warning of a flood when it had never even rained on the earth before? The laughter and derision must have grown so wearisome as year after year went by, but she and her family faithfully carried out God's instructions. Eventually, the ones who had mocked them would have jumped at the offer of a seat on the ark.

Sometimes we look foolish to others when we're pursuing a dream. If other people don't have the vision for what we hope to achieve, our efforts appear to be a waste of time. Even when we're doing God's work, there is no guarantee that our friends will understand. It takes trust in God and commitment to his will to stay on course when others are ridiculing us, but it's always worth it. After all, we wouldn't want others' opinions to make us miss the boat.

> *The message of the cross is foolishness to those who are perishing.*
> *1 Corinthians 1:18 (NKJV)*

August 26

Living in a Zoo
NOAH'S WIFE

Genesis 7:1-10

Glancing at the clock, Tracey groaned. Still another half hour before Dustin would get home from work. She finished cutting up the chicken and shooed Robbie and his friend away from the cookie jar and into the backyard. Sitting down to nurse the baby, Tracey realized that the dog was scratching at the door to be let out, and the cat was weaving itself around her ankles begging for supper. "You two will just have to wait your turn," she told them. Just then the phone rang, the potatoes started boiling over, and the baby began to wail. Tracey looked at the ceiling. *My life is a zoo!*

Noah's wife knew the feeling. For a year, she lived on a huge boat filled with thousands of animals and all their necessary supplies. Mealtimes took on a whole new meaning for Noah's wife and her three daughters-in-law, but that must have seemed minor in comparison to their other chores. How did these women stand such a living arrangement, as month after month passed by? They must have wondered if their ordeal would ever end, if they would ever stand on land and breathe fresh air again.

Sometimes, as homemakers, our lives seem like a zoo, especially when it's feeding time. It seems that all we're doing is feeding people and cleaning up their messes. We may start to wonder how much longer we can stand it. Will things ever change? The answer to our situations is the same as for Noah's wife. God is with us in every circumstance in every season of our lives. He will give us the strength to keep on plugging away at our chores even when they seem like drudgery. More than that, he will use those times to help our faith grow as we find blessings among the messes. Later, we will look back and know that he was the One who kept us afloat.

My times are in your hands.
Psalm 31:15 (NIV)

August 27

A Fresh New World
NOAH'S WIFE AND DAUGHTERS-IN-LAW

Genesis 8:1-19

Although the missionary organization had tried to prepare them for their new lives, the overwhelmed mother and her children kept their faces pressed against the car windows during the long ride from the airport. Such wonderful sights—the rows of painted houses, the park with expanses of colorful flowers, and trees of all shapes and sizes. But the tall buildings and wide spaces were a little frightening, too. The family felt worlds away from their little village of thatched huts.

Noah's family must have felt that they were stepping into a new world as they left the ark after living on it for almost a year. It must have been a huge relief to stand on land again and gaze at open spaces, and yet a little frightening, too. This was the same world they had known before, but it was different. The flood had washed away all traces of the former inhabitants and their wickedness, leaving the earth clean and fresh, but also strangely quiet. Since it was not a perfect world like the Garden of Eden, the world was still decaying and sin would soon pollute it again. But Noah's family thanked God for the opportunity to begin a new life.

When we become God's children, we enter a new world unseen by human eyes. We live in the same aging physical bodies, but Christ has washed away our sin, leaving us clean and fresh. We still exist on the same earth, but spiritually we belong to a new Kingdom with values that are opposed to those of the world. Our challenge is to live in the world without conforming to its attitudes. Through prayer, Bible study, and fellowship with other believers, God can transform our thinking so that we reflect his values. Then we may look around and see the same old world, but we will be living a new life.

> *Don't copy the behavior and customs of this world, but let God transform you into a new person by changing the way you think.*
> *Romans 12:2*

August 28

The First Rainbow
NOAH'S WIFE AND DAUGHTERS-IN-LAW

Genesis 9:1-17

The young mother walked through the apartment with an open mouth, scarcely comprehending what the pastor was telling her. She knew that his church had promised to find her a job and provide a home for her family. But could this place really be hers—with the clean carpets, soft beds, running water, and a refrigerator packed with food? All she had ever known was living on a mud floor, carrying water from a dirty river, and scratching out a living from a small vegetable plot. Surely this was some mistake—and yet the man was smiling and holding out a set of keys.

After the flood, Noah's wife and family may have wondered if their home was secure, or if God would repeat the flood in the future. God assured them that he would never again send floodwaters to destroy all life. As a sign of his promise, he placed the first rainbow in the sky. How did Noah's wife and daughters-in-law feel as they gazed at the very first rainbow? Such brilliant colors arcing across the sky, put there just to assure them that their home was safe from destruction. Each time a rainbow appeared, their hearts swelled with renewed wonder at God's goodness and provision.

God has given us a promise even greater than the pledge of the rainbow. Jesus promised that someday those who believe in him will move into an eternal home, free from decay, sorrow, trials, and death. Our new home will be so wonderful that we can't even imagine it right now, yet it will be perfectly suited to us. Best of all, God will live among us. Living in his glorious presence will make even the richest mansion on earth seem like a hut with a mud floor.

> *No eye has seen, no ear has heard, and no mind has imagined what God has prepared for those who love him.*
> *1 Corinthians 2:9*

August 29

A Reason to Go On
JOB'S WIFE

Job 1:13-19; 2:7-10
It all seemed so unreal. The woman stood by the pile of debris that had once been her home. As she looked up and down the street, she felt as if she were dreaming—or rather, having a nightmare. Her neighborhood had been demolished by the hurricane and the flood that followed it. Houses, stores, the school, and her church—all gone. Worst of all, her husband had died of a heart attack during the storm. Although emergency workers and volunteers surrounded her, the woman ignored their offers of help. She saw no hope of rebuilding her uninsured home, and no reason to rebuild her life.

Job's wife also knew how it felt to suddenly lose everything. When Satan claimed that Job worshiped God only because God had prospered him, God gave Satan permission to test Job with adversity. In one day, Job and his wife lost their livestock, their servants, and their ten children. Then Job's body became covered with painful sores. The grief of losing her children and then seeing her husband suffer made Job's wife lose all hope. Her life as she had known it seemed to be over. She saw no reason to go on. In her despair, she blurted out a suggestion that Job curse God and die. Death seemed preferable to such unbearable pain.

When sudden disaster strikes, we may deal with similar feelings. From a human perspective, it may look as if we have no reason to go on. Why bother trying to rebuild our lives when we have nothing left to work with? Even in the midst of our bewilderment that God has allowed such suffering, we can cling to the truth that he is also responsible for all the good in our lives. Everything that he allows to touch us has a purpose, and he promises to see us through it. That's reason enough to go on.

"I know the plans I have for you," says the LORD. "They are plans for good and not for disaster, to give you a future and a hope."
Jeremiah 29:11

August 30

New Vision
JOB'S WIFE

Job 42:7-17

The Bible doesn't tell us anything about Job's wife except for her comment to him in Job 2:9, but at the end of the book, we see that her life did change for the better. After Job's time of testing, God gave him and his wife twice as much wealth as before. Their relatives and friends showered them with love and comfort. According to Job 42:13, we assume that Job's wife gave birth to ten more children. The memory of her terrible heartache and suffering must have softened over the years as she discovered new joy in God's abundant blessings.

By the end of their trials, Job had acquired a new vision of God. While he knew *about* him before, he now felt that he knew God on a more personal level. Did Job's wife also gain a deeper understanding of God through her suffering? Did she learn to trust him to walk with her through the tough times of life? Did she feel closer to the God who forgave her for words spoken in bitterness and grief? Perhaps Job's wife knew God more intimately after the tragedy that stripped away everything except for God's presence in her life.

Sometimes we suffer as a consequence of our sinful choices; at other times, suffering results simply from our living in a sinful world. God sometimes uses trials to test and strengthen our faith, to give us a powerful witness to the world, or to help us become more like Christ. We may not understand God's purpose in allowing hard times, but we can count on him to help us endure them. After the trial ends, we'll discover that we know God better than before. When we're hurting, we can think only about what we've lost. But if we hang on to our trust in God, we'll find that we've gained a new vision of him and deeper spiritual insight.

> *I had only heard about you before, but now I have seen you with my own eyes.*
> *Job 42:5*

August 31

Temporary Shelter
WOMEN LIVING IN TENTS

Leviticus 23:33-43

Linda gritted her teeth as she pulled on the tent peg with all her might.
Since going home was her favorite part of a camping trip, she had been
glad to stay behind and take down the tent while Paul and the kids got in
one last hike. Linda tried to be a good sport, but she just didn't understand
why people would want to spend a week in a dome of thin fabric when
they could be in a house with solid walls—and a bathroom. She also didn't
understand how this big pile of material and metal stakes could possibly fit
into that small drawstring bag.

Many Bible women knew the experience of living in tents, some of
them for most of their lives. One of the yearly observances celebrated by the
Israelites was the Festival of Shelters, also known as the Festival of Taberna-
cles. For seven days, the people lived outside in small temporary shelters, or
booths, as a reminder that their ancestors had lived in tents after God rescued them out of Egypt. Some of the women in later generations may have
resented the inconvenience of spending a week in an outdoor shelter when
they had a house, but God knew the importance of special observances that
would help them remember what he had done for them.

Passages in the New Testament compare our earthly bodies to tents.
What a perfect word picture to help us remember that our lives here are
temporary. No matter what kind of house we live in, we inhabit bodies that
are fragile and susceptible to disease, aging, and death. Someday, it will be
time to take down our earthly tents and move into permanent homes. God
promises to give us new bodies, free from the defects of our old ones. We
will be glad to put away our flimsy tents and move into permanent shelter.

We know that when this earthly tent we live in is taken down (that is,
when we die and leave this earthly body), we will have a house in heaven,
an eternal body made for us by God himself and not by human hands.
2 Corinthians 5:1

September 1

Renewing Our Love for Christ
WOMEN IN EPHESUS

Revelation 2:1-7

We can imagine the women waiting eagerly for the apostle John's letter to be read. Through a vision, John had been given a specific message for each of the seven churches in Asia. This precious letter contained words from the Lord Jesus Christ directed to their group of believers. The women must have felt a warm glow as the letter opened with praise for their church. Jesus acknowledged their hard work and their patient endurance through hardships. They had resisted sexual sin in a city famous for immoral practices connected with worship of the goddess Artemis. They had exposed the lies of false prophets.

At first it sounded as if the church at Ephesus was doing everything right. But then Jesus exposed their serious flaw—"You don't love me or each other as you did at first!" (Revelation 2:4). The Ephesian believers had been so caught up in doing the right things that their passion for Christ had cooled. They were motivated by a sense of duty rather than fervent devotion to Christ. He urged them to remember how they had felt when they first met him and to regain the enthusiasm they felt then.

The warning to the church at Ephesus gets to the heart of true Christianity. Many religions emphasize works, but Christianity is based on a love relationship with God through Jesus Christ. Sound doctrine and service for God are vital, but we can get so caught up in Bible knowledge and activities that a legalistic attitude replaces our desire to simply be with him. Sometimes we need to stop and remember why we love God and how we felt when we first understood his sacrifice. When he lived on earth, Jesus' harshest criticisms were of people who were religious but not in love with God. If we've left our first love, we need to do whatever it takes to get back to it.

> *I have this against you, that you have left your first love.*
> *Revelation 2:4 (NASB)*

September 2

An End in Sight
WOMEN IN SMYRNA

Revelation 2:8-11

As I walked across my parents' small farm, one thought kept coming to my mind: *Only for a little while.* I saw where I had spent hours as a child, sitting on a clump of tree roots jutting out of the pond and pretending that I was on an island. All that remained was a dry depression in the ground. Then I walked through what used to be cotton fields, where my family had worked long days in the hot sun all summer. Growing up, I felt as if the dust, blisters, and backaches would go on forever. From the perspective of my present age, it seems that those days lasted for only a little while.

The women in Smyrna needed a reminder that all our earthly experience is temporary. These believers had endured extreme poverty and intense persecution from Gentiles and from Jews who were hostile to Christianity. Jesus warned them that more suffering would come: Satan would have some believers thrown into prison. Others would face death. But Jesus urged them not to be afraid of the suffering since it would not last. The phrase "ten days" indicated a limited period of time. The believers' suffering would have a definite end determined by God.

We may not always understand the reason for our troubles, but we can be certain that suffering will come and that it will end. Although we go through painful experiences, they pale in comparison to the future glory of being in Jesus' presence, free from sin and sorrow. Jesus knew that he faced an excruciating death by crucifixion, but he also knew that the pain would be temporary. He looked ahead to his resurrection and glorious ascension to heaven. From an eternal perspective, any pain we suffer is brief, and it prepares us for the everlasting joy of heaven.

> *Our present troubles are small and won't last very long. Yet they produce for us a glory that vastly outweighs them and will last forever!*
> *2 Corinthians 4:17*

September 3

Neglected Faith
WOMEN IN SARDIS

Revelation 3:1-6

After she got home from the doctor's office, Renee stared at her right arm in the mirror. No one would ever guess that she had done strength training for two years. The arm that had done bicep curls with fifteen-pound dumbbells now hung flabby and almost useless at her side after four weeks in a cast. Renee now understood what the doctor meant by muscle atrophy.

Jesus' message to the church at Sardis accused those believers of being as lifeless as an atrophied muscle. He acknowledged that they had a reputation for being active and effective, so those hearing the letter must have been shocked by Jesus' evaluation: "You are dead." The believers hadn't exercised their spiritual muscles by developing the disciplines of the Christian life or by fighting against sin. As a result, they were "soiled . . . with evil," except for a small group whose lives were pleasing to God. Jesus sent the believers in this church a wake-up call, telling them to strengthen their faith by remembering and obeying the basic truths of the gospel.

If we don't nurture our faith, it doesn't stay the same—it weakens, leaving us vulnerable to sin's influence. In order to grow spiritually, we have to practice habits of prayer, worship, Bible study, and obedience. God's Holy Spirit works with our personal discipline to help us make godly choices. As we obey God's commands, we become more like Christ. But if we go through the motions of the Christian life while neglecting to deepen our relationship with God, that relationship will deteriorate. We may look good on the outside, like the church at Sardis, but that doesn't fool God. Sooner or later, he will send us a wake-up call.

Wake up! Strengthen what little remains, for even what is left is almost dead.
Revelation 3:2

September 4

No Audition Required
YOUNG WOMEN IN PERSIA

Esther 2:1-4, 12-13

The young woman fought back tears as she responded to the interviewer's questions. All her life, she had dreamed of being a recording artist. Now, she had quit her job and borrowed money for a long bus ride, all for the chance to audition for the new season of *American Idol*. Behind that young woman sat hundreds of other young men and women, trying not to look nervous as they waited for their names to be called. Their future plans rested on the opinions of the three judges in the next room and what happened during their brief moments behind the closed doors.

The young women in today's passage must have struggled with similar feelings. When King Xerxes wanted a new queen, his officials searched the vast empire for beautiful young women. After receiving beauty treatments for a year, each woman spent one night with the king. Her future depended on whether or not she could impress the king enough that he would choose her out of the rest of the throng as his new queen. After the months of preparation ended, each woman nervously awaited her turn to see if she would succeed during her one night behind closed doors.

How blessed we are that our God is not like a Persian tyrant or an *American Idol* judge. We don't have to audition to see if we're good enough to become his children. He accepts us just as we are, blemishes and all. And he doesn't offer us just one chance to know him. Out of his great love for us, he continually places people and circumstances in our lives to draw us toward a relationship with him. Even if we reject him, he keeps on wooing and pursuing us. How can we *not* respond to such great love?

> *He is patient with you, not wanting anyone to perish, but everyone to come to repentance.*
> *2 Peter 3:9 (NIV)*

September 5

Losers
YOUNG WOMEN IN PERSIA

Esther 2:12-14

When she gazed at her reflection in the mirror, she hardly recognized her face. The corners of her mouth turned down, her eyes showed more red than white, and the dark circles under her eyes testified to another sleepless night. She had seen the telltale scowl on her husband's face and had known what to expect. Whenever he had a bad day at work, he took it out on her. Oh, he never hit her, but she felt beaten up. "Why did I marry a loser like you? You can't do anything right!" His words echoed inside her head and made her wonder why she had even been born.

Many of the women in ancient Persia must have also felt like losers. After each of the women in today's passage (except Esther) had her chance to impress the king, she moved to the second harem, where all the king's wives and concubines lived. She never went into the king's presence again unless he remembered her and specifically requested her by name. These women never had the chance to enjoy life as real wives with families of their own. It's hard to imagine how they felt about being confined to the king's harem for the rest of their lives, just another face in a huge crowd of women rejected by the king.

Women feel like losers for a variety of reasons. They may suffer verbal or physical abuse, be overweight, have a physical handicap, go through divorce, deal with problem children, or be poor and homeless. The bad news is that we are all losers—which is why we need a Savior. Jesus gave his life to win the battle for our souls so that we could be accepted by the King and not live as rejects. The antidote to feeling like a loser is to focus on what God says about us. When we lose ourselves in his love, we know we are winners.

My victory and honor come from God alone.
Psalm 62:7

248

September 6

From Nobody to Somebody
WOMEN LIFTED UP FROM OBSCURITY

God delights in taking "nobodies" and transforming them into special "somebodies." He took a young orphaned girl from a conquered race and made her the queen of the world's most powerful monarch. Because of Esther's faith in God and her humble obedience to her adoptive father, Mordecai, God used her to save the Jewish race from annihilation.

Rahab was a prostitute in a pagan city marked for judgment. When she trusted in the God of Israel, she saved the lives of herself and her family members and later became a prominent Israelite leader's wife. Abigail was married to a man despised by others as a stupid, drunken fool. After risking her life to save her husband and others, she became the wife of the man who would become one of Israel's greatest kings.

These women and others in the Bible rose from obscurity to take prominent roles in history. They didn't reach a higher position in life because they chased after riches, fame, or popularity. God raised them up because of their humility and their willingness to follow his leading. Rather than seeking the spotlight for their own glory, they deliberately made honoring and obeying God their first priority.

Our society pushes a different formula for success than the one that God proposes. Books and classes teach us how to influence people, market ourselves, and move up in the world, but God says that to be great, we must seek him above all else. One day, when God judges all hearts and rewards those who serve him, many who appeared obscure and lowly on earth will be lifted up. For now, even if the world sees us as nobodies, when we do our best to follow God's will, we can know that he is making us into very special somebodies.

He has brought down princes from their thrones and exalted the humble.
Luke 1:52

September 7

Protective Mother
JOCHEBED

Exodus 2:1-10

In the twenty-first century, mothers often fear for their children's safety. School shootings such as the 2007 tragedy at Virginia Tech in Blacksburg, Virginia, which left 32 people dead, make even classrooms seem dangerous. Many of us are afraid to let our kids play in neighborhood yards or parks because of the child kidnappings we see in the news. While we may struggle with fear and uncertainty, death was certain if the Egyptians discovered Jochebed's son.

Pharaoh had ordered his people to "throw every newborn Hebrew boy into the Nile River" (Exodus 1:22). Jochebed was able to hide Moses from the Egyptian guards for three months, dreading the day when that would become impossible. When she could no longer hide him, she waterproofed a basket, put her son in it, and set it among the reeds in the Nile where the pharaoh's daughter and her attendants usually came to bathe.

Jochebed had no choice but to trust her baby's life to God. Although her people were slaves, she knew that Yahweh was ultimately in control of her family's fate. Yet she did more than pray and wait—she took action. Jochebed used her common sense and her resources to protect her son.

There is nothing more important we can do for our children than to cover them with prayer. We can also take commonsense steps to ensure their safety by checking out their environments and friends, reviewing safety rules with them, and becoming involved in their activities. After we've done all that we humanly can, we have to entrust our children into the hands of God—the same God that Jochebed trusted to watch over her baby as he floated in a basket on the Nile River.

Spread your protection over them.
Psalm 5:11

September 8

Compassion International
PHARAOH'S DAUGHTER

Exodus 2:5-10

Courtney smiled as she opened the envelope and studied the crayon drawings. In a couple of years, Pedro would be able to write letters that would be translated and sent to her. Until then, she received updates on his life from the agency. As Courtney stuck a drawing on the refrigerator, she gazed into the large brown eyes of the smudged face that had stirred her compassion at first sight. How she wished that she could sponsor all the children on Compassion International's Web site. But at least she knew that her thirty-two dollars a month made a world of difference in one child's life.

The Egyptian princess in Exodus 2 also showed compassion for a child of another race. One day, when she went to bathe in the Nile River as usual, she found a little basket floating among the reeds. Imagine her surprise when she opened it and found a baby boy. The princess knew instinctively that the baby boy was one of the Hebrew babies marked by her father for destruction. The doomed infant's cries wrenched her heart. She defied the pharaoh's edict and lovingly adopted the boy as her own son.

The Bible says that God "showers compassion on all his creation" (Psalm 145:9). That compassion moved him to lay down his life for a sinful world. Believers are now called to lay down their lives in love and service for others. The Christian life demands more than expressions of sympathy and promises of prayer; it requires compassion in action. If we see people in need and we have the means to help them, God expects us to demonstrate our love in more than words. We can't help every needy person in the world, but we can show compassion for whomever God floats down the rivers of our lives.

> *If someone has enough money to live well and sees a brother or sister in need but shows no compassion—how can God's love be in that person?*
> *1 John 3:17*

September 9

When Opportunity Knocks
MIRIAM

Exodus 2:4, 7-8

Once upon a time, a man climbed onto his roof to escape rising floodwaters and prayed for God to rescue him. In a little while, a man passed by in a rowboat and tried to rescue him. The man on the roof declined, believing that God would rescue him. Later, a helicopter hovered overhead and dropped down a rope. The man refused to take it, preferring to wait for God's help. Eventually the man drowned, and in heaven he asked why God hadn't answered his prayer. "What do you mean?" replied God. "I sent you a rowboat and a helicopter. What more did you want?"

Moses' sister displayed more intelligence than the man in this joke. When the Egyptian princess found the basket, Miriam boldly offered to find a Hebrew woman to nurse the baby. We can only wonder how this little girl of ten or younger felt as she approached the daughter of the cruel pharaoh who hated her people and had ordered the murder of their newborn boys. Because of her devotion to her baby brother, Miriam didn't allow the situation to intimidate her. She seized the opportunity, and as a result of her alertness and quick action, Moses spent the first few years of his life with his own family.

How often have we missed God's answers to our prayers because they didn't take the shape we expected? Sometimes we miss his deliverance from difficult situations because we don't watch for the opportunities that he sends. After we have prayed to God for help, the next step is to demonstrate our trust by expecting him to act. By staying alert and taking advantage of his provision even when it comes in unexpected ways, we'll be more like Miriam and less like the man on the roof.

Make the most of every opportunity in these evil days.
Ephesians 5:16

September 10

Protected by the Blood
WOMEN AT THE FIRST PASSOVER

Exodus 12:1-13

The young woman squinted at the document in her hand. Just ten months ago she thought she'd found the perfect boyfriend. That was before she discovered how violent he was when he drank. After he lost his job, his temper flared up more than ever. She still had a bruise from the last time she'd talked about leaving him. But it was the way he had erupted when her toddler walked into the room that finally made her decide to get the court order of protection. Now, she wondered if a piece of paper could really protect her and her son.

Did the Hebrew women who celebrated the first Passover wonder if their families would really be protected? God had told each Hebrew family to slaughter an unblemished lamb and smear some of the blood on their doorframe. Later that night, he judged Egypt by killing every firstborn son. But when the angel of death saw the blood on the Israelites' doorframes, he passed over their homes. God accepted the substitution of the lambs for their firstborn sons. Although Moses had passed along God's words, many mothers must have watched their oldest sons anxiously that long night, especially as the wails arose from grief-stricken Egyptian mothers.

Court orders are often effective, but unfortunately, they can't guarantee safety. God is the only One who can truly protect us. Being his children doesn't mean that nothing bad will ever happen to us, but it does mean that he is in control of our lives even when we face dangerous situations. It also means that we are protected from eternal judgment for sin. If we have accepted Christ as our perfect Passover lamb, then we have God's promise for the eternal protection of our souls—and that promise is written with the blood of his Son.

> *Since we have been made right in God's sight by the blood of Christ,*
> *he will certainly save us from God's condemnation.*
> *Romans 5:9*

September 11

Seeing God's Presence
WOMEN IN THE EXODUS

Exodus 13:17-22

As the sun began to sink, so did my spirits. I had decided to try a different route on this trip since the printed directions seemed easy enough. Suddenly, the road had divided, and I now realized that I had chosen the wrong side. After stopping twice for directions and driving in circles for twenty-five minutes, I still wasn't on the road I needed. Now, I sat in my car trying not to cry like a baby. I had no idea which direction to take.

The Hebrew women coming out of Egypt didn't have to wonder which way to turn. God led them by a pillar of cloud during the day and a pillar of fire at night. All these women had ever known was slavery and oppression; now, they had the all-powerful God of the universe visibly assuring them of his presence, love, and guidance. As they journeyed through the wilderness on the way to the Promised Land, one look at the cloud or the fire ahead of them confirmed the direction they should take.

We don't have these visible signs from God, but we have two blessings that the Hebrews did not have. We have God's Spirit living in us permanently, which became possible after Jesus' death and resurrection. God's Spirit confirms that we belong to him and directs us toward godly choices when we remain sensitive to his leading. The second blessing is the Bible, which assures us of God's love and also offers divine guidance. When we have tough choices to make, we may wish that God would write directions on a sticky note and post them on our refrigerators. But he *has* promised to lead us on our life journeys by internal signs.

Seek his will in all you do, and he will show you which path to take.
Proverbs 3:6

September 12

Trapped, with No Way Out!
WOMEN IN THE EXODUS

Exodus 14:5-14

The Hebrew women who left Egypt knew what an emotional roller coaster felt like. They must have been thrilled when God sent Moses to deliver them from slavery. Although God sent plagues on the Egyptians, he clearly demonstrated that the Israelites were his chosen people. The Israelites didn't suffer swarms of flies, hail, or the death of their livestock. When the Egyptians endured three days of darkness over their land, the part of Egypt where the Israelites lived had light as usual. When God devastated the Egyptians by killing the firstborn male in each family, the Israelites were protected.

At last, the day of their freedom arrived. The Israelites walked out of Egypt as free people—and wealthy ones at that. God had caused the Egyptians to shower them with fine clothing, silver, and gold. Then he provided visible signs of his presence to lead his people to a wonderful new land of their own. Suddenly, their celebratory mood changed as someone spotted the Egyptian army in hot pursuit. The Israelites were trapped, with the Red Sea in front of them and hundreds of chariots and troops coming up behind. As Pharaoh's immense forces closed in, the Hebrews responded in the normal way—they panicked. It looked as if their glorious escape from Egypt would end in death.

We all feel trapped sometimes, hemmed in by problems, failures, fear of what might happen, or ghosts from our past. Sometimes it seems there is no way out of our predicaments. At those times, it is best to ignore the adage, "Do *something*—even if it's wrong!" God may show us how to resolve an impossible situation, or his instructions may be the same as Moses'—to stay calm and watch God rescue us. At those times, we'll have an idea of how the Hebrew women felt so long ago.

Stand firm and you will see the deliverance the LORD will bring you today.
Exodus 14:13 (NIV)

September 13

How Did I Get Through That?
WOMEN WALKING ACROSS THE RED SEA

Exodus 14:15-31

Shannon collapsed into the recliner and reviewed the past week's events. Monday morning had started off like any normal day—until she got the call about her mother's stroke. In about an hour, Shannon had briefed a coworker about the big presentation, arranged after-school child care, packed, and started the three-hundred-mile drive to her hometown. The rest of the week had revolved around talking with doctors, visiting her mom at the hospital, and caring for her father, who was sick at home with pneumonia. *How in the world did I get through that?* she wondered.

The women in Exodus 14 must have wondered the same thing. When the Egyptians chased and trapped the Israelites, God sent a powerful wind to open a path through the Red Sea. The women must have nervously watched the walls of water and wondered if they would come crashing down on them. Perhaps some of them kept their eyes fixed ahead of them. After the two million people, along with their livestock, finished crossing, they surely looked back in wonder at what they had just done.

When God divided the sea for the Israelites, he demonstrated his power and protection for his people. He does the same today. We all experience difficult times, which often arise unexpectedly. God promises to give us the strength and wisdom we need when we turn to him in a crisis and ask for his help instead of trying to handle it in our own strength. Even when we feel trapped in a situation with no way out that we can see, God can make a way. Later, when we look back at what we've gone through, we'll understand that it's not a matter of how we made it, but of who walked us through it.

> *When you go through deep waters, I will be with you. When you go through rivers of difficulty, you will not drown.*
> Isaiah 43:2

September 14

One Plan, Many Roles
WOMEN IN MOSES' LIFE

God allowed Moses to accomplish amazing things when he confronted the powerful pharaoh of Egypt and then led an estimated two million people and their livestock on a journey through the desert. Although Moses was the Israelites' guide, primary judge, and spiritual leader, God assigned crucial roles to several women as he carried out his plan to deliver his people from slavery.

When Pharaoh ordered the death of all newborn Hebrew males, the Hebrew midwives refused to obey. Jochebed, Moses' mother, devised an ingenious plan to save her infant son. Pharaoh's daughter defied her father's decree when her compassion was moved by the baby floating on the Nile. Thanks to Miriam's courage and quick thinking, Moses' own mother was assigned to nurse him. This gave her the opportunity to influence her son during his early years before he went to live in the palace with Pharaoh's daughter, where he received the best education available.

Each of these women played an important part in the process that prepared Moses to be Israel's deliverer. Probably none of them realized that their actions were helping to set in motion a plan that would change world history. Later, when the dramatic events unfolded, did they look back in amazement at how God had involved them in his work?

Sometimes it may not seem that we fill an important role among Christ's followers, but there are no insignificant assignments in God's work. When we are faithful in carrying out the tasks he gives us, we play a key role in his unfolding plan even if our part is invisible to the world. It doesn't matter if we play a starring role or a supporting role, as long as we act as he directs.

> *All of you together are Christ's body, and each of you is a part of it.*
> *1 Corinthians 12:27*

September 15

Giving God 100 Percent
MIRIAM

Exodus 15:20-21

As I looked over my daughter's first-grade progress report, I beamed with pride. She excelled in each of the academic areas and had high marks in social skills. But the handwritten note at the bottom reminded me of one of her most endearing qualities—her enthusiasm. Beside a smiley face, her teacher had written, *Whatever we do in class, Holly always gives 110 percent of herself.*

Miriam shines as a biblical example of a woman who gave herself to God, 100 percent. As the first female prophet mentioned in the Bible, she was entrusted by God to share his wisdom with the people. Miriam also displayed other gifts after the miraculous crossing of the Red Sea. Although she was probably at least ninety years old, Miriam grabbed a tambourine and continued the song of praise that Moses had begun, leading the women as they danced to the Lord. Whether using her gifts as a prophet, leader, singer, or perhaps a poet, Miriam served God with enthusiasm and joy.

If we're honest, we have to admit that we don't always give God our best. It's tempting to throw ourselves into work, family matters, hobbies, or the pursuit of pleasure and to slack off in spiritual things. We may spend hours crafting a business letter or a presentation, but offer God only quick "bless me" prayers or a few memorized lines before meals. We may take a class to improve our leadership skills, but open God's Word only on Sunday mornings. While it's commendable to pursue professional and personal excellence, only our relationship with God and our service for him have eternal value. Whatever we do for him deserves 100 percent of our effort and enthusiasm—or even 110 percent.

Whatever your hand finds to do, do it with all your might.
Ecclesiastes 9:10 (NIV)

September 16

The Green-Eyed Monster
MIRIAM

Numbers 12:1-15

Miriam must have been a strong, intelligent woman since she had an unusual position of influence as a prophet and leader among the Israelites. God later included her name when he declared through Micah that he "sent Moses, Aaron, and Miriam" to bring his people out of slavery (Micah 6:4). Yet even as Miriam worked faithfully alongside Moses, something deadly began to develop in her character. Miriam and Aaron used the fact that the widowed Moses had married a Cushite woman as a basis for criticizing him. But their words reveal their underlying motive: "Has the Lord spoken only through Moses? Hasn't he spoken through us, too?"

Their jealousy over Moses' influence and power had probably been growing for some time; now it burst forth in open rebellion against his authority. After all, Miriam had worked tirelessly in helping to lead their people through the desert. Perhaps she had ministered among them during the years that Moses lived in the pharaoh's palace and the forty years that he'd spent as a shepherd in Midian. Didn't she deserve as much recognition as he did?

Miriam's jealousy against her brother endangered her family relationships and threatened the unity of her nation. God struck Miriam with leprosy for instigating the rebellion but graciously removed her punishment after seven days. His swift judgment shows how serious envy can be.

It's only natural to want to be appreciated and recognized for our efforts, but when that desire develops into jealousy, the results can be disastrous. Envy of others is a danger in our relationships with family and friends, in work settings, and in our service to God. Unfortunately, we're often unconscious of its beginnings until it breaks out in rebellion or in criticism of others. The only safeguards against jealousy are honest self-examination of our attitudes and then asking God to remove any traces of resentment before it grows into something deadly.

> *Anger is cruel, and wrath is like a flood, but jealousy is even more dangerous.*
> *Proverbs 27:4*

September 17

Seeing the Invisible
WOMEN AND THE GOLD CALF

Exodus 32:1-5

Jessica was enjoying her walk and the beautiful day until she turned the corner. She always dreaded passing by the neighbor's house with the two pit-bull terriers in the yard. Jessica knew that an invisible fence surrounded the yard, but she couldn't help feeling anxious as she walked by. As soon as she heard the dogs barking their heads off, her shoulders automatically tensed up.

The Israelites also found it difficult to trust in something they couldn't see. Although God had displayed his power before them in astounding ways, they grew tired of worshiping an invisible God. When Moses didn't return from Mount Sinai right away, the people decided that he wasn't coming back. They wanted gods they could see. This may have seemed natural to them, as they came from a country that worshiped idols. They may have felt comforted by having a tangible object to adore, but when Aaron melted their gold earrings and formed a gold calf, the Israelites broke the second commandment that God had given them.

It's not always easy to trust in Someone who is invisible. We may have witnessed the power of God in our lives in amazing ways, but sometimes that doesn't seem like enough. When confronted with circumstances that fill us with fear, we may search for something tangible to comfort us. God has given us a visible image of himself through the life of Jesus Christ as recorded in the Bible. Jesus revealed God's love when he healed a crippled woman, his mercy when he forgave a woman caught in adultery, and his anger at sin when he cleared the Temple of those who took advantage of the worshipers. When we read about Jesus, we're reading about God; when we worship Jesus, we're worshiping our invisible Father.

> *Christ is the visible image of the invisible God.*
> *Colossians 1:15*

September 18

A Bitter Drink
WOMEN AND THE GOLD CALF

Exodus 32:1-20

Nicole touched a drop of the prescription medicine to her tongue and immediately gagged. How on earth would she get this bitter-tasting stuff down? She always had trouble swallowing medicine, but she needed something to ease her symptoms. Then Nicole remembered a song from the movie *Mary Poppins* about a spoonful of sugar helping medicine go down. Nicole slept better that night after learning the trick of chasing medicine with a spoonful of honey.

The women in today's Bible passage had to swallow a bitter drink with nothing to help it go down. After Aaron crafted the gold calf, he announced that the next day would be a "festival to the LORD." Perhaps the Israelites thought that they were worshiping God as they sacrificed offerings, but their festival soon dissolved into blatant immorality.

When God sent Moses back to deal with the situation, Moses angrily smashed the stone tablets on which God had written his commandments. He then burned the calf, ground it into fine powder, put it in water, and forced the people to drink it. As the women choked down the liquid, were they flooded with regret at this reminder that they had to bear the consequences of their sin?

Just as the natural world operates according to laws such as gravity, there are spiritual laws that also carry consequences when they are broken. Partying our way through life without giving a thought to God will result in an eternity of regret and separation from him. Mixing our faith with worship of other things is also dangerous. When we choose to do things our own way rather than God's way, sooner or later we will bear the consequences of our foolishness. No matter how enjoyable sin appears at first, it eventually turns into a bitter drink that doesn't go down easily.

> *They must eat the bitter fruit of living their own way, choking on their own schemes.*
> *Proverbs 1:31*

September 19

Going in Circles
WOMEN WANDERING IN THE WILDERNESS

Numbers 14:26-35

At last! thought Alisa. *I'm finally getting somewhere.* She finally understood why the park ranger had tried to discourage her from hiking this particular trail alone. At some point, she had left the trail. Now she had used up her water and most of her energy, but at least she was back on track. Suddenly, Alisa felt sick as she recognized the same spot where she had stopped for a break two hours before.

The Israelite women knew the feeling of going in circles. God had brought the people of Israel to the rich land he had promised to give them, but they had allowed fear and disbelief to keep them from entering it. Although God had revealed his power and presence to them in numerous ways, the people refused to trust in his promises. God judged their disobedience by giving them another route to follow that forced them to wander in the wilderness for forty years.

How these women must have despaired as the years passed by, filled with endless traveling and the knowledge that their own lack of faith had doomed them to this lifestyle. They must have spent a lot of time imagining how their lives might have been if only they had stepped over into the Promised Land in faith (see Numbers 13:25-33).

It's not pleasant to know that we have just wasted our time and effort by covering the same ground again instead of moving closer to our destination. The same thing can happen in our spiritual lives, although this is often not obvious to us. God has given us his Word to guide us on our journeys of becoming more like him. When we refuse to follow his instructions for godly living, we find ourselves wandering aimlessly through life instead of enjoying the blessings of obedience. If we feel that our lives are going in circles, we don't have to wonder why—it's because we have wandered away from him.

I used to wander off until you disciplined me; but now I closely follow your word.
Psalm 119:67

262

September 20

Misunderstood
HANNAH

1 Samuel 1:9-14

As she prepared for her parents' visit, Ella felt torn in two. She loved her family—she just wished they understood her new love for Jesus. During family devotions or prayers before meals, her parents looked at Ella and her husband as if they were fanatics. Her father questioned them about the money they gave to church, naming other "more sensible" uses for it. *I wish they could understand that we haven't joined a cult,* Ella thought.

Hannah was also misunderstood. She yearned to become a mother with every fiber of her being. Knowing that God alone could grant her desire, she poured out her anguish to him. As she cried and silently prayed to God for a son, the priest at the Tabernacle angrily rebuked her for being drunk. His accusation must have mortified Hannah, who did her best to live a godly life. Eli accepted her explanation, but Hannah knew that God understood her heart even if no one else did.

As followers of Jesus, we will be misunderstood. Just as people misinterpreted Jesus and his mission, there will always be some who question our motives, sincerity, and maybe even our sanity. The early Christians called their weekly gatherings "love feasts," and some people thought that they were orgies of immorality and lust. Since the believers celebrated the Lord's Supper with bread that represented Jesus' body, some accused them of being cannibals.

The world is not capable of understanding women who devote their lives to loving God and making him their first priority. When we live by his guidelines instead of by the world's standards, some will see us as fanatics, weirdos, or worse. How comforting it is that God knows us even better than we know ourselves. Whatever the world thinks of us, we never have to worry about his misunderstanding us.

He made their hearts, so he understands everything they do.
Psalm 33:15

September 21

Ultimate Healing
EYEWITNESSES TO JESUS' HEALING POWER

Matthew 15:29-31

The women present in today's Bible passage enjoyed a celebration like none they had ever seen before. When Jesus sat down on a hill near the Sea of Galilee, an immense crowd gathered around him. The people had brought all their sick relatives, friends, and neighbors for Jesus to heal. For the next three days, Jesus healed every single person who needed his touch. Women in the crowd were overjoyed to be healed or to see their loved ones restored to health—blind people seeing, deaf people hearing, lame people walking, weak and suffering people now strong and healthy. The crowd praised God for these miracles.

When someone we love goes through a serious illness, we suffer, too. We desperately long for God's healing touch. Although James 5:16 instructs us to pray for one another's healing, God gives no guarantees. Sometimes he miraculously heals the sick, while at other times he chooses not to. Although he always has a reason for his actions, we can't help asking "why" when God doesn't heal us or our loved ones. God wants to know if we will keep trusting him when our prayers aren't answered in the way that we want. Do we love him for his miraculous powers, or do we love him for who he is?

Regardless of whether God grants physical healing, he has already provided spiritual healing for all who will accept it. We were all born suffering from the deadly disease of sin. Jesus died so that we can escape everlasting punishment and separation from God. Instead of separation, God gives us the opportunity to spend eternity with him, enjoying perfect bodies free of aches, pains, and illness. In the meantime, even if disease destroys our bodies, sin has lost its power to destroy our souls.

They laid them before Jesus, and he healed them all.
Matthew 15:30

September 22

Only Two Choices
TWO WOMEN AT THE MILL

Matthew 24:37-44

Marilyn sat in the coffee shop and restlessly fingered the half-carat diamond on her left hand. *What have I gotten myself into?* she wondered. Sure, Rick was a great guy and they'd had a lot of fun the past year. He wanted to settle down and start a family. But now that the wedding loomed only two months away, Marilyn was having second thoughts. She had always enjoyed the freedom of going out with a lot of different guys. *Am I ready to give that up? How can I say "I do" when a part of me is shouting "I don't"?*

A marriage proposal requires a "yes or no" answer. We are also required to give an answer to God. In the passage from Matthew 24, Jesus told several stories to show how critical it is for every person to make a choice about following him. When Jesus returns to earth, people will be going about their usual business, like the two women grinding flour at the mill. Suddenly one woman will be taken and the other will remain. The separation of those who know God from those who have rejected him will be swift. At that point, there will be no second chances.

These days, we admire people who keep an open mind, accept all viewpoints, and explore all their options. Many people try to take a middle-of-the-road stance regarding Jesus, but Jesus taught that we have only two choices: to receive him as our Savior and follow him as our Lord, or to reject him and be an enemy of God. Looking for an alternative choice is dangerous. Someday, our time will be up and it will be too late for second thoughts. By not saying "I do" to God, we will have said "I don't" to him.

> *[Jesus said,] "He who is not with me is against me."*
> *Matthew 12:30 (NASB)*

September 23

For Better *and* Worse
MICHAL

1 Samuel 19:1-17

Natalie wiped the cereal from her husband's chin and wondered if he would recognize her today. Sometimes she felt that Alzheimer's had robbed her of her husband and of her own life as well. When was the last time she had slept all night or spent the day with girlfriends or . . . ? As she helped her husband into the recliner, her eyes fell on their wedding picture, taken thirty-six years earlier. *Now I remember why I do this.*

Michal's feelings for David turned out to be more superficial than Natalie's self-sacrificing love. When Saul sent men to kill David, Michal helped him escape through a window and told the soldiers that he was sick in bed. When Saul discovered her deception, she claimed that David had forced her to help him by threatening to kill her. Instead of reminding her father of David's innocence, as her brother Jonathan had, Michal's lie fueled the fire of Saul's jealous rage. Immediately after saving David's life, she endangered it. The way she handled the situation was in her own best interest, not David's.

Some of us might have second thoughts about getting married if we could see into the future. Would we be willing to accept our husbands "for better or for worse" if we knew just how bad the worst could be? Our circumstances change and people change, not always for the better. That's when we face the real test of love. Will we hold fast to our commitment to our spouses, always seeking their best interests above our own?

When God accepts us as his children, he does see the future. He knows that at times our devotion to him will cool and we'll return to serving our own interests instead of his. He knows that our behavior will sometimes disappoint him. In contrast, his love for us never wavers. God displays the ultimate in self-sacrificing love.

> *[Love] is not self-seeking.*
> *1 Corinthians 13:5 (NIV)*

September 24

Killing Words
MICHAL

2 Samuel 6:9-23

Michal must have felt like a Ping-Pong ball. When David fled for his life, Saul spitefully gave Michal away to be another man's wife (see 1 Samuel 25:44). Years later, David became king of Israel and sent for Michal. Her second husband, Palti, followed along behind her, crying (see 2 Samuel 3:14-16). Considering the attitude toward women at the time, it's impossible to tell whether David wanted Michal back because he loved her or because he saw her as a possession that rightfully belonged to him.

David and Michal couldn't possibly return to the relationship they had known as young newlyweds. They had spent many years apart. Michal had been the wife of a man who apparently loved her, and David had added other wives. Still, Michal was David's first wife. Unfortunately, Michal's attitude toward God and her husband killed the possibility of forging a new relationship.

When David brought the Ark of the Covenant to the capital city of Jerusalem, people streamed into the streets. David joined the procession, not as king, but as a servant of God. Overwhelmed with joy and gratitude, he danced through the streets to express his feelings to God. As Michal looked out the window, she despised her husband for what she saw as a loss of dignity. Michal didn't try to understand David's motivation. She went out to meet him with sharp sarcasm. Her remarks probably hurt David and caused a permanent separation between them.

Even when another person controls the circumstances of our lives, we control our attitudes and words. We can blurt out any criticism or sarcastic comment that comes to mind, or we can try to understand the other person's motivation and emotions. When we feel contempt for someone, we can ask God to help us change our attitude. That way, we won't be guilty of killing with words.

> *The tongue has the power of life and death.*
> *Proverbs 18:21 (NIV)*

September 25

Checking Our Wardrobes
SEDUCTIVE WOMEN

Proverbs 7:4-21

This passage in Proverbs describes a type of woman that men are warned to avoid. Although this woman pretended to be religious, her behavior betrayed loose morals. The woman dressed in such a way as to attract men's attention. Her movements were sensual and her conversation seductive. She had no interest in domestic pursuits, preferring to be out on the town looking for a man to entice. Rather than developing godly qualities, this woman concentrated on making herself attractive to men. She thrived on their admiration and desire for her.

Janet Jackson's famous "wardrobe malfunction," when Justin Timberlake grabbed at her bodice and exposed her breast, shocked most of the people who watched the Super Bowl game in 2004. If our senses hadn't grown so dull, we would be shocked every time we turn on the television or walk into a store. With women's clothing getting shorter, lower, sheerer, and tighter, not much is left to the imagination. Even much of the clothing for little girls seems designed to look seductive. Many magazines and television shows promote everything from liposuction to breast enhancement by conveying the message that we must do whatever it takes to look sexy.

It's sad that many Christian women are falling for the lie that we need to make ourselves look enticing to men. Whether we're single or married, we need to be very careful in our relationships with men. When cultural influences seep into our thinking, our movements or words may be seductive without our even realizing it. God's Word can help us guard our attitudes so that we dress and behave in a way that pleases God. There's nothing wrong with being attractive, but God wants his daughters to dress modestly, not in clothing that arouses lust in men. When we dress to impress the opposite sex, we give the wrong impression of our Father.

I also want women to dress modestly, with decency and propriety.
1 Timothy 2:9 (NIV)

September 26

Building a Home
THE WISE WOMAN

Proverbs 14:1

I walked through the house, in awe of what my friend had accomplished. When her two children entered middle school, she went back to school herself—for a degree in construction management. This house was the culmination of her program. Of course, some of the work was done by contractors, but my friend planned and supervised the project and did much of the work with her own hands. The result of her labor was a two-story home that was beautiful and exhibited quality construction.

At any stage of life, every woman is in the process of building a "home." If we want to be like the wise woman in Proverbs, we'll build our "homes" according to God's blueprint. The foundation of our lives will be the gospel of Jesus Christ, the only foundation guaranteed to last for eternity. We'll put up thick walls of prayer to surround our lives with protection. Studying God's Word will provide a roof over our heads when the storms of life beat down on us. We need to furnish our "homes" with godly characteristics such as love, joy, self-control, peace, and patience.

Regular home inspections and spring cleanings are also important. Are the attics of our minds cluttered? Are our roofs leaking? Could our chimneys use cleaning so that we can safely let off steam from the pressures of life? Do we need to shake off the mat at the front door and welcome friends into our hearts more often? Constructing and maintaining our "homes" require a lot of hard work, but the effort will be worth it when time reveals that we've built lives that are beautiful in God's eyes and exhibit quality construction.

A wise woman builds her home.
Proverbs 14:1

September 27

Tearing Down a Home
THE FOOLISH WOMAN

Proverbs 14:1

Myra stared at the empty trash can and gulped. *It wasn't supposed to turn out like this.* The day before, she and Anthony had their first fight as newlyweds. When Anthony clammed up, Myra stalked to their bedroom seething with resentment and frustration. Her eyes fell on his wedding ring, sitting on the dresser as usual instead of on his finger. She had a sudden impulse to drop the ring in the trash can. *When he sees it, he'll realize how hurt I am, and we'll talk it out.* Unfortunately, Myra didn't consider the possibility that Anthony might empty the trash. The ring was lost.

Sometimes we can be like the foolish woman in Proverbs who tears down her home with her own hands. Destructive choices such as an extramarital affair can be the wrecking ball that does permanent damage to our lives. More often, our habits and attitudes do less obvious harm over time. Attitudes of self-centeredness, jealousy, and criticism chip away at relationships with family and friends. If we neglect to nurture a daily relationship with God, every area of our lives will begin to erode.

By filling our lives with God's wisdom and looking to him for guidance, we will realize when we're doing something foolish and destructive. We may have some home repairs to make, such as offering apologies or dropping harmful habits. We may need to do some serious remodeling. Thankfully, God offers help when we need to rebuild our lives. And in case you're wondering, Myra and Anthony are still married today. As a matter of fact, she gave him a wedding band as a Valentine's Day gift in 2005. I know this because my first name is Myra and I'm married to Richard Anthony Matthews.

A foolish woman tears [her home] down with her own hands.
Proverbs 14:1

September 28

Secret Places
MARY MAGDALENE

Mark 16:9; Luke 8:1-3

Although a lot has been written about Mary Magdalene, little of it is based on fact. Some traditions identify Mary as the "sinful woman" of Luke 7, although the writer knew her personally and referred to her by name in the next chapter. Many people believe that Mary was a former prostitute, although the Bible gives no indication of this. Many legends about Mary Magdalene are based solely on imagination or questionable ancient documents. The fourteen times that the Bible mentions Mary tell us what we need to know.

The only clue the Bible gives concerning Mary's early life is that Jesus cast out seven demons from her. Some people interpret this to mean that Mary was completely demon possessed; others think that it refers literally to seven evil spirits. We can only wonder how Mary looked and acted before Jesus freed her from demonic bondage. Did she resemble the violent, demon-possessed men in Matthew 8 who lived in a cemetery? Was she disheveled and wild-eyed? However the possession manifested itself, Jesus' power transformed Mary into a strong, clear-thinking woman who became his devoted follower.

Even believers in Christ can suffer from Satan's influence. We've all been shocked when an apparently model mother suddenly kills her children, or a woman who seemingly enjoys life commits suicide. Most of us have inner "demons" that torment us—sinful urges, painful past experiences, recurring thoughts of guilt or worthlessness. We may be able to hide things from other people, but God wants us to open these areas to him so that he can free us from bondage. Mary of Magdala changed from a demon-possessed woman to the first person privileged to see Jesus after his resurrection. We can't live the transformed life that God intends for us until we give him access to our secret places.

> *"Can anyone hide from me in a secret place? Am I not everywhere in all the heavens and earth?" says the LORD.*
> *Jeremiah 23:24*

September 29

It Never Hurts to Ask
ACSAH

Joshua 15:13-19

Sherri gritted her teeth as she started up the stairs to tuck her sons into bed. Same routine every evening—make dinner, clean the kitchen, throw in a load of laundry, help with her fourth-grader's homework, give her toddler a bath, read a bedtime story, then back to the kitchen to pack lunches for the next day. *Is it too much to expect a little help around here?* She seethed as she passed through the den. Tom lay asleep on the couch, with the newspaper spread across his chest and the television blaring.

Acsah didn't hesitate to ask for what she needed. She already had a brave husband who had won her hand by conquering a city, and a generous dowry of land from her father. But since the land was arid, Acsah urged her husband to ask for additional land with springs for irrigation. Othniel seemed reluctant to ask for anything more, but as the only daughter of a loving father, Acsah felt comfortable in making the request. When she met her father, Caleb, she got off her donkey as a sign of respect. "Give me another gift," she boldly requested. "Please give me springs of water, too." Her father granted her request without hesitation.

Most women find it difficult to ask for help. Often, we think that our husbands and families should know what we need without being told. Unfortunately, people (especially men) can't read our minds. How often have we made our lives harder than necessary because we wouldn't ask for something? Why do we choose to nurse our resentments instead of making requests?

We also sometimes hesitate to ask God for things, although he urges us to bring our requests to him. Like Acsah, we have a loving Father who wants us to feel comfortable about asking him for what we need. If our requests are legitimate, we can never ask for too much from him.

You do not have, because you do not ask God.
James 4:2 (NIV)

272

September 30

Desperate Women
WOMEN DURING FAMINE

2 Kings 6:24-30

We've all been haunted by images on television and in newspapers of people who suffer from starvation. Especially heart wrenching are the pictures of babies and young children with huge eyes and swollen bellies. Sometimes they're shown lying against their mothers, too weak and lethargic to lift a hand and shoo the flies away from their faces. The eyes of the parents always look empty and hopeless.

The women in today's passage knew the horrors of starvation. When Samaria suffered severe famine because of a siege, the people became so desperate for food that some resorted to killing and eating their children. One woman persuaded another mother to kill her son so they could eat him, promising that they would eat her son the next day. When the first woman hid her son, the woman who had killed hers appealed to the king. At that moment, all this mother could think of was the broken promise of a second meal. How can we imagine her feelings after the famine ended and the horror of what she had done sank in?

Even if we don't live in an area affected by famine, people around us are desperate for spiritual food. Everyone longs for answers to life's problems, and many are searching for something to give meaning to their lives. Many people have rejected God's Word as a source of truth and look for other ways to feed their souls. When Israel began to ignore God's Word, God warned that if they didn't repent, they would soon not hear from him at all. As children of God, we need to point people to God's Word, where they will find what they're looking for before they suffer the worst kind of famine.

> *"The time is surely coming," says the Sovereign LORD, "when I will send a famine on the land—not a famine of bread or water but of hearing the words of the LORD."*
> *Amos 8:11*

October 1

Pick Me, Pick Me!
"CHOSEN LADY"

2 John 1:1-3

PE was never my favorite class, and I especially dreaded the days when we divided into teams. Two girls were appointed as team captains, and one by one, they chose girls for their groups, starting with the most athletic ones, which did not include me. I stood in a line with the rest of the class, shifting from foot to foot. We tried to look unconcerned as we desperately hoped that we wouldn't be chosen last.

The ancient letter of 2 John is addressed to "the chosen lady and . . . her children." Scholars have debated what this phrase means. Some think that the term refers to a particular woman in a local congregation. Others speculate that John wrote to a woman whose name was similar to the Greek words for "chosen" or "lady." Many people believe that the phrase refers to the local church and its members.

Whether John was addressing one woman or all believers, the word "chosen" must have had a nice ring to the women who heard the letter read as it made the rounds of the churches. They knew that at one time only the nation of Israel could claim to be God's chosen people. Now, Jesus Christ had opened the way for all people to come to God on the basis of faith alone. These women knew that whatever the world thought of them, they were God's chosen ones.

None of us want to be chosen last. It makes us feel that we're not valued. Thankfully, God is not an earthly team captain. He's not picking the most athletic or the most popular. When we accept God's truth, we become his chosen women. It's not a question of how long it will be before our names are called out, but of how long before we call on his name.

You are a chosen people.
1 Peter 2:9 (NIV)

October 2

Misplaced Worship
QUEEN OF HEAVEN

Jeremiah 7:16-20; 44:15-17

I was actually sorry when the light turned green because I hadn't finished reading all the bumper stickers plastered on the car in front of me. *In Goddess We Trust. Born Again Pagan. Goddess is alive and magic is about!* The last sticker led me to do a little online research. I discovered that in 1975, The Covenant of the Goddess was incorporated as a nonprofit religious organization. Since then, some sources claim that neo-paganism has become one of the fastest growing religions in our country. The word *goddess* is used casually in media and advertising, but real goddess worship is very much alive today.

When Jeremiah was God's prophet, people in Judah had adopted goddess worship. The planet Venus represented Ishtar, the Babylonian goddess of love and fertility. Women baked cakes, poured out drink offerings, and burned incense to the "queen of heaven." Instead of worshiping the Creator, they worshiped the sun, moon, planets, and constellations. Although God warned them of his judgment, their idolatry had confused their thinking. They believed that their problems were caused by slacking off on their cult rituals rather than by turning away from God in the first place.

From the beginning of time, people have tried to worship something else besides God. God warns that this degrades us. Today, many people have distorted the responsibility to care for God's creation into a worship of nature. Some even see humans as the enemies of the earth. Other people replace God's truth with astrology. Reading daily horoscopes may seem harmless, but such activities can affect our thinking. God is the only One with the power to control our lives, and only he deserves to be worshiped. Anytime that we honor something other than him, we hurt ourselves.

> *They traded the truth about God for a lie. So they worshiped and served the things God created instead of the Creator himself, who is worthy of eternal praise!*
> *Romans 1:25*

October 3

Approaching God
THE WOMAN WHO TOUCHED JESUS' ROBE

Mark 5:24-34

Darla peeked at her friend Jan, who was praying before their lunch. *Every time she prays, it sounds as if she's talking with a close friend,* Darla marveled. Darla was a Christian, but she never felt that she was in the actual presence of Jesus, as Jan seemed to. She wanted that more than anything, but how could she feel close to God when she had so many sleazy habits that she needed to clean up?

The woman in Mark 5 also had a problem with approaching Jesus. A medical condition had caused her to bleed constantly for twelve years. After spending all her money on doctors, she must have despaired of ever enjoying a normal life. Then she heard about Jesus' miracles and healings. Finally, she felt a glimmer of hope once again. But according to Jewish law, her condition made her unclean and she would also make anyone that she touched unclean.

As she mingled with the crowd, the woman slipped behind Jesus and touched his robe. Her bleeding immediately stopped, but her thrill turned into terror when Jesus demanded to know who had touched him. The trembling woman fell at his feet and confessed. Jesus addressed her with a term of endearment, assuring her that her suffering was over because her faith had healed her.

The woman wanted to touch Jesus' robe and slip away, but he wanted a personal relationship with her. He wanted to express his love and comfort her, face-to-face. He desires the same for us. If we have trusted in Jesus Christ as our Savior, then we are always invited to come face-to-face with our heavenly Father. We can confess our sins; confide our worries; and find mercy, comfort, and healing. No matter how unclean or sleazy we feel, we don't need to slip behind our Savior and touch his robe—we can run right into his arms.

Because of Christ and our faith in him, we can now come boldly and confidently into God's presence.
Ephesians 3:12

October 4

You *Can* Go Home Again
NAOMI

Ruth 1:1-7

Brandy checked the odometer and rubbed her neck—two hundred miles left to go. *My life could be a country song,* she thought. As the car sped down the interstate, her mind sped through the past eight years. She'd taken off for New York fresh out of high school, bursting with the dream of a dancing career. Now, after too many failed auditions and failed relationships, money worries and lonely nights, Brandy was fresh out of dreams and was headed back to her hometown. She didn't know what her future held, but at least she would be in a place where people knew her name.

The woman in today's Bible passage made the same decision as Brandy. When a severe famine struck Israel, Naomi and her husband had moved to Moab, probably intending to stay for just a while. Ten years later, Naomi's husband and two sons had died, leaving her a destitute widow with no means of support and protection. Naomi must have regretted their decision to move to a culture filled with the detestable heathen practices of idol worship. Would God ever bless her again? When she heard that back in Israel the famine had eased, she knew what to do—she would take the road home.

Sometimes our decisions don't turn out as we plan, even though they seem like the best course of action at the time. We wake up one day and realize that we've moved away from God and his ways. Even if we're fresh out of hope, God waits for us to repent of our rebellious ways and place ourselves under his authority again. Then he will restore us and give us new dreams. When it looks like the end of the road for us, it's time to turn around and take the path home. Someone there waits for us, and he knows our name.

> [The Lord said,] *"If you return to me, I will restore you so you can continue to serve me."*
> *Jeremiah 15:19*

October 5

Looking Out for Others
NAOMI

Ruth 1:8-13

The young mother mentally calculated the cost of the diapers and food in her cart to make sure that she had enough money. She noticed the older woman in front of her glance back at her again. *Yes, I know I look like an awful mess,* the young woman thought. Or was her fussy baby with an ear infection bothering the woman? A few minutes later, she walked out of the store, wishing she could thank the older woman who had paid for her groceries.

Naomi also cared deeply about the well-being of others. If Naomi hadn't loved her daughters-in-law as her own children, Orpah and Ruth would not have decided to return to Israel with her. On the way, however, Naomi began to have second thoughts. Was it in the girls' best interest to move to a country where Moabites were despised? Remarriage was their only chance for security, and the opportunities for that would be slim in Israel. Despite the comfort she received from their presence, Naomi urged Orpah and Ruth to return to the security of the familiar. She would make the long, dangerous journey alone in order to protect them.

This selfless attitude seems rare in our looking-out-for-number-one, dog-eat-dog world. Our me-first mentality is exposed by the shock expressed when someone returns lost money to its rightful owner or refuses pay for helping a stranded motorist. God wants us to rise above our self-centeredness to do what's in the best interest of others. This often requires sacrifice on our part. Christ was the supreme example of this attitude when he died on the cross, because he was looking out for our interests rather than his. Whether we give up our desires, time, or material possessions, we won't ever come close to what Christ gave up for us.

> *Let each of you look out not only for his own interests, but also for the interests of others.*
> *Philippians 2:4 (NKJV)*

October 6

Defining Moment
ORPAH AND RUTH

Ruth 1:8

While traveling down the road that led to Judah, Orpah and Ruth came to a crossroads in their lives. Naomi began to have second thoughts about taking these young Moabite women to live in Israel with her. Maybe it wasn't fair to take them away from their families and the opportunity to remarry among their own people. Even after Orpah and Ruth tearfully insisted that they wanted to go with Naomi, she urged them to go back, explaining why it would be better for them to stay in Moab. As the three women stood crying, Orpah and Ruth faced a defining moment in their lives.

The road ahead stretched to a distant, unknown destination. They didn't know what life would be like in Israel. Looking down the road behind them, the women could see the land of their birth. But Naomi and her sons had shown them something better than they had known. Naomi worshiped a God of love and compassion, totally different from the gods of the Moabites. Still, the easiest choice would be to return to the security of their familiar lives. The road Orpah and Ruth chose to follow would determine the direction of their lives.

We all come to crossroads at different times in our lives. God leads us in new directions, but he always lets us choose whether to follow him or not. We get stuck between the pull of the familiar and the urge to forge ahead toward the unknown. Should we really quit a job to enter full-time ministry? Can we really find the courage to end an abusive relationship? If we share our faith with a neighbor, will it ruin the friendship? Our willingness to follow God down a strange road to an unseen destination reveals our level of trust in him.

What new direction does God have in mind for you?

October 7

Staying in Our Comfort Zones
ORPAH

Ruth 1:6-14

Once again, I pulled out the conference brochure. All my life I had fantasized about being a writer, but I had no idea why this had come in the mail.
I alternated between excitement and fear. It would mean driving over a
hundred miles by myself to an unfamiliar area, which I'd never done before.
What if I got lost? At the workshop, I would turn in a writing sample to be
evaluated. What if I was told I was a terrible writer? Then I wouldn't have
even the dream anymore. I took a deep breath when I noticed that the dead-
line was the next day. Time to make a decision.

Orpah also knew how it felt to be torn between staying with the safety
of the familiar or exploring new territory. When Naomi was ready to return
to her own country, she urged her two daughters-in-law to return to their
families. Orpah dearly loved her mother-in-law and insisted that she would
go with her. But when Naomi urged her again, Orpah relented and tearfully
kissed her good-bye. Orpah's decision appeared reasonable, since it seemed
to be the only way for her to remarry and have a family, but in later years,
did she wonder what the other life might have been like?

God often calls us to leave our comfort zones to serve him in some
new way. Then we have to decide whether we will allow our shyness, our
lack of confidence in our abilities, or a fear of the unknown to keep us from
following him. When God leads us into new territory, we can be sure that
a great adventure lies ahead. If I hadn't stepped out in spite of my fears to
attend my first writers' conference, I would have missed the blessings of a
new ministry. And you wouldn't be holding this book in your hands.

God has not given us a spirit of fear and timidity, but of power, love,
and self-discipline.
2 Timothy 1:7

October 8

Unwavering Loyalty
RUTH

Ruth 1:1-18

These days, people often give up when the going gets tough. If a job is too demanding, we quit. When a friend is going through a horrible time, we may be tempted to "disappear" for a while. If a marriage becomes difficult, there's always divorce. If it would be too inconvenient to raise a child, we can abort the pregnancy. Babies, young children, and the elderly are sometimes abandoned.

People have loved the story of Ruth for centuries, partly because of Ruth's beautiful expression of unwavering commitment to her widowed mother-in-law. When Naomi prepared to return to her own country, she implored Ruth to go back to her family. Ruth chose instead to bind herself to her destitute mother-in-law. We can only imagine her anxiety as she faced a future of poverty among people who despised her native country. We have to admire the great love for Naomi that trumped all Ruth's fears.

Sometimes following God seems too hard. He asks us to give up our old lives so that we can be conformed to the image of Jesus Christ. We may sometimes be tempted to return to old habits, comfortable relationships, and former pleasures that conflict with our new lives. But if we love God, we willingly bind ourselves to him. There is no turning back.

Because of her love for Naomi, Ruth didn't take the easy way out by returning to Moab. God's love for us gives us, too, the courage to choose what seems to be the harder road. We may not clearly see where God is leading us, but we can be sure that it's someplace we'll want to be. Like Ruth, we will be rewarded beyond anything we can imagine.

[Ruth replied,] "Wherever you go, I will go."
Ruth 1:16

October 9

Traveling Companions
NAOMI AND RUTH

Ecclesiastes 4:9-12

"Forget it—I won't take no for an answer. I'm going to drive you to every one of your chemo treatments."

"But it's forty miles each way. What about your job?"

"I've cleared it with my boss. I'll make up the hours by doing some work at home."

"What about your kids?"

"All set. Francine, next door, will come over whenever I need her. Meredith, I've already decided—I'm going to walk through this with you."

Meredith opened her mouth, but no words came out.

"When Naomi saw that Ruth was determined to go with her, she said nothing more" (Ruth 1:18). Sometimes, it's hard to speak when our hearts are full. Naomi urged Ruth to return to her own people because she thought this would be best for her daughter-in-law. How glad she must have been when Ruth vowed that she would go wherever Naomi went. The road back to Judah was long and hard, but what a comfort to be traveling with a friend. Ruth also accepted Naomi's God as her own. However uncertain their future, the women would face it together, looking out for each other as they looked to God for guidance.

Busy women sometimes neglect to nurture their friendships with other women, especially when they're caring for young children. But when hard times come, we need a friend to go through them with us. We need someone to help us carry our burdens when they get too heavy for us to manage alone. A sister in Christ can pray for us and help us keep our eyes on God. As we follow him together, we can help one another grow into the persons God created us to be. As we go through life, what a comfort to have traveling companions who share our burdens!

Share each other's burdens, and in this way obey the law of Christ.
Galatians 6:2

October 10

Call Me Bitter
NAOMI

Ruth 1:19-20

One of my least favorite sayings is based on a quote from Nietzsche: "Whatever doesn't kill us makes us stronger." There are other responses to adversity besides dying or growing stronger. One of the most popular options is bitterness. Medical professionals recognize a bitter spirit at the root of many physical and emotional problems. A cynical attitude is bad for our health, harmful to our relationships, and a hindrance to our spiritual lives.

Naomi's life became so bitter that she asked people to call her Mara ("bitter") rather than Naomi ("pleasant"). Naomi and her husband had been prominent, well-respected citizens of Bethlehem, but now Naomi was returning to her hometown as a poor widow. She expressed her grief and resentment over the tragic deaths of her husband and sons, even knowing that God was in control of her life. Naomi saw only a bleak future of poverty ahead. In her grief, she couldn't fully appreciate the blessing of a daughter-in-law who was willing to give up everything for her. Naomi also didn't know that God would soon restore her joy and her zest for life.

It's natural to struggle with discouragement when we go through a trial or a loss. The grieving process takes time, but eventually we need to move past our hurt and accept healing from the only One who can give it. We don't have to shy away from being honest with God when we feel resentful toward our circumstances, other people, or him. The longer we allow bitterness to grow, the harder it is to get rid of it. If we accept God's leadership over our lives and ask for his help, we don't have to live with the crippling effects of bitterness. And we won't feel the need to change our names.

> *Watch out that no poisonous root of bitterness grows up to trouble you, corrupting many.*
> *Hebrews 12:15*

October 11

Gleaning
RUTH

Ruth 2:1-3

Just as she'd done every morning for two weeks, Jana sat down at the kitchen table with the classified ads, a highlighter, and a determined look on her face. The plant closing had hit without warning and affected many people in her town. With a school-age son, Jana couldn't waste time in finding another job. She didn't have a college degree, but she was young, healthy, and willing to work hard. Jana had gratefully accepted public aid the year following her son's birth, but now she had resolved to take any job that would support the two of them.

As a widow with no means of support, Ruth took advantage of an Israelite way of providing for the poor. According to laws established by God, landowners didn't harvest the corners of their fields, and the reapers left any grain that they dropped on the ground. Ruth immediately went out to find a barley field where she could work as a gleaner, following the harvesters and gathering grain along with other poor people. Although she was an outcast in a foreign land, Ruth found relief in hard work as well as comfort in knowing that she had found a way to help her mother-in-law.

Many people mistakenly believe that the Bible says, "God helps those who help themselves." God makes it clear that salvation is a gift, not something that we earn (see Ephesians 2:8-9). When it comes to our spiritual growth, however, we have work to do. We can't just sit back and hope that we become like Christ; we are responsible for feeding ourselves from God's Word, seeking him in prayer, disciplining our wills to obey him, and serving others. If we don't seem to be growing, maybe we need to get up and get to work.

> *Work hard to show the results of your salvation, obeying God with deep reverence and fear.*
> *Philippians 2:12*

October 12

Right Field
RUTH

Ruth 2:3-18

Help, Lord! Farrah silently prayed as she boarded the plane. She just realized that she left her papers in the taxi. She desperately needed the address of her new apartment and the name and phone number of the contact person from her new company. Three hours later, on the plane, Farrah had made friends with a secretary from her new company—who lived in Farrah's apartment building. Farrah knew it wasn't coincidence that had put her in that particular airplane seat.

It wasn't coincidence that led Ruth to one of Boaz's fields, either. As a close relative of Elimelech, Boaz appreciated Ruth's loyalty to Naomi and admired her willingness to work hard. Boaz greeted Ruth warmly and invited her to work alongside his servant girls for the entire harvest season. She wouldn't have to wait until a field had been harvested to move in, as the other gleaners did, and she wouldn't have to draw her own water. Boaz had even instructed his men to be respectful to her. Such special treatment must have overwhelmed Ruth.

Coincidence doesn't exist for God's children. Although he allows us choices, he controls every area of our lives. God puts us into just the right places and circumstances that will help us to become more like Christ and to bless other people by our faith. Sometimes he directs us to just the right Bible verse we need for our situation. At other times, he guides us to the perfect person or resource that will meet our need.

If we turn away from God's leading, we will wander away from his plan for our lives. But when we do our best to obey his commands and follow his Spirit's guidance, he will lead us back to where we need to be. We don't want to let sin lead us way out into left field; we want to be like Ruth and stay in the right field.

> *The LORD directs the steps of the godly. He delights in every detail of their lives.*
> Psalm 37:23

October 13

Helping Others
NAOMI

Ruth 2:19–3:4

As Kathleen pulled into the parking lot, she once again silently thanked her friend for butting into her life. When her husband died suddenly of a heart attack, Kathleen felt something inside her die too. For two long years, she lived inside a wall of darkness and pain, feeling cut off from life. Eventually, she checked out the volunteer literacy program just to make Alice quit nagging her. Now Kathleen couldn't imagine missing her time at the center helping a sixty-year-old woman learn to read. Kathleen still missed her husband, but this work had brought her a new joy.

Naomi returned to Bethlehem as a destitute, grief-stricken woman who had lost her husband and both sons. Her spirits revived when Ruth brought home much more grain than a gleaner would normally gather in one day. Her depression lifted more when she learned that God had led Ruth to the field of Boaz, a close relative of her husband, who showed unusual kindness to Ruth. But Naomi really perked up when she decided to do a little matchmaking. Boaz evidently needed a nudge to fulfill the role of family redeemer and marry Ruth. With a goal, Naomi now had plans to make. By helping Ruth find a better life, her thoughts moved away from her own sadness.

Severe trials and loss can make us self-preoccupied, unable to focus on anything except our own pain. We may feel that we'll never be able to enjoy life again. As we move through the normal grieving process, one of the best ways to help ourselves is to reach out to others in need. Helping others draws our attention away from our own problems, and we discover the joy that comes from meeting others' needs, whether we're working as a literacy volunteer or a matchmaker.

Remember the words of the Lord Jesus: "It is more blessed to give than to receive."
Acts 20:35

October 14

Trust and Obey
RUTH

Ruth 3

In 1996, aerialist and acrobat Montana Miller accepted a rare invitation to become one of the first five women to participate in the world cliff-diving championships. The competition took place in Acapulco, Mexico, where an elite group of professional cliff divers have amazed tourists for several decades. These divers plunge more than a hundred feet into a narrow inlet of the Pacific Ocean, and their timing is crucial. They must begin their fall *before* the waves come in so that the water will be there when they reach it. If I were learning to dive off a cliff, I would probably wonder about my instructor when he told me to jump at the moment the water was out of the inlet.

When Naomi decided to secure Boaz as a husband for Ruth, her instructions probably didn't make much sense to her daughter-in-law. As a foreigner, Ruth wasn't accustomed to the Hebrew law that required a close relative to marry the widow of a deceased man in order to continue his name and property rights. She did know that her mother-in-law was trustworthy and had her best interests at heart. Her faith in Naomi's character overcame any confusion she may have felt, and she willingly agreed to follow Naomi's directions. Ruth felt safe in her mother-in-law's hands, even when she didn't understand why Naomi wanted her to do things that seemed strange to her.

We may not always comprehend something that God is calling us to do. Loving our enemies and turning the other cheek sound strange to us because they clash with our human way of thinking. God's Kingdom operates on an entirely different set of laws and principles than those of the world we live in. If we trust God's character and feel safe in his hands, then we can follow his leading even if it doesn't make sense to us. Obedience doesn't necessarily require understanding; it does require trust.

> *"My thoughts are nothing like your thoughts," says the* LORD. *"And my ways are far beyond anything you could imagine."*
> Isaiah 55:8

October 15

Redeemed
RUTH

Ruth 4:1-12

Naomi probably suspected that Boaz had admired Ruth from the first moment he saw her, but apparently he needed help in taking action. Perhaps he hesitated because he was much older than Ruth. *No matter,* Naomi must have thought. *I know how to get him to carry out his responsibility. Besides, this will bring happiness to both Ruth and Boaz.* So she coached Ruth in how to propose marriage to him. Boaz answered yes, sort of. He explained that there was a closer relative who had first rights to be her family's redeemer. But Boaz assured Ruth that if the other man wasn't interested, he certainly was.

When Ruth returned home early the next morning, she found Naomi eager to hear all the details. Naomi joyfully predicted that Boaz would settle the matter that very day. Did time drag by as the two women waited to hear the outcome? Meanwhile, the nearer kinsman jumped at the chance to buy back land that had once belonged to Elimelech. With no surviving heirs, the land would permanently become his. But when he learned that he would also be required to marry Ruth and produce a son who would inherit the land, the man lost interest. So Boaz was free to marry Ruth.

As the years went by, Ruth's gratitude and love for Boaz must have grown as her understanding of the role of kinsman-redeemer deepened. Boaz became her protector and provider. She found a new life as a wife and mother, and it all started when she asked Boaz to spread his covering over her.

God came to earth as Jesus Christ in order to become our kinsman-redeemer. Through his death, he bought us back from sin and claimed us as his own. He willingly fulfills the role of protector and provider and makes a new life possible for us. And it all begins when we ask him to spread his covering over us.

Spread the corner of your covering over me, for you are my family redeemer.
Ruth 3:9

October 16

Restored
NAOMI

Ruth 4:13-22

Olivia turned off the Tinkerbell lamp and tiptoed out of the room. Stooping to pick up a stuffed elephant, she smiled as she remembered Grace's excitement at the zoo that afternoon. *I never dreamed I could feel this happy again.* When a car accident took her son and daughter-in-law, Olivia felt dead inside. While she began making the funeral arrangements, doctors worked to save her newly delivered granddaughter. Against all odds, little Grace clung fiercely to life. Finally, Grace came home, and when she did, she gradually restored Olivia's zest for living.

When Naomi returned to her hometown, she must have felt dead inside. She had lost her husband and both sons, and in addition, her means of support and her role in society. But Naomi never lost her faith in God even when it looked as if he had turned against her. She recognized his hand in the meeting between Ruth and Boaz. When Boaz married Ruth and redeemed Elimelech's family, Naomi no longer had to worry about loneliness or poverty.

After Ruth gave birth to a son, she allowed Naomi to be his nurse and care for him. The townswomen rejoiced with Naomi that God had restored her life through a daughter-in-law's love, a kinsman-redeemer, and the birth of a grandson. Naomi would have rejoiced even more if she'd known the rest of the story: that little Obed would be the grandfather of the great king David, through whose line the Messiah would come.

Tragedy can drain all the life out of us. We don't think we'll ever have a reason to smile again. But we don't know the rest of the story. If we don't turn our backs on God, he will bring great blessings even out of tragedy and sorrow. We might not understand why he allows us to suffer, but we can trust that he will provide the grace to restore our lives again.

> *You have allowed me to suffer much hardship, but you will restore me to life again and lift me up from the depths of the earth. You will restore me to even greater honor and comfort me once again.*
> *Psalm 71:20-21*

October 17

A Powerful Ingredient
A WOMAN MAKING BREAD

Luke 13:20-21

One day as a newlywed, I decided to make chicken and dumplings. I carefully mixed the flour, baking powder, and other ingredients for the dumplings, then dropped spoonfuls into a saucepan of boiling water. After leaving the kitchen for a couple of minutes, I returned to find the dumplings pushing the lid off the pan and trying to crawl out. I transferred them to a larger pan, only to have the same thing happen. Finally, I cooked the dumplings in my largest stockpot. The next time I made the recipe, I spooned in smaller amounts of the dough, since I knew how much it would expand.

Jesus told a parable about the leavening power of yeast. He said that the Kingdom of God is like the yeast a woman used to make bread. She mixed only a little yeast with a large amount of flour, but the yeast permeated every part of the dough and made it expand. This illustration has been interpreted in different ways. Since the Bible often uses yeast as a metaphor for sin, some people believe that Jesus referred to the power of evil to influence whatever it comes in contact with. Others interpret the yeast as the gospel, quietly spreading through the world and transforming people's lives.

If we think of the yeast as sin, the parable warns us not to tolerate even what we consider an insignificant sin, since it can spread and become pervasive in our lives. If we think of the yeast as the gospel, the parable reminds us of the gospel's power to transform our lives in every respect. Our faith may seem small at times, but God's presence will permeate and transform us. When we understand how much we "knead" God's truth instead of our own half-baked ideas, we will rise to any occasion.

> [Jesus said,] "I tell you the truth, if you had faith even as small as a mustard seed, you could say to this mountain, 'Move from here to there,' and it would move."
> Matthew 17:20

October 18

A Bountiful Harvest
WOMEN BRINGING IN THE CROPS

Psalm 126:5-6

All summer, I impatiently watched my backyard. Because of rainy weather and family obligations, my husband and I had been late in getting our garden planted. Then, an unusually dry summer made for slow growth. I bought fresh vegetables in the grocery store and at the local farmers' market, but I couldn't wait to pick them from our own garden. Finally, the tomatoes turned red, the squash turned yellow, and the green peppers grew big enough to pick. It had been a long time coming, but the harvest was worth the wait.

Harvest must have been a special time for the women in Bible times too. They couldn't just run to the grocery store to pick something up for a meal. Since they had no refrigerators or freezers, they had to gather and preserve as much food as they could during the harvest. Women worked in the fields to reap barley and wheat. They must have looked forward to the joyful celebration that accompanied the harvest.

Sometimes we get tired of waiting for a spiritual harvest. We ask God over and over to resolve a difficult situation, but nothing seems to happen. We do our best to overcome a sinful habit and get discouraged when we slip once again. We spend years trying to share our faith with a neighbor but get no response. It's hard to keep praying and living a godly life when we don't see results. But God promises that if we keep on trusting him, he will send a bountiful harvest at the right time. We will reap some blessings in this life, but the full harvest will come when we stand before Christ's judgment seat to receive our rewards. Right now it may seem a long time in coming, but it will be a harvest worth waiting for.

> *Let's not get tired of doing what is good. At just the right time we will reap a harvest of blessing if we don't give up.*
> *Galatians 6:9*

October 19

Misplaced Hatred
HERODIAS

Mark 6:14-20

Every time Herodias thought about John the Baptist, she seethed with hatred and a desire for revenge. How dare he rebuke her and her husband in public? Herodias must have known that her marriage with Herod was unlawful; they had both left their spouses. But since Herod ruled over two provinces in Israel, it's likely that no one dared to point that out until this outspoken prophet came along. To make matters worse, Herod had some strange fascination with John. He actually liked listening to him. Herod had finally thrown John into prison, but he still refused to execute him. We can imagine Herodias gritting her teeth and thinking, *Imprisonment is not enough to pay him back for the embarrassment he caused me. I'll find a way.*

Instead of hating the sin in her life, Herodias hated the one who pointed it out to her. John's words troubled what remained of her conscience. Rather than face the truth of his reprimand, she wanted to shut him up. John's willingness to be bold in speaking God's message about her life offered Herodias the opportunity to seek forgiveness from God and make a correction in her behavior. But she poured all her attention and energy into devising a way to get rid of the messenger.

When someone criticizes our behavior, we usually respond defensively. We find it easier to get angry at the person than to evaluate the message to see if it's true. We may not realize that our anger is merely covering up our guilty consciences. Instead of instantly reacting on the basis of our emotions, a much wiser response would be to examine our lives prayerfully in light of the criticism. God sometimes uses other people to get our attention and point out areas in our lives that need correction. We don't want to be like Herodias and hate the wrong things.

If you listen to constructive criticism, you will be at home among the wise.
Proverbs 15:31

October 20

A Better Life
HERODIAS

Mark 6:21-24

Nothing had prepared the young woman for the feelings that flooded through her each time she looked at her newborn daughter. With all her heart, she wanted to be a good mother, but could she? She had run away at age sixteen to escape an abusive home. For several years she had lived hand to mouth, proud of her independence, but not always proud of what she had to do to get by. Now, there was someone else to think about. *I don't know how, but I promise you this—I'm going to make a better life for us,* she vowed to the sleeping baby.

Apparently Herodias didn't harbor such maternal thoughts for her daughter. Herodias came from a messed-up family background. Herod had divorced his first wife to marry Herodias, the daughter of his half brother Aristobulus. At the time, Herodias was married to Philip, Herod's other half brother, who was also Herodias's half uncle. The family had a reputation for cruelty and depravity. Instead of wanting a better life for her daughter, Herodias used her to take revenge on John the Baptist. When she sent the teenage girl to dance before Herod and his drunken birthday guests, did she suspect that he would offer to reward her?

Good parents willingly make sacrifices so that their children will have the best lives possible. We want them to be well-fed, comfortable, and well-educated. We try to shield them from hurtful experiences. Our heavenly Father also wants his children to have the best lives possible. We may feel like prisoners of our lifestyle, unable to rise above a sinful habit or addictive behavior such as promiscuity, drugs, or alcoholism. Jesus sacrificed himself to shield us from sin's harmful effects. No matter what has a grip on us, God wants to give us better lives.

> *We are confident that you are meant for better things, things that come with salvation.*
> Hebrews 6:9

October 21

One Wish
HERODIAS'S DAUGHTER

Mark 6:25
"Don't forget to make a wish!"

Where do I begin? Chloe wondered. Should I choose a new car to replace my old clunker, or a new man to replace my klutz of a boyfriend? She sighed and took a deep breath. Too bad this birthday wish thing doesn't work—if it did, I'd wish for fewer candles on this cake that's lighting up the whole house.

Herodias's daughter had the opportunity to have a wish come true. She knew that her stepfather's offer to give her anything up to half his kingdom wasn't literal; he meant that he would give her anything in his power to grant. She also knew that she needed to give Herod an answer right away, while he was in a party mood and wanting to impress his important guests. When she hurried to ask her mother's advice, Herodias had a ready answer. She instructed her daughter to ask for the one thing *she* desired most—the death of John the Baptist.

If we could choose one wish to have granted, our answer would reveal a great deal about us and our values. Would we immediately think of something we needed such as a new car? Or would we ask for something intangible such as having a relationship restored? Of all the things we could choose, our answer would reveal what we most desired at that moment.

Every day, our mind fills with needs and wishes, sometimes crowding out the one thing we should desire most—a closer relationship with our Creator. We can't help being concerned with our legitimate needs, but when we spend time getting to know God through his Word, our Spirit begins to long for him more than anything else. The more we understand God's character, the more we see he's what we really wish for.

As the deer longs for streams of water, so I long for you, O God.
Psalm 42:1

October 22

Getting Our Own Way
HERODIAS

Mark 6:26-29

When Herodias's daughter followed her mother's advice to ask Herod for John's head, Herodias finally got her own way. Herod had refused to kill the prophet, but now Herodias had him trapped. Herod couldn't back down from his rash promise in front of his party guests, so he immediately sent soldiers to the prison to behead John. When Herodias's daughter handed her the platter bearing John's head, did Herodias feel a thrill at the grisly sight of her conquered enemy? Did she sigh with relief, thinking how much better her life would be now that she had rid herself of the one who seemed to delight in pointing out her sin?

As Herodias celebrated her victory, she had no idea how much she had lost. God had sent John to proclaim the truth to Herod and Herodias and to urge them to turn from their sin. When Jesus later appeared before Herod for trial, Jesus didn't say a word to him. Was it because Herod and his wife had been given a chance to hear from God through John, and they had thrown it away?

Our human nature screams out to get its own way. We think we know what we need and what will make us happy, but our minds are easily deceived and influenced by the world's thinking. Our desires often conflict with what God wants for us. Sometimes he allows us to have our own way, always hoping that we will learn that he knows what's best for us. Each time we "win" by getting our own way, we lose something precious—an opportunity to follow God's perfect plan for our lives. As we deliberately place our will under his control each day, we won't be so demanding about getting our own way. We'll understand that God's way is always best.

Teach me your way, O LORD, and I will walk in your truth.
Psalm 86:11 (NIV)

October 23

Rescue Mission
AHINOAM AND ABIGAIL

1 Samuel 30:1-18

As the police officer helped Crystal into the patrol car, she felt as if a week had passed instead of thirteen hours. Her ordeal had begun that morning when her estranged husband showed up at her office waving a gun. After ordering everyone out, he shut Crystal and himself in a workroom. Crystal had feared for her life as his moods swung back and forth from apologetic and remorseful to angry and threatening. Finally, when her husband had demanded food, an officer used the opportunity to overpower him. *It's really over!* she realized, as she collapsed against the officer's shoulder.

Abigail and Ahinoam, two of David's wives, knew how it felt to be captured and rescued. When Amalekite forces raided their town, they were carried off with the rest of the women and children. As the miles passed by, the women's hearts must have grown heavier as they wondered what the future held for them. One night, their captors feasted and danced to celebrate their plunder. Suddenly, David and four hundred of his men rushed upon the camp. The women's hearts surely leaped for joy when they saw their rescuers coming to free them.

All of us have been captured, whether we know it or not. God created us to be in a relationship with him, but sin has distorted that perfect relationship and allowed Satan to have power over us. Satan desperately wants us to remain unaware of the rescue mission that God has carried out on our behalf. Jesus Christ died to set free those held captive in the grip of sin. When we believe in Jesus, God delivers us from Satan's kingdom of darkness and transfers us to our rightful place, the Kingdom of Christ. When we read the story of our rescue in the Bible, our hearts should leap for joy.

> *He has rescued us from the kingdom of darkness and transferred us into the Kingdom of his dear Son.*
> *Colossians 1:13*

October 24

Limiting Our Blessings
THE PROPHET'S WIDOW

2 Kings 4:1-7

As the opening credits appeared on the screen, my eyes strayed to my friend's bowl of popcorn. I had never come to one of these free afternoon movies before. It wasn't a first-run film, but I hadn't seen it. To top it off, the theater offered free popcorn if we brought our own containers. My friend had showed up with a bowl at least twice the size of mine. I found it difficult to concentrate on the movie—I was thinking of all the bigger containers I had at home and wondering why I had limited myself.

The woman in 2 Kings must have been glad that she hadn't limited her blessings to one small container. When her husband died, his creditor had threatened to seize her two sons as payment for debts. She told the prophet Elisha that all she had was a little oil, probably olive oil that she used for fuel, light, and cooking. Elisha instructed her to borrow a lot of empty jars from her neighbors and pour the oil into them until they were full. The woman obeyed, and as soon as she filled the last container, the oil stopped flowing. How overjoyed she must have been to see that she now had enough oil to sell and pay her debts as well as to support herself and her sons!

The widow demonstrated her faith by the number of jars she collected and by her willingness to follow the prophet's instructions. Although God promises to meet all our needs, his provision works in the same measure as our trust and obedience. How often do we limit the blessings we receive by our lack of faith and our refusal to follow his instructions? God wants us to dream big and expect miraculous things from him. If we are open to all he has in store for us, there won't be a container anywhere big enough to hold the blessings.

> *[He] is able to do immeasurably more than all we ask or imagine,*
> *according to his power that is at work within us.*
> *Ephesians 3:20 (NIV)*

October 25

Not Too Timid to Speak Up
A YOUNG ISRAELITE MAID

2 Kings 5:1-19

Arlene saw the ambulance pull into her neighbors' driveway. Had something happened to their son? Everyone knew that the little daredevil was always pulling crazy stunts. Only two days ago, Arlene had seen him climbing on his roof while his parents were at work. She had thought about calling his mom, but she didn't. Suddenly, she gasped. *What if . . .* Arlene stood with her eyes strained toward her neighbors' front door.

The girl in today's passage wasn't too afraid to speak up. She'd been taken from her home in Israel and given to the wife of Naaman, the king of Aram's army commander. When Naaman contracted leprosy, the girl remembered the prophet Elisha and the miracles he had performed. But would a powerful army captain listen to the suggestion of a young slave girl? Besides, Naaman worshiped other gods, not the God of Israel. The girl's longing to help her master overcame any intimidation she felt, and she told her mistress about Elisha. Her boldness led to Naaman's healing and to his new faith in God. The event must have influenced many others as the story spread throughout Israel and Aram.

It's easy to feel intimidated about talking to other people about God because we don't know how they'll react. Will they be offended, mock us, or accuse us of trying to cram our beliefs down their throats? If they are highly educated or in prominent positions, we may wonder why they would listen to us at all. The same God who gave boldness to a young Israelite slave girl wants to help us overcome our timidity. Each of us comes in contact with people who need to hear the good news of God's love and forgiveness. If we ask God to give us the right words, we may be surprised at what happens when we speak up.

> *Pray also for me, that whenever I open my mouth, words may be given me so that I will fearlessly make known the mystery of the gospel.*
> *Ephesians 6:19 (NIV)*

October 26

Not Too Proud to Listen
NAAMAN'S WIFE

2 Kings 5:1-19

The mother sat in the waiting room, anxiously hoping for news about her son's surgery. She couldn't help feeling responsible for the accident. It had been only a month since his babysitter had told her that Nathan was out of control and needed professional help. The mother cringed as she remembered her response. She hadn't seen the wild behavior described by the girl, and the thought of being given parenting advice from a teenager had angered her. Now, she wished she had listened to the babysitter instead of firing her.

Naaman's wife wasn't too proud to listen to the advice of a young slave girl. As the wife of a powerful army commander, she enjoyed a position of wealth and prominence. Her maid came from a different culture, where the people worshiped a God who seemed strange to her. Many women in her situation would have indignantly brushed off a servant's opinion. But because Naaman's wife longed for her husband to be cured of his leprosy, she told him what her maid had said. Her willingness to listen to someone in a humble position brought her the reward of her husband's being healed of a serious disease.

We all have our own ideas about the right way to do things, but sometimes pride causes us to miss out on the *best* way to handle our problems. We rarely hesitate to seek advice from professionals or experts in the areas of health, finances, technology, or decorating. But in everyday life we may ignore the suggestions of others, especially if we think they're not qualified to offer an opinion. The Bible says that wise people listen to the advice of others. Although God's Word is our best source of advice, we never know when someone else's ideas or experiences may benefit us, or even save us from serious consequences—as long as we're not too proud to listen.

> *Fools think their own way is right, but the wise listen to others.*
> *Proverbs 12:15*

October 27

New Beginnings
PRISCILLA

Acts 18:1-4, 18-21

Priscilla's life as she knew it came to an abrupt end when Emperor Claudius expelled all the Jews from Rome. She and her husband faced an uncertain future in the thoroughly wicked city of Corinth, but she didn't waste time dwelling on what she had left behind. Priscilla and Aquila took up their trade of tent making, and when they met the apostle Paul, they invited him to live and work with them. We don't know when Priscilla became a Christian, but she took full advantage of Paul's presence and the opportunity to learn about Christ from such an excellent teacher.

Eighteen months later, Priscilla faced another new beginning when she and Aquila accompanied Paul to Ephesus. Although Paul left soon after their arrival, he trusted the couple to continue the work of spreading the good news about Jesus Christ. Priscilla had made the most of her time under Paul's training. She and Aquila planted a new church in Ephesus and equipped the new believers until God led them back to Rome after Claudius's death. After they returned to Rome, they opened their home as the gathering place for believers there.

We all face times when our lives take an unexpected turn. Job changes force us to move, relationships end, best friends move away, or our financial situations drastically change. At times like these, it's hard not to get stuck in the past, remembering how things used to be. Priscilla's life encourages us to look around and make the most of every opportunity God sends—new friends and relationships, new ministries, new opportunities to learn. Because of her attitude, Priscilla's life influenced countless people. She reminds us that under God's leadership, when one thing comes to an end, we can always expect to find a new beginning.

Make the most of every opportunity.
Colossians 4:5

October 28

Using Tact
PRISCILLA

Acts 18:24-28

Dora's friends looked away in embarrassment. They enjoyed her company for the most part, but they always hesitated to invite her to dinner parties. Everyone could see that Dora was highly intelligent and educated, but they didn't appreciate the way she flaunted her knowledge. She never hesitated to correct anyone, and she did it immediately and loudly. Tonight, her husband had been her victim, and Dora seemed oblivious to the hurt look on his face.

The woman in today's Bible passage was more tactful than Dora. Since Priscilla's name is sometimes put before her husband's, many believe that she was more educated or had a stronger personality than Aquila. In any case, Priscilla was tactful and considerate as she ministered with her husband. When a famous, gifted speaker came to Ephesus, Priscilla and Aquila went to hear him. Although Apollos preached about Jesus accurately, he didn't know the full story. Rather than correct him in public, the couple invited him into their home and shared the news of Jesus' death, burial, and resurrection, which made salvation possible. They wanted to share their knowledge, not show it off.

Sometimes we get so carried away with the desire to share information that we forget to be sensitive to other people's feelings. If we need to correct someone, it's always best to do it in private. We also need to watch our tone and our words. People don't appreciate being made to look or feel foolish. It's especially important to be careful in sharing truth about God. Just because we've been Christians for a long time or studied the Bible for years doesn't mean that we know it all. Jesus never made anyone feel stupid, and we are accountable for how we talk about him. If we're not interested in other people's feelings, they won't be interested in hearing what we know.

> *While knowledge makes us feel important, it is love that strengthens the church.*
> *1 Corinthians 8:1*

October 29

Obeying the Law
WOMEN WHO HEARD PAUL'S LETTER

Romans 13:1-5

Tara snatched the ticket from the officer's hand and stuffed it into the glove compartment. *So what if I didn't come to a complete stop?* she fumed as she drove away. *Nobody was coming from either direction, and what a stupid place for a stop sign, anyway.* It seemed unfair for her to get this ticket so soon after the two speeding tickets earlier this month. Calming down, she pulled into a handicapped spot to make a quick run into the drugstore. As she walked past the rear of her car, she paused to wipe the dust off her fish symbol.

If the women who lived in first-century Rome felt that it didn't matter whether or not they obeyed the law, the issue was cleared up when they received Paul's letter. It must have been hard for them to hear the instruction about submitting to governing authorities at a time when a madman such as Nero ruled the city. Many of these women probably had family members who had been tortured or murdered by the evil emperor. How could they be expected to submit to such an authority? But Paul wrote that when they rebelled against the government, they were rebelling against God, who establishes the ruling authorities.

We might not think that it's a big deal to disregard laws that seem minor or inconvenient. But even though believers are citizens of Christ's Kingdom, we are expected to be good citizens on earth, too. Even if we can't respect the character of a person in authority, we can acknowledge that God has allowed that person to hold the position. Even when we disagree with a particular law, we are responsible to submit to it as long as it doesn't contradict God's laws. It may go against our nature, but if first-century women could recognize Nero's authority, surely we can submit to a stop sign.

> *Everyone must submit himself to the governing authorities, for there is*
> *no authority except that which God has established.*
> Romans 13:1 (NIV)

October 30

Breaking the Law
PUAH AND SHIPHRAH

Exodus 1:11-21

Denise gripped the steering wheel tightly as she drove home from work. Being a nurse had been her dream since childhood, but now it had become a nightmare. She had been devastated to learn that her hospital performed late-term abortions, leaving the babies who survived the procedure to die alone on a table. Now, a change in policy required all nurses to assist doctors in the abortions, regardless of their beliefs. Denise faced a tough choice. Her family desperately needed her income, and if she refused to obey the ruling, she would certainly lose her job.

Today's Bible passage focuses on two women who faced a tough choice about obeying the law. Alarmed at how the enslaved Israelites kept multiplying, the ruler of Egypt commanded the two principal Hebrew midwives to kill any boys they helped deliver. Puah and Shiphrah knew that if they were caught disobeying an order from Pharaoh, it meant certain death; they also knew that God forbade murder. Their decision may have required soul-searching to reach the point where they were willing to risk their lives in order to follow God. He protected Puah and Shiphrah and rewarded them for their choice.

God instructs us to respect the government and obey its laws even if we don't agree with them. That loyalty ends, however, when an earthly law requires us to do something contrary to God's commandments. Our first allegiance belongs to him. It meant that Puah and Shiphrah might be forfeiting their lives, but they recognized God's authority above that of the powerful tyrant who ruled their people. If following God means that we have to disobey human authority, we must be prepared to accept the consequences of those choices and trust our lives to the One who protected two Hebrew midwives so long ago.

> *Peter and the apostles replied, "We must obey God rather than any human authority."*
> *Acts 5:29*

303

October 31

Feeling like Outcasts
WOMEN WITH LEPROSY

Leviticus 13:45-46

The young woman sat on the bench with her head hanging down. The park bustled with people jogging, families picnicking, and friends laughing, but the woman didn't notice. Two weeks earlier, her world had turned upside down when she'd tested positive for the virus that causes AIDS. *Should I tell my family and friends?* she debated. She needed all the support she could get, but she also dreaded their reactions. Would they avoid her? Would they act as if she were contagious? Dealing with the symptoms would be bad enough without being treated like an outcast.

In Bible times, a diagnosis of leprosy struck fear in people's hearts. Lepers knew that they would become outcasts. In the Bible, *leprosy* refers to a number of serious skin diseases. Since some of them were extremely contagious, people who exhibited such symptoms had to be isolated from the rest of the population. Lepers had to warn anyone who came close to them by crying out, "Unclean! Unclean!" Women with leprosy faced a grim future— they would know the anguish of being cut off from family and friends as the disfiguring disease slowly destroyed their bodies.

Ever since sin entered the world in the Garden of Eden, we are all born as outcasts. Our inherent sinful nature cuts us off from the God who created us to have an intimate relationship with him. Jesus' death on our behalf freed us from the terrible diagnosis and grim future that Satan had planned for us. When we accept God's gift of salvation, nothing can ever make us outcasts in his eyes again. In Bible times only the priest had the authority to declare a person cured, or clean. Similarly, only God has the authority to declare someone clean from sin. After he does that, even if the world treats us as outcasts, nothing will ever separate us from his love.

I am convinced that nothing can ever separate us from God's love.
Romans 8:38

November 1

A Time to Party
ISRAEL'S FESTIVALS

Leviticus 23

I sank into a kitchen chair, with a stack of bills to pay, a growing to-do list, and a brain swirling with worries. As I gazed absentmindedly out the big window, something grabbed my attention. A little wren was splashing around in the water-filled gutter spout. Hopping around and shaking its wings, the bird seemed to be having the time of its life enjoying the sunshine, which I had failed to notice. I smiled, but a pang of guilt shot through me—that tiny bird was enjoying life more than I had been lately.

This chapter in Leviticus summarizes the annual festivals that God planned for the Israelites. Although these observances included solemn times of introspection, mostly they were occasions for rejoicing in God's provision and goodness. I like to imagine how the women felt about the celebrations built into their nation's calendar. These breaks from the burden of their daily chores reminded them that the God they worshiped wanted them to have joy-filled lives.

We have conveniences that the Israelite women didn't dream of, but our lives are crammed with responsibilities and distractions that can rob us of joy, if we let them. Along with taking care of ourselves, our families, and our jobs, we need to schedule times to celebrate the good things in life. That may seem self-indulgent, but God has asked us to do it, as long as we keep a healthy balance.

Some people act as if it's more spiritual to be solemn and gloomy all the time, but God loves to hear his children laugh. He wants us to have times of self-examination when we grieve our losses and sinfulness, but he also encourages us to express joy. When we reflect on how much God loves us, we always have a reason to celebrate.

> *For everything there is a season, a time for every activity under heaven.*
> *Ecclesiastes 3:1*

November 2

Journey to Wisdom
QUEEN OF SHEBA

1 Kings 10:1-9

The queen of Sheba was hungry for wisdom. She had probably often heard that Solomon was the wisest man who ever lived. She had probably also heard that this king attributed his immense wisdom and wealth to his God, Yahweh. Although it meant a long, arduous journey, the queen determined to see for herself whether these reports were true. During the many weeks she spent on camelback, perhaps the queen of Sheba mentally prepared the questions she would ask King Solomon. Could his wisdom be as great as people said, or had the reports been exaggerated? She may have hoped rather than believed that she wouldn't be disappointed. Either way, she would find out.

Arriving in Jerusalem, the queen put off examining the magnificent Temple and palace until she had first satisfied her curiosity about Solomon. What a conversation they must have had. The queen asked all the questions that were on her mind, and Solomon answered every one. To her amazement, she found that nothing was too hard for him to explain. The queen of Sheba realized that the reports about Solomon had minimized his wisdom rather than exaggerated it.

Centuries after this remarkable visit, Jesus commended the queen of Sheba for her willingness to travel so far to encounter Solomon's wisdom (see Matthew 12:42). He contrasted her with the Pharisees and other Jews who refused to listen to him even though he was right there with them. Too often, we go searching for wisdom in some source other than God even though we have access to his written Word. God wants us to share all the questions on our minds with him and then prayerfully study his Word to gain understanding and insight. We may not immediately find all the answers we want, but the search will lead us to the wisdom that we need.

If you need wisdom, ask our generous God, and he will give it to you.
He will not rebuke you for asking.
James 1:5

November 3

The Greatest Offering
QUEEN OF SHEBA

1 Kings 10:10-13

Patsy looked at the huge floral arrangement in the Waterford crystal vase. *I'd trade that for a five-minute phone call in a heartbeat.* Every birthday and most holidays were the same—she could expect flowers, a fruit basket, and maybe a gift certificate from an expensive boutique, but no personal contact. It wasn't as if her daughter couldn't afford to fly in for a visit; she obviously didn't want to take the trouble. *I'd rather be shown a little attention than showered with expensive gifts that I don't really need,* Patsy thought.

Although the queen of Sheba saw that Solomon was the richest man on earth, she showered him with gifts from her own wealth, including four tons of gold, huge quantities of spices, and precious jewels. The queen followed the usual custom in offering tribute to the king of another country; she also wanted to honor Solomon for the wisdom he had shared with her. King Solomon bestowed generous gifts on his royal guest, too, and gave her whatever else she asked for.

Many of us wish that we could afford to buy more expensive presents for those we care about, but the price tag isn't what's important. An expensive anniversary gift doesn't mean much to a wife whose husband never shows affection the rest of the year. Fancy toys won't make children feel loved if their parents don't spend time with them. Thoughtful gestures and acts of kindness linger in our memories long after flowers wilt and checks are cashed and spent.

Similarly, God is more concerned with our attitudes than with the amount of our offerings. Giving a lot of money to his work doesn't mean anything if we don't spend time with him. We honor God by obeying his Word and giving loving service to others. We can't impress him with material wealth, but we can shower him with expressions of our love.

> *I want you to show love, not offer sacrifices. I want you to know me more than I want burnt offerings.*
> *Hosea 6:6*

November 4

What Did She Find?
QUEEN OF SHEBA

1 Kings 10:8-9

Danielle likes to tell people that she always finds more than she's looking for. When her dog ran away, Danielle walked through the park near her house calling him. On her way back, she found a man's wallet under a tree. When she went to drop the wallet by the elderly owner's home, she had trouble finding his house. The man's good-looking young neighbor offered his assistance, and ten months later, he and Danielle married. Danielle ended up with her dog, a cash reward, and a husband.

Did the queen of Sheba find more than she went looking for? She returned to her country with her mission successfully completed. She had seen the famous King Solomon for herself and had found that his wealth and wisdom far exceeded the reports she had heard. During their visit, they had also established trade agreements between their countries.

But did the queen go home with something more valuable than the riches carried on her camels' backs and the satisfaction of having her questions answered? Did her deep conversations with Solomon open her eyes to the source of his wisdom? On the long trip home, did the queen's mind dwell on statements Solomon had made about the one true God of heaven?

Many traditions and legends focus on the queen of Sheba's visit to Solomon, but the Bible doesn't give us many details. If the queen returned home with only material wealth and intellectual knowledge, her trip was a miserable failure. In the same way, our life journeys are unsuccessful if we pursue only worldly riches and wisdom. At the end of our lives, the most important consideration will be whether or not we have a relationship with God through Jesus Christ. Perhaps the queen of Sheba came to place her faith in God. If so, she found much more than she was looking for during her famous visit.

What do you benefit if you gain the whole world but lose your own soul?
Mark 8:36

November 5

Going Above and Beyond
REBEKAH

Genesis 24:1-27

The young single mother listened as her first grader bubbled over about her day. Could this be the same pouting child she had dropped off that morning? Darla had understood Abby's disappointment. Darla, too, was upset at having to miss the special parent-child lunch at school. But since she'd been on the new job for only a few days, she couldn't ask for time off. Now, Darla wished she could hug the lunch lady who had showed up with three sacks from McDonald's, two for herself and her little girl, plus one for Abby.

Rebekah also went beyond what was expected of her. It was customary for women drawing water from a well to offer a drink to a traveler, but Rebekah offered to water Eliezer's camels as well (see Genesis 24:19). She had no idea that she'd just fulfilled the sign Eliezer had requested from God in his search for Isaac's bride. It was hard work to draw enough water for ten thirsty camels, but Rebekah welcomed the chance to serve someone in need. Her kind and generous spirit won her the privilege of being the grandmother of twelve men who would become the nation of Israel.

Many people concentrate on getting away with the least possible amount of work. Even hard workers often ask, "What's in it for me?" How refreshing it is when we find someone who goes beyond the bare minimum to pursue excellent service. Even when their extra efforts aren't recognized by the world, God sees them. That kind of servant heart is just what he uses in his work. We never know what kind of reward God has waiting for us when we go above and beyond the call of duty to serve others—not because we should, but just because we want to.

> *Even the Son of Man came not to be served but to serve others and to give his life as a ransom for many.*
> *Matthew 20:28*

November 6

Defining Moment
REBEKAH

Genesis 24:50-61

Abraham and his servant had prayed for God's guidance in finding a wife for Isaac, and God had obviously led the servant to Rebekah as the chosen woman. Her brother, Laban, had the authority to negotiate the marriage contract, and he had consented. The plan was not complete, however, until Rebekah answered the question posed by her family: "Are you willing to go with this man?"

This was a defining moment of Rebekah's life—a decision that would determine her future. Was she willing to go with this stranger to a country she had never seen, to marry a man she had only heard about? Did she stop to think that if she left, she would probably never see her relatives again? Rebekah was not given time to ponder her decision, but she didn't seem to need it. Although she didn't know what lay ahead, Rebekah must have believed that this unexpected offer revealed God's direction for her life.

Each of us faces a similar choice. God has made all the arrangements for us to become his children. He created us and sent a Savior to pay the price for our sins so that we can be free of our old nature. Although he has the right to control our lives, he leaves the choice to us as his Spirit poses the question: "Are you willing to go with this Man?"

Our decision will determine our future for all eternity. Are we willing to leave behind the world that we know and venture into unknown territory? Will we step out in faith and follow the leadership of a Man we've never seen? None of us knows how much time we have left to ponder our answer, but when we understand how much God loves us, we will answer firmly, as Rebekah did, "Yes, I will go."

Will you go where Jesus Christ leads you today?

November 7

Playing Favorites
REBEKAH

Genesis 25:19-28

Maria looked at the birthday card propped up on her mother's mantel. *No surprise there,* she thought. Maria's card to her mom lay in the pile of mail on the desk, while her brother's stood proudly displayed. Childhood memories suddenly flooded back—Maria being teased in band about her tarnished old saxophone, when her brother had a brand new trumpet; Maria's disappointment at being told that her family couldn't afford dance lessons, although they managed her brother's tae kwon do classes; Maria performing in a class play while her parents cheered for her brother at one of his many basketball games. *Nothing's changed,* thought Maria. *She doesn't even try to hide her favoritism.*

Rebekah and Isaac's family illustrates the problems and conflicts that arise when parents are partial to a certain child. Isaac preferred the rugged, outdoorsy Esau, while Rebekah favored the quiet, homebody Jacob. We don't know how much Rebekah's preference for Jacob was based on his temperament, and how much on God's prediction before the twins' births that the older would serve the younger.

After being unable to conceive for twenty years, Rebekah must have rejoiced when she learned that she carried twins. God's promise that her sons would become two great nations thrilled her, and she probably never forgot his statement that the younger son would become the stronger nation. Her jealous love for Jacob overpowered her maternal instincts for Esau.

Thankfully, God does not play favorites among his children, although it may appear that way to us at times. Favoritism is not a part of his character. Every believer has been given spiritual gifts and the power of the Holy Spirit to accomplish great things for God's Kingdom. Although he plans different roles for each of us, he desires the same thing for every person—a close relationship with him.

> *God does not show favoritism.*
> *Romans 2:11*

November 8

Teaching to Deceive
REBEKAH

Genesis 27:1-29

"Mom, phone's for you! It sounds like Helen!" called Tim. Suzanne rolled her eyes. *Oh no, not again.* Helen was an old friend, but Suzanne dreaded her phone calls. They typically came close to dinnertime and dragged on and on and on. It was hard to end the conversation politely.

"Tell her I just left for the grocery store," Suzanne whispered.

"But, Mom . . ."

"Just do it!" snapped Suzanne. *It's better this way,* she assured herself. *At least I won't have to be rude to her.*

Suzanne didn't realize it, but she was training her son to be deceptive. In Genesis 27, we see another mother very deliberately teaching her son to deceive. God had already declared that Jacob would be the family leader instead of his older brother, but Rebekah decided to help Jacob get the blessing that Isaac had just promised to Esau. Using Esau's clothes and covering Jacob's smooth arms with goatskins, she instructed Jacob to trick Isaac into thinking that he was his brother. Focused only on her goal, Rebekah ignored the possible consequences of her actions as she carried out this ancient case of identity theft.

Few of us will ever devise such a detailed plan to trick someone, but if we examine our behavior, we may find subtle habits of deception—little white lies to avoid someone we don't want to see or phony excuses to get out of doing something we don't have time for. Or we may fudge the facts a bit just to make ourselves look better. These things don't seem so bad until we remember that others are watching our behavior. More important, God sees us. He desires that we be honest and truthful all the time—and goatskins don't deceive him.

> *You desire truth in the innermost being.*
> Psalm 51:6 (*NASB*)

November 9

I Did It My Way
REBEKAH

Genesis 27:41–28:5

Did Rebekah feel guilty about deceiving the husband she had lived with for so many years? Was she ashamed of taking advantage of his advanced age and poor eyesight? Or did she excuse her deception as a means that justified the end? Did she really believe that she was helping God work out his plan for Jacob to have precedence over his older brother?

Whatever Rebekah's feelings or intentions, she got what she wanted. Isaac gave Jacob the blessing usually reserved for the firstborn son. Rebekah "won" in the sense that her plan worked, but she soon learned how much she had lost. When Esau threatened to kill Jacob, she had to send Jacob away to wait until Esau's jealous anger cooled.

As she watched her favorite son leave home, probably with hot tears stinging her eyes, did she wonder if she would ever see him again? By the time Jacob returned twenty years later, Rebekah would be buried beside her mother-in-law, Sarah, who also suffered from taking matters into her own hands instead of waiting for God to carry out his plan in his way.

People are no different today than in Old Testament times. Like Rebekah, we still struggle with the desire to do things our own way, even when it comes to God's work. When we are focused on a problem, we may forget to look for God's will in the situation and resolve it by any means possible.

God is no different today than he was in Rebekah's time. His intentions and purposes will stand, with or without our cooperation, and often despite our interference. Even when it looks as if God's plan needs our help, it's best to concentrate on his will, not on our own ideas of how things need to be done. We win only when God gets *his* way.

The Lord's plans stand firm forever; his intentions can never be shaken.
Psalm 33:11

November 10

Standing Firm
PERSECUTED WOMEN

2 Thessalonians 1:3-8

Noviana Malewa still suffers physical and emotional pain as the only survivor of a radical Muslim attack on her and three of her friends in Indonesia. On October 29, 2005, Noviana and three other Christian high-school girls were walking home from school when they were assaulted by a group of jihadists with machetes. The attackers beheaded three of the girls, but Noviana survived the slash to her head and neck. Her extensive medical treatment was provided by The Voice of the Martyrs, one of several organizations dedicated to ministering to persecuted Christians worldwide.

The women in the church at Thessalonica also experienced persecution because of their Christian beliefs. After accepting the gospel through the apostle Paul's preaching, these early believers faced severe hostility from Jews and Gentiles. The Bible commends them for their response. Instead of running away from the situation, they accepted the suffering as something that God had allowed for his purpose and glory. They made a conscious decision to endure the persecution through God's strength. In the midst of their suffering, their faith flourished and their love for one another grew.

When we face hostility because of our Christian beliefs, our first instinct may be to avoid it at all costs. We may be tempted to lash out in anger at the unfairness of our situation. Although we may want everyone to like us, as followers of Christ we can expect to be misunderstood, ridiculed, criticized, discriminated against, and even hated. Whenever we take a stand for him, we face the possibility of persecution to some degree. The Bible warns that this will worsen as we move toward the end of time. God promises to give us the strength that we need to endure. In the meantime, we can look forward to the day when God will dole out justice and end all persecution of his children.

Everyone who wants to live a godly life in Christ Jesus will suffer persecution.
2 Timothy 3:12

November 11

Standing in the Gap
WOMEN WHO INTERCEDED FOR OTHERS

Two of the most admirable women in the Old Testament interceded for others. Abigail intervened when her drunken husband insulted David and his men after they had generously protected Nabal's flock. Knowing that David would avenge the offense, Abigail rode out to meet him. Her gifts of food and soothing words persuaded David to turn aside from his anger. Abigail's wise actions saved the lives of many and protected the next king of Israel from unnecessary bloodshed.

When one of the Persian king's advisors got him to set a date for the extermination of Jews in his kingdom, Queen Esther risked her life to intercede for her people. Esther patiently waited on God's timing to plead her cause. In the meantime, God arranged circumstances to make King Xerxes favorable toward Esther's request. Esther's courage and dependence on God saved the Jewish people and destroyed the man who had tried to annihilate them.

Christians have the great privilege and responsibility of interceding for one another before God's throne. Although we are blessed with being able to approach God directly, James 5:16 makes it clear that we sometimes need to confess a sin to a fellow believer and ask that person to pray for us. We can request prayer for others' material needs, relationship problems, healing, or spiritual growth. We also have the privilege of praying for persecuted believers throughout the world.

In our ministry of intercessory prayer, it's encouraging to remember that Jesus does the same thing for us. Although we are freed from the condemnation of sin by trusting in Jesus' death and resurrection, Satan is still our accuser. Jesus is the defender who presents our cases before God. The One who hears our intercessory prayers for others also intercedes for us.

> *Christ Jesus, who died—more than that, who was raised to life—is at the right hand of God and is also interceding for us.*
> Romans 8:34 (NIV)

November 12

Dealing with Resentment
MARTHA

Luke 10:38-40

Ruth lay in bed, staring at the ceiling and listening to her husband's snoring. *Oh great!* she thought. *It's not enough for him to ruin my day; he has to ruin my night, too!* First, he'd forgotten to pick up milk on his way home from the office. Then he spent the evening watching the football game with his brother when he knew perfectly well that she wanted his help painting the spare bedroom. Her muscles tensed up just thinking about him—and he'd wondered why she wouldn't say good night.

When Jesus and his disciples visited Martha's house, we don't know what she was cooking, but we know that she began to stew. As a meticulous hostess, Martha wanted everything to be perfect for her guests. She didn't mind being in charge, but did her sister plan to just sit there and leave all the dinner preparations to her? It wasn't fair. Everyone could see how busy Martha was. Why didn't Jesus say something to Mary about helping out? As the minutes dragged by, Martha's irritation grew until finally she decided to say something.

By the time Martha spoke up, her resentment had grown to the point that she didn't consider Mary's feelings when she rebuked her in front of everyone. In our desire to please, we often repress our feelings about situations that we consider unfair. As our resentment grows into anger, it can erupt in sudden outbursts, or we may turn it inward and get depressed. It's healthier to express our feelings with others when we can do so calmly. God also wants us to talk with him openly about our frustrations. He doesn't want us to repress or ignore unpleasant feelings; he wants to help us deal with them. God knows that if we keep simmering, we'll eventually boil over.

"Don't sin by letting anger control you." Don't let the sun go down while you are still angry.
Ephesians 4:26

November 13

Focused on Details
MARTHA

Luke 10:41-42

Donna fell into bed, exhausted. *What a week this has been!* she moaned to herself. Rehearsals with her third-grade class for the special program, parent-teacher conferences after school, and the twins' science-fair projects she was helping with—on top of her usual running around. If she worked all day tomorrow, she would just be able to finish the preparations for hosting her in-laws' anniversary celebration on Sunday. As she drifted off to sleep, still mentally checking things off her list, Donna had the vague feeling that she had forgotten something.

Martha was focused on serving a wonderful meal for Jesus, but she had no clue that she had left out the main ingredient. As she appealed to Jesus to make Mary help her with the work, Martha never dreamed that she could be the one in the wrong. Jesus gently chided Martha for being so distracted by all the dinner details. He told her that Mary had chosen the single most important thing—listening to him. Jesus' words must have gone straight to Martha's heart as she understood that she had let her service get in the way of simply loving him.

We have more modern conveniences today than Martha had, but we're still busy. As women's roles have expanded, so has our stress level. It's easy to get so caught up in the details of running our homes, nurturing our families, or advancing our careers that we leave God out of our lives. The work we're doing may be meeting others' needs, but we pay a price when we neglect our own spiritual well-being. Sometimes it seems that we can't spare even a few minutes for prayer or reading the Bible, but Jesus' statement is still true today. We may have to let go of some details, but we'll find fulfillment only when our main focus is the one thing that truly matters.

[Jesus said,] "There is only one thing worth being concerned about."
Luke 10:42

November 14

Paying Attention
MARY OF BETHANY

Luke 10:38-42

"You're not listening to me!" Norma accused her husband as they sat at the kitchen table.

"Sure I am," Chip protested, dropping the sports pages. Norma continued telling him her plans for the next day, but she noticed that his eyes had already slipped back toward the paper.

"Then I thought I would buy something in black leather so I can hitch a ride across the country with a guy on a Harley and join the circus. Does that sound like a good idea?"

"Sounds fine," Chip mumbled.

Mary of Bethany was a better listener than Norma's husband. She sat on the floor, gazing up at Jesus' face and listening to him talk. How Mary must have loved these relaxed visits when she and her siblings had Jesus in their home, away from the noisy crowds. Jesus' words would have stirred her spirit and stayed in her mind and heart long after the conversation ended. As Mary soaked up every word, she didn't hear anything but Jesus' voice. Martha's sudden outburst probably filled her with guilt for not helping and embarrassment at being accused in front of their guests. But those feelings quickly evaporated as Jesus defended her by saying that she had chosen the most important thing.

Unfortunately, we don't always give God our full attention. How many times have we mentally planned the day's activities or meals during the Sunday morning service? Haven't we all struggled with thoughts of our to-do list during our daily prayer time? It's hard to give God our undivided attention when so many concerns bombard our minds. But nothing is more important to our spiritual growth than developing the discipline of shutting out the world and worshiping God with wholehearted devotion. Then we can choose the most important thing, as Mary did.

> [Jesus said,] "Mary has discovered it, and it will not be taken away from her."
> Luke 10:42

November 15

It Takes All Kinds
MARTHA AND MARY

1 Corinthians 12:12-21

As Alison drove home, she couldn't wait to call Kelli. The seminar on personalities had let her see her sister in a new light. Alison had immediately pegged herself as a Choleric, a born leader who was always taking charge, always achieving. She'd also recognized Kelli, a quiet, analytical introvert, in the discussion of the Melancholy personality. *All these years I've been criticizing what I thought were weaknesses—just because she's not like me,* Alison thought. *I owe my sister a long-overdue apology.*

Martha and Mary also experienced conflict because of personality differences. Martha had an active personality, always busy and fussing over details. Mary was quieter and more contemplative. When Jesus dropped by, Martha immersed herself in preparations that would make his visit the very best it could be. Mary fastened her full attention on Jesus, drinking in his words and making the most of the opportunity to learn from him. While the two sisters had different approaches to showing devotion to Jesus, they both loved him deeply. Jesus loved and appreciated both women. He was very gentle in rebuking Martha when she took her gift of practical service to an extreme and it became a weakness instead of a strength.

God's love for variety can be seen in his creation, in the vast array of animals and flowers and in the fact that no two snowflakes are alike. He also gave each of us a unique personality. We all have different combinations of natural talents, abilities, personality traits, and spiritual gifts. While these differences sometimes cause conflicts among believers, God planned our diversity so that we would depend on one another and enrich one another's lives. When we remember that we all serve the Lord Jesus, we'll appreciate how another's personality complements our own instead of trying to change that person.

In his grace, God has given us different gifts for doing certain things well.
Romans 12:6

November 16

Time Management
THE IDEAL WOMAN

Proverbs 31:10-27

Maeve did a double take at the clock as she hung up the phone. *Where does the time go?* She *had* to call her best friend when she learned that Brian, not Stephen, was the father of Kirsten's baby. She hadn't meant to discuss today's episodes of those other soaps too. Maeve looked around at the unfolded laundry and dirty dishes. They'd better have pizza delivered tonight so she could catch up on things. *Thank goodness I know how to multitask,* she thought as she turned on *Oprah.* Reaching into the laundry basket, Maeve dug out the bottle of Disco Pink, her favorite color for toenails.

The ideal woman described in Proverbs 31 is at the opposite extreme from Maeve. She works from before dawn until late into the night, and her accomplishments are extraordinary. Not only does she meet all her family's needs and conduct profitable business ventures, but this superhuman woman also serves the needy in her community. Her hands are always busy, either at home or in the business world. It makes me tired just to read about her!

Most of us fall somewhere between Maeve and the woman in Proverbs 31, and most of us are looking for improvement. Time-management seminars promise to help us accomplish more each day. Stores are stocked with day planners, electronic gadgets, and books on the topic. Sometimes the very things designed to save us time, such as computers, also encourage us to waste it.

God holds us accountable for how we spend the limited time we have on earth. The wisest use of our time is to do the important work that God has planned for each of us. If we let him guide our daily activities, we will make a difference in other people's lives—and we'll resemble the Proverbs 31 woman more than Maeve.

> [Jesus said,] *"As long as it is day, we must do the work of him who sent me."*
> *John 9:4* (NIV)

November 17

A Wise Planner
THE IDEAL WOMAN

Proverbs 31:15

The woman in Proverbs 31 discovered two keys to making the most of her time: planning and delegating. Although she gets up early to make breakfast, she allows extra time in the morning for planning her day's activities. Rather than start the day in a rush, she schedules a quiet time to prayerfully reflect on the needs of her family and herself and to set priorities for the day. After she determines what needs to be accomplished, she delegates some assignments to her servant girls.

Many women find that getting up a little earlier in order to plan the day helps them to get much more done. If we start the day at a hectic pace, we may end it feeling exhausted and wondering why we didn't accomplish more. Sometimes we're worn out because we try to do everything by ourselves. We may need to practice delegating some chores to family members. Even if we can't hire housekeepers, we all have "servant girls" in our homes—washers and dryers, dishwashers, slow cookers, food processors, bread makers, and other handy appliances. We get the most from these helpers when we plan their use.

Planning is important in our lives as well as in managing our homes. If we don't know what we want to do with our lives, we'll wear ourselves out for nothing. Our goal as believers is to honor God by using the gifts, abilities, and resources he has given us. All our activities can be evaluated on the basis of whether or not they help us toward that end. We might not be morning people like the Proverbs 31 woman, but it pays to have a consistent time each day for prayer, reading God's Word, talking to him about our plans, and listening for his voice. When all our activities line up with God's agenda for our lives, we will have found an ideal, no-fail plan.

Commit your actions to the LORD, and your plans will succeed.
Proverbs 16:3

November 18

Trustworthy
THE IDEAL WOMAN

Proverbs 31:11-12

Mercedes tapped her pencil against the notepad. *Hmm, what story can I use this time?* She didn't enjoy lying to her husband—there were just some things he was better off not knowing, such as the cost of her new outfit. By pretending that the washer repair cost twice as much as it did, she'd managed to keep peace in the house. "Gone to watch Betty's kids while she's at her night class." If Antonio knew she was out with her old high-school friend, he would overreact the way he did about everything. It wasn't that anything was going on between her and Alan, but still . . . it was better to keep Antonio in the dark.

The ideal woman described in Proverbs 31 is more trustworthy than Mercedes. Her husband knows that he can rely on her to handle the family finances without overspending or wasting money. She makes the most of their resources while making the family's well-being her first priority, rather than selfish interests of her own. She never gives her husband a reason to be suspicious of her behavior. He has complete confidence in how she conducts herself in every situation. Because of her faithful and honorable lifestyle, he knows that his heart and his life are safe in her hands. The ideal woman brings good, not harm, into her husband's life.

Do our family members, friends, and neighbors see us as a source of good in their lives? Can they depend on us to be honest and sincere and to always do what's best for them? Or are we focused on our own desires and looking for ways to hide our ulterior motives from those we secretly wrong by our behavior? If we want to please God, we will always keep our lifestyle worthy of trust—his and others. That's the ideal way to live.

The trustworthy person will get a rich reward.
Proverbs 28:20

November 19

A Wise Investor
THE IDEAL WOMAN

Proverbs 31:16-18, 24

When Sabrina opened the closet door, her eyes fell on a strange-looking contraption pushed toward the back. *What in the world?* she thought. *Oh yeah—what a waste of money!* For only four easy payments of $19.99 plus shipping and handling, this thing was supposed to flatten her tummy, trim her waistline, tighten her rear, and give her muscular legs—in only a few minutes a day. It hadn't taken Sabrina long to realize that she had fallen for another worthless gimmick. "Not one of my smartest investments," she said aloud.

The ideal woman described in Proverbs 31 invests her time and money wisely. She's an excellent homemaker and a successful business-woman. She buys and sells property. She uses her sewing skills to make extra clothing to sell to merchants. She invests part of her earnings in a vineyard and starts a side business. Whether she's pursuing home- or business-related interests, this woman ensures that everything she does is profitable. Rather than carelessly waste her resources, she invests them wisely, always expecting and getting a return on her efforts.

We may not all work in the business world, but we make daily invest-ments of our time, money, energy, and abilities. We can waste what God has given us if we get lazy or if a self-centered attitude leads us to pursue goals that have no lasting value. At the end of our lives, God expects us to show a profit in how we have handled the resources he gave us. Investing in God's work means using everything we have to build relationships and create opportunities to share his love and forgiveness. That's the ideal way to invest our lives.

> *She makes sure her dealings are profitable.*
> *Proverbs 31:18*

November 20

A Helping Hand
THE IDEAL WOMAN

Proverbs 31:20

Although Imelda Marcos came from an impoverished background, she lived a lavish lifestyle as the wife of the Philippine president. Some sources estimate that she and Ferdinand embezzled billions of dollars while he was in office. Imelda reportedly owned more than a thousand pairs of shoes. She was widely criticized for her decadent lifestyle as her country sank deeper into debt and crushing poverty. In the documentary *Imelda,* she defended her extravagant spending by saying that she needed to be a role model and "a star for the poor people."

The ideal woman described in Proverbs 31 takes the opposite approach to the poor. Although she has a family to care for, a household to run, and businesses to manage, this woman also looks out for the needy in her community. She doesn't just mail a check to an organization or treat needy people kindly when she passes them on the street, she is actively involved in meeting their needs. Perhaps she shares some of the cloth she weaves, the clothing she sews, or the food that she so carefully prepares (see Proverbs 31:14-15). Rather than treat the poor as a cause, she "opens her arms" to them and cares for them as individuals.

We have an overwhelming number of opportunities to help the poor. God may be calling us to become personally involved with a needy individual or an organization that ministers to the poor. When he calls us to make monetary donations, it's hard to choose which organizations to support. It's also difficult to decide how much we can spare when we need to be building up a nest egg for the future. But God has such deep compassion for the needy that when we help them, he regards it as an action done for him. He promises to reward our generosity—and that's the ideal nest egg.

If you help the poor, you are lending to the LORD—and he will repay you!
Proverbs 19:17

November 21

A Sharp Dresser
THE IDEAL WOMAN

Proverbs 31:22-26

As I sat in the doctor's waiting room, I felt like a slob. In comparison to the woman sitting across from me, I looked as if I had rolled straight out of bed and into the car. The woman wore wool pants with a beautiful plaid jacket. Her purse, shoes, scarf, and jewelry all picked up the hot pink in the jacket's pattern. As she reached for a magazine, her sleeve moved, revealing a watch with a hot-pink band. I felt sure that she was also wearing hot-pink underwear.

The ideal woman in Proverbs 31 isn't obsessed with clothes, but neither does she neglect her appearance. She gives the same careful attention to her appearance that she does to her home and to her family's well-being. In keeping with her family's status, she wears dresses made of linen and colored with an expensive purple dye made from shellfish. More important, she makes sure that her grooming, her demeanor, her words, and her behavior all project an air of dignity and self-respect. Her appearance and dignified behavior contribute to her husband's reputation as a respected community leader.

Christian women often feel pulled in two directions. We like pretty clothes and want to make ourselves look as nice as possible, but it seems ungodly to be preoccupied with our external appearance. The Proverbs 31 woman shows us that it's okay to dress nicely. The way we care for ourselves reflects on the reputation of our Creator, just as our words and behavior do. As long as we don't go overboard, we don't have to feel guilty about paying attention to our appearance. But God doesn't want us to forget to dress in the dignity that comes from knowing that we are his dearly loved daughters. That's the ideal wardrobe that will make us stand out in any crowd.

> *She is clothed with strength and dignity.*
> *Proverbs 31:25*

November 22

Sense of Humor
THE IDEAL WOMAN

Proverbs 31:25

As we read through the description of the ideal woman in Proverbs 31, we may picture her as a solemn, serious person who is always intent on a project. She seems to be going in a dozen different directions and working day and night. Thank goodness for Proverbs 31:25, which tells us that she laughs. It's good to know that although the ideal woman is industrious and hardworking, she makes time to relax and enjoy life. The verse also tells us why she laughs: She has no fear of the future. She knows that she has faithfully fulfilled her God-given roles to the best of her ability. Because she has done her part and the rest is in God's hands, she can look toward the future with optimism.

The Bible emphasizes the importance of working hard, but it also recognizes our need for optimism and laughter. Modern scientific research has confirmed that a cheerful outlook is powerful medicine (see Proverbs 17:22). Laughter promotes healing, eases pain, lowers blood pressure, boosts immune-system functioning, relieves stress, and promotes a general sense of well-being. A sense of humor is important for our physical and emotional health, and it is an important asset in relationships.

With our busy schedules, it's difficult to make time to relax, unwind, and simply laugh; and with today's headlines, it may seem impossible to laugh "without fear of the future." As Christians, we have more reason to laugh than anyone. Our past has been forgiven and God has promised us a glorious future. We are loved and protected by our Creator. When we do our best to fulfill our God-given roles, we can leave the rest in God's hands. Trusting our lives to our heavenly Father leaves us free to enjoy his blessings, laughing and looking to the future without fear. That's the ideal attitude.

A cheerful heart is good medicine, but a broken spirit saps a person's strength.
Proverbs 17:22

November 23

Appreciated or Not
THE IDEAL WOMAN

Proverbs 31:28-30

Keri stood at the kitchen sink, surveying the damage. *Why do I even bother?*
She'd wanted only to make the school holiday special for the boys. Each had
chosen a friend to invite for a sleepover, and also a favorite food to have for
dinner. What she had planned and worked on for two days had disappeared
within minutes. Now the boys were in the basement playing video games,
and her husband was in his home office filing reports. Keri had been left to
face the mess alone without a word of thanks.

The ideal woman in Proverbs 31 gets more appreciation from her
family than many wives and mothers do. Her children stand up and bless
her for her hard work. Her husband praises her and says that she surpasses
all other virtuous and capable women. This woman must feel warmed and
honored by her family's compliments. Love for her family and a desire to
honor God are what motivate her to be the best that she can be, but she
must be glad that her efforts are appreciated.

Few women receive such recognition. Instead of standing up and calling us blessed, our children may just sit down and ask what's for dinner.
Our husbands are usually oblivious to all that we do behind the scenes. Our
employers and coworkers may have no idea how much extra effort we put in
on that last project. Even when others don't appreciate us, God sees everything we do and will acknowledge our efforts someday. The ideal situation
would be for others to thank us for our hard work, but that won't always
happen. When we're feeling unappreciated, we can look forward to God's
promised rewards.

> *The Lord will reward each one of us for the good we do.*
> *Ephesians 6:8*

November 24

Actions Speak Louder Than Words
THE IDEAL WOMAN

Proverbs 31:31

Taylor heard a loud voice and glanced across the crowded room. *Oh no! I was hoping she wouldn't be here!* She had to endure the woman's conversation at work, but being around her at parties was too much. It wasn't that her coworker had no good qualities; she'd be great company if she could just stop talking about herself so much. Every other word seemed to be *I* or *me.* Every story she told had an undercurrent of boasting, even when she talked about her problems. As Taylor crept toward the door, she heard a loud voice. "Yoo-hoo! Taylor, over here!"

The ideal woman in Proverbs 31 didn't need to boast about her accomplishments. She didn't plan and work diligently so that she could brag about her home, family, or business successes. She acted from a motivation to honor God and serve others. No one who observed her lifestyle could fail to recognize her godly character. She lived with the quiet confidence that whatever others thought of her, her actions spoke for themselves.

Sometimes we get caught up in other people's opinions. If they don't notice our abilities and accomplishments, we may feel the need to fill them in, especially if we have low self-esteem. An air of boasting can creep into our conversations without our noticing. It's gratifying when others praise us, but we won't feel it's necessary if we remember that our actions speak for themselves. When we focus on honoring God and serving other people instead of seeking our own glory, our lifestyles will speak volumes to anyone who observes us. That's the ideal praise.

> *Let her deeds publicly declare her praise.*
> *Proverbs 31:31*

November 25

Giving Thanks
WOMEN AT THE WALL'S REDEDICATION

Nehemiah 12:27-43

Doreen closed her journal and looked at the clock. It was hard to believe that in just twenty minutes, her mood had shifted from one end of the spectrum to the other. She'd started the morning feeling gloomy and grumpy, without even noticing the beautiful sunshine. She'd tried to shake off the mood, with no luck. Finally, she remembered her friend's telling her she could improve her attitude by listing fifteen things that she was thankful for. In spite of all the problems Doreen was dealing with, she managed to list twenty-two blessings in her life. Looking out the window, she wondered, *Now why didn't I notice that gorgeous sky before?*

The women in the passage from Nehemiah also experienced the joy of thankful hearts. When the people in Jerusalem finished rebuilding the city wall, everyone gathered for a dedication ceremony. Nehemiah organized two large choirs to march on the walls in opposite directions, singing and praising God. Some priests played trumpets and other musical instruments. As the people thanked God for the blessing of having a secure wall around their city again, their joy was so great that the sound "could be heard far away."

God's instruction to be thankful in all circumstances sounds strange to us. Surely he means for us to be thankful when we feel like it? It may seem hypocritical to thank God when we have a negative attitude, but we soon discover the benefits. According to Philippians 4:6-7, we receive God's peace when we tell him our needs along with thanking him for what he's already done for us. Concentrating on our blessings pulls our focus away from what we need or want and places it on God's love and goodness. And that's always a reason to give thanks.

> *Be thankful in all circumstances, for this is God's will for you who belong to Christ Jesus.*
> *1 Thessalonians 5:18*

November 26

Betrayed
TAMAR

2 Samuel 13:1-14

The young woman unlocked her apartment door and collapsed on the sofa. *I can't believe I've done it again,* she thought. After several dates, they'd already discovered many common interests, and they enjoyed each other's company. But as usual, when a relationship started to get serious, she broke it off. It wasn't Josh's fault—he was always kind and considerate. Oh, how she wanted to trust him! But she couldn't stand being touched. It always brought back those childhood memories . . . those evenings her mom worked the night shift . . . her stepfather's footsteps coming toward her room. . . .

Tamar also knew how it felt to be betrayed. When her half-brother Amnon became infatuated with her, he pretended to be sick in order to get close to her. He even involved their father David in his scheme. Out of concern for Amnon, Tamar came to his house to make his favorite food. Amnon ordered the servants out and grabbed Tamar. Although Tamar pleaded with him not to do such a wicked thing, Amnon raped her. Tamar came to Amnon's house to do something considerate for a sick brother. Instead, she'd ended up being violated as Amnon used her to satisfy his lust.

The Rape, Abuse, and Incest National Network (RAINN) estimates that one in six American women have been victims of attempted or completed rape. Many women experience abuse at the hands of the very people who should protect and care for them. Memories of rape or sexual abuse often cause women to lose trust in other people, which makes healthy relationships impossible. Although professional help may be needed, we can find comfort in being loved by a God who will never break our trust. Jesus Christ experienced betrayal, torture, and a horrible death on our behalf. Because of his love for us, we can always trust God with our lives, even when others turn out to be untrustworthy.

Even my best friend, the one I trusted completely, the one who shared my food, has turned against me.
Psalm 41:9

November 27

False Guilt
TAMAR

2 Samuel 13:15-22

Her hands trembled as she dropped the phone on the counter. She hadn't meant to do this over the phone. For several weeks, she had been thinking about telling her mother. Then tonight, her mom had called and started drilling her again with questions about why she didn't visit. Somehow, it all came out in a rush. She hadn't known what reaction to expect, but why was her mom's anger directed at her instead of at her stepfather? Did her mother really believe that it was her fault? She hung her head and wondered, *How could a ten-year-old girl have "asked for it"?*

As soon as Amnon finished raping Tamar, his lust turned into hatred and disgust. He ordered his servants to throw her out of his house. Tamar tore her royal robe and put ashes on her head to show her extreme grief at what had been done to her. When her full brother Absalom learned what had happened, he told her to keep quiet about it. Although Absalom harbored a desire for revenge and had Amnon killed two years later, at the time, it probably seemed to Tamar that he treated the crime lightly. Her sorrow and confusion must have intensified when King David, their father, heard about Amnon's offense and refused to take action.

In cases of rape or molestation, women are often hurt by others' reactions in addition to the pain of the abuse. Some people refuse to acknowledge what has happened and accuse the woman of making the story up. Or they may treat her pain lightly or accuse her of exaggeration. In some cases, the victim even becomes the target of anger instead of the perpetrator, and she feels as if she were the one at fault. Even when others try to burden us with false guilt, God knows the truth. We can trust him to punish the guilty and prove our innocence, in his time.

> *He has seen my innocence.*
> *2 Samuel 22:25*

November 28

Self-Imprisonment
TAMAR

2 Samuel 13:20

The young woman hesitated, then signed and sealed the letter. As she walked out to the mailbox, she wondered if it would change anything. Her counselor had urged her to write a letter to her stepfather, telling him that she forgave him for the years of abuse. Would this really help her to move on with her life? She hoped so, but she didn't feel any different yet. Shutting the mailbox, she took a deep breath. She didn't know how her stepfather would react to the letter, but one thing she knew for certain—she was tired of being a prisoner of her past.

Did Tamar live as a prisoner of her past after being raped by her half brother? In that culture, loss of virginity was considered a disgrace. Tamar was probably no longer considered marriageable. To make matters worse, God forbade incestuous relationships (see Leviticus 20:17). The only information we have about Tamar's later life is that she "lived as a desolate woman in her brother Absalom's house" (2 Samuel 13:20). We can only wonder if Tamar ever forgave her brother for violating her so cruelly, and her father for not punishing the crime.

Tamar lived under the old law of "an eye for an eye" (see Leviticus 24:20), before Jesus taught that we should forgive anyone who hurts us. That command seems impossible when someone has committed a heinous crime against us or a loved one. While it *is* impossible in our human strength, God will give us the power to do it if we make the difficult choice to obey him in this area. Refusing to forgive someone who has wronged us hurts us more than the other person. It also hinders our prayers and stunts our spiritual growth. When we remember that God forgives us, we'll be motivated to ask for his help in forgiving others.

The Lord forgave you, so you must forgive others.
Colossians 3:13

November 29

Broken Hearts
HURTING WOMEN

The woman sat at her kitchen table, staring out at the gray November day and feeling numb. She'd hoped that the move to a small town would mean a fresh start for herself and her children after the divorce. But just when she thought her son seemed to be adjusting, he'd been arrested for selling drugs. When her daughter hadn't come home two nights ago, she found a note in her room. The tenth grader had dropped out of school and moved in with an older man. The mother's eyes fell on the bare branches of the maple trees, broken and twisted from the previous year's ice storm. She thought, *That's exactly how I feel.*

The Bible includes many stories of women whose hearts were broken. Tamar was raped by her half brother. After moving to a strange country, Naomi lost her husband and both sons (see Ruth 1:1-15). The mother in Matthew 15 watched her daughter being severely tormented by a demon day after day. Job's wife lost all ten of her children and all of her possessions in one day.

Living in a world warped by sin can break our hearts. Sometimes we're hurt by our own mistakes, and sometimes by the choices of people close to us. Many women carry deep wounds from abuse or hurtful words in their childhoods. When the hurt seems too much to bear, we may respond by shutting down emotionally. That numbness in our spirits makes us wonder if our hearts will ever be whole again.

God wants to heal our broken hearts, if we'll let him. It may be difficult to face what seems unbearable, but we must be totally honest with him. Trying to hide our pain is unhealthy physically, emotionally, and spiritually. Even when it seems impossible, God can mend the broken pieces of our lives and our hearts.

> *The LORD is close to the brokenhearted; he rescues those whose spirits are crushed.*
> *Psalm 34:18*

November 30

Comforting Others
COMPASSIONATE WOMEN

2 Corinthians 1:3-7

The mother sat in her family room, looking around the room with dazed, empty eyes. In the past twenty-four hours, her world had changed forever—with the call about her son's car accident, the hours spent in the intensive-care waiting room, the devastating news from the surgeon. Friends had rallied around her, but how could they know how she felt? She heard the doorbell ring and hoped that her husband wouldn't answer it. She heard footsteps, and the next minute, she found herself wrapped in the embrace of a woman she barely knew—a mother who had lost her daughter in a car accident the year before.

Many women who have experienced tragedy reach out to others in similar situations through organizations such as hospice groups, rape-counseling hotlines, or bereavement support groups. The women in Bible times didn't have these outlets, but many of them surely ministered to other individuals. Tamar probably had a heart for other women who had experienced the horror of rape. Perhaps Naomi reached out to other widows after she returned to Israel. The mother in Matthew 15 would have been able to support other mothers with seriously ill children. Perhaps Job's wife had a special sensitivity for people who felt that God had abandoned them.

One result of suffering is that we develop a new awareness of others who are hurting. Since God has comforted us and helped us endure, we are able to reach out and minister to others in similar situations. People in the middle of a tragedy need someone who has lived through a similar experience to come alongside them. As women who have been there, we can identify with their feelings and offer comfort as no one else can. If we accept the comfort that God gives us in painful situations, tragedy won't make us bitter; it will make us more compassionate.

> *He comforts us in all our troubles so that we can comfort others. When they are troubled, we will be able to give them the same comfort God has given us.*
> *2 Corinthians 1:4*

December 1

Disgraced, but Not out of Grace
SAMSON'S MOTHER

Judges 13:2-5; 16:21

We don't know if Samson's mother was alive when her son ended up grinding grain in a Philistine prison. If so, she must have been grief-stricken. Her mind undoubtedly strayed back to earlier, more joyful days. After not being able to have children, she had been elated when an angel announced that she would have a son. Even more thrilling, this son was to be set apart for special service to God as a Nazirite. God had appointed him to begin Israel's deliverance from their Philistine oppressors.

As Samson grew up, his mother must have impressed on him the privileges and responsibilities of his special calling. Despite his supernatural strength, however, Samson operated out of his weaknesses. Samson allowed his physical desires and his feelings to control him. He violated his Nazirite vows, broke God's laws repeatedly, and used his special gifts to play practical jokes and exact personal revenge. Samson's behavior must often have disgraced his mother and made her heart ache as she pondered his wasted potential.

Sometimes we feel disgraced by the behavior of someone we love. We may consider that person's sinful actions to be a result of failure on our part. Maybe we feel disgraced because of our own ungodly choices and wasted opportunities. We may wonder if we will ever get back what we have lost.

Any disappointment that Samson's mother felt would have turned to praise if she had known that his name would be included in the Hebrews 11 list of faith heroes. Despite Samson's grievous mistakes, God allowed him to fulfill his life's purpose through one last heroic act before his death (see Judges 16:30). God can bring victory out of failure in our lives too. Even when we feel disgraced, he still offers us his grace.

> [The Lord said,] "My grace is all you need. My power works best in weakness."
> *2 Corinthians 12:9*

December 2

Looking for Perfection
EVE

What a perfect gift for Carolyn! I thought, as I picked up the framed print of the famous poem about footprints in the sand. As I stood in line to pay, I noticed a tiny scratch on the frame. The imperfection was barely visible and could be seen only when I held the frame at a certain angle. But it was enough to send me back to the shelf to examine each of the framed prints until I found the most perfect one.

While it's only natural to want the nicest gift for someone, that incident started me thinking about my drive for perfection, which seems to grow stronger during the holidays. I want the perfect Christmas tree to decorate, and I knock myself out to make my house look picture perfect. I expect every dish of my Christmas meal to be cooked to perfection. My unrealistic expectations have ruined more than one special occasion for myself and for others.

Eve was the only woman who ever experienced perfection. God created a perfect environment for Adam and Eve to live in. Eve represented perfect womanhood, and she and Adam enjoyed an ideal relationship based on love and respect. Eve had the privilege and joy of an intimate relationship with her Creator. She lived in a perfect world, and she still ruined it by her disobedience to God's single command.

Perhaps our drive for perfection stems from a longing to get back what was lost in the Garden of Eden. In any case, we'll never know perfection in our environment or in ourselves as long as we live on earth. But as we allow God's Spirit to transform us into becoming more like Christ, we move closer to that day in heaven when all imperfections will fade away. In the meantime, I'm definitely imperfect, but with God's help, I'm improving.

> *I don't mean to say that I have already achieved these things or that I have already reached perfection. But I press on to possess that perfection for which Christ Jesus first possessed me.*
> *Philippians 3:12*

December 3

Recognizing the Truth
DAMARIS

Acts 17:16-34

Chloe looked at the clock, punched her pillow a couple of times, and flopped over onto her stomach. She wanted to be a good citizen, but she hadn't expected her first turn at jury duty to keep her awake at night. They were just three days into the trial, and they'd already heard totally different accounts of what had happened. All the witnesses seemed convincing to Chloe, but they couldn't all be giving accurate testimony. *How will we ever sort out such a mess?* she wondered. *How are we supposed to decide who is telling the truth?*

Damaris may have had similar feelings at some point in her life. She lived in ancient Athens, regarded as the intellectual capital of the world at that time. The people loved to discuss and debate all the latest ideas. The apostle Paul took advantage of this openness to present the gospel to the city's prominent council of philosophers. When Paul finished speaking, some laughed at him, others expressed an interest to hear more later, and a few believed his message. We don't know what drew Damaris to Paul's words, but we do know that she responded to God's Spirit. In a culture that took pride in its diversity of beliefs, Damaris recognized and embraced the life-changing truth of the gospel.

We live in an atmosphere similar to the one that Damaris lived in. Our culture prides itself on being open to new ideas and philosophies. One set of beliefs is considered as good as any other. But without a thorough knowledge of what God says in his Word, we can easily be deceived. Paul warns us not to be pulled into "empty philosophies and high-sounding nonsense that come from human thinking" (Colossians 2:8). Only God's Word and Spirit will help us recognize the truth when we hear it.

> *[Jesus prayed,]* "Make them holy by your truth; teach them your word, which is truth."
> *John 17:17*

December 4

Crafty Women
SEWING FOR THE TABERNACLE

Exodus 35:20-29

When God gave Moses detailed instructions for building a house of worship, the Israelite community came together to offer the needed materials and services. Women took an active part in preparing the special place where God's glory would reside. Those skilled in sewing and spinning made yarn from goat hair, and they made cloth from fine linen and blue, purple, and scarlet thread. Eager to help in this important work, these craftswomen offered their talents as gifts to God. Imagine their joy when they saw the completed Tabernacle and knew that their very own hands had contributed to its beauty and glory!

Women have always used their handiwork to make their homes, work environments, and churches more beautiful. Even pioneer women who had few resources found ways to make basic necessities such as quilts and clothing beautiful. Today, interest in knitting, weaving, and spinning has revived. Many women enjoy hobbies such as sewing handmade clothes, doing needlework, and making jewelry. Although any of these items can easily be purchased at stores, women take pleasure in making them with their own hands. Another popular craft that women are enjoying is compiling gorgeous scrapbooks of family photos and mementos for their children.

All the beauty in the world around us is part of God's handiwork, but our own bodies display his most awesome craft. Before we were born, God "knit" together (literally "embroidered") all the intricate parts of our bodies. But even if we are handmade, we are not yet finished projects. Although it doesn't always seem like it with untidy ends dangling, God is busy crafting our lives into a reflection of his glory. Handmade projects can get messy, but when God finishes his work one day, we will see that his hands have made our lives beautiful.

You created my inmost being; you knit me together in my mother's womb.
Psalm 139:13 (NIV)

December 5

Kindred Spirits
NAOMI AND RUTH, MARY AND ELIZABETH

Ecclesiastes 4:7-12

During the darkest time of my life, one friend especially went out of her way to reach out to me. In the winter, I accompanied Kathy on an overnight trip when she had a teachers' conference. In the spring, she unexpectedly received two concert tickets and invited me to go with her. In the summer, she planned a picnic for our families. In the autumn, we enjoyed our usual trip to a fall festival. My friend for all seasons made sure that I had some good times even during the bad ones.

We all need a friend who is willing to share our good times and our bad times. When Naomi lost her husband and both sons, her daughter-in-law's loyalty and friendship gave her courage and strength to face an uncertain future (see Ruth 1). Instead of traveling the road back to her native country alone, Naomi had the joy and comfort of a companion. Since Ruth had come to believe in God, she and Naomi were kindred spirits.

A few days after the angel announced to Mary that she would give birth to the Messiah, Mary went to visit an older relative (see Luke 1). Elizabeth had also miraculously conceived a baby, whose birth had been announced by an angel. What a comfort Mary and Elizabeth must have been to each other during their three-month visit, as they shared their joy, their hopes, and their anxieties.

God designed us to enjoy relationships that offer mutual help and encouragement. Having a close friend to share the times of our lives eases our burdens and increases our joys. With today's fast-paced and often transient lifestyles, it can be difficult to develop friendships. Many people live with feelings of alienation and loneliness because they lack companionship. God wants us to discover the joy of sharing life with a kindred spirit.

Two people are better off than one.
Ecclesiastes 4:9

December 6

A Desperate Housewife
POTIPHAR'S WIFE

Genesis 39:6-12

The television series *Desperate Housewives* premiered in 2004. Its official Web site describes the show as a "primetime soap" that "takes a darkly comedic look at suburbia, where the secret lives of housewives aren't always what they seem." According to the show, the secret life of a housewife includes promiscuous sex. Sadly, this series became an immediate hit.

Potiphar's wife would have felt right at home on Wisteria Lane. Here was a woman with too much time on her hands. Married to a wealthy, important man with plenty of servants, she had nothing better to do than consider how to seduce the handsome new teenage slave. Mrs. Potiphar would have been better off spending her time dusting instead of lusting.

Perhaps Potiphar was so busy and preoccupied that his wife was desperate for male attention. Maybe she was having a midlife crisis and longed to feel desirable again. Perhaps she struggled with unresolved childhood issues, unfulfilled needs, or an addictive personality. Whatever her reason for trying to get Joseph to sleep with her, she had no excuse for her behavior.

As our society moves away from objective standards of right and wrong, adultery begins to seem acceptable. Magazines and tabloids chronicle the affairs of stars and other famous people, and the public devours the details. Movies and television shows often portray extramarital relationships as beautiful. They almost never show the ugly truth.

God warns against committing adultery for good reasons. Affairs break the bond of trust between husband and wife and destroy many of the marriages and families they touch. They usually leave the spouse feeling empty and unfulfilled. When we feel a strong attraction toward a male friend, neighbor, or coworker, we need to limit our interaction with him. And we need to tell God that we're really desperate for his help.

Listen to my cry, for I am in desperate need.
Psalm 142:6 (NIV)

December 7

Defining Moment
POTIPHAR'S WIFE

Genesis 39:12

Potiphar's wife was used to getting what she wanted when she wanted it. But Joseph refused to sleep with her even though she tried day after day to wear him down. Finally, she arranged to be alone with him, grabbed his cloak, and demanded that he go to bed with her. Joseph instantly fled from the house, leaving her stunned and holding his cloak. Potiphar's wife faced a defining moment in her life. She could admit that Joseph had been right about her sinful behavior and change her ways. Or she could do whatever it took to get herself out of this sticky situation, no matter who got hurt in the process. Would Potiphar's wife choose to get moral or get even?

When things are going our way, it's easy to look good. When we don't get what we want, our true character is revealed. How do we react when our friends turn down our suggestions for a restaurant choice, when our families refuse to go along with our plans for the holiday, or when we don't get the promotions we want so badly? Each time our desires are frustrated, we make a choice to accept it gracefully and make the best of the situation or to use whatever means we have to get what we want.

Not getting our own way offers us an opportunity to examine our behavior and consider whether our wishes are reasonable. We may discover an attitude or an area of our lives that needs changing. Being frustrated also gives us a chance to mature in our relationships with other people and with God. If we fully trust him with our lives, can we believe that even when we don't get what we want, he makes sure we get what we truly need?

How do you react when you don't get what you want?

December 8

False Accusations
POTIPHAR'S WIFE

Genesis 39:13-20

She rolled over in bed, then sat upright with a gasp. This wasn't her apartment—how in the world . . . Suddenly it all came rushing back—the fight when her husband left to play poker, her trip to the bar, the guy who kept buying her drinks and offering a sympathetic ear. She'd been mad at Jim, but she sure hadn't meant to let things go so far. *If Jim finds out, he'll leave me in a second,* she realized. She moaned. Her panic eased as an idea came to her mind. Reaching for the phone, she pushed 911.

When Joseph refused her sexual advances, Potiphar's wife probably reacted with anger, humiliation, and perhaps a little shame. Indignation that a Hebrew teenager had rebuffed her advances was soon replaced by worry as to how her husband would react if he heard about her conduct. She decided to accuse Joseph of attempted rape in order to cover up her own sinful behavior. His leaving the cloak in his hurry to get away from her made the accusation easier. She used the evidence of his innocence to accuse him of a crime.

When we're in danger of having our wrongdoing exposed, we have a choice as to how we will react. We can admit our fault, accept the consequences, and learn from the mistake, or we can try to avoid being caught. Unfortunately, some of us use false accusations against other people to cover up our own shame. Doing this increases our guilt and hurts the innocent. Whether we're the one making a false accusation or the one being wrongly blamed, we can be sure that God sees the truth. He will judge the guilty and vindicate the innocent in his time.

> [The Lord said,] *"You must not testify falsely against your neighbor."*
> Deuteronomy 5:20

December 9

Nourishing Words
WOMEN AND FOOD

As I finished cleaning up the kitchen, I wondered why I felt so stuffed. Had I really eaten that much at dinner? Then I started adding up all the little extras—nibbling while cooking, testing the food before serving it, scraping the yummy gooey stuff off the dessert server, and "cleaning up" my children's leftovers. No wonder I hadn't lost weight even though I'd been controlling my portion sizes at meals.

Most women spend a lot of time thinking about and dealing with food. We plan meals, shop for groceries, cook the food, and take care of the leftovers—one way or another. The women in Bible times also spent much of their time planning and preparing meals, particularly during special feasts and observances. Martha was especially consumed with food preparation when Jesus visited her home in Bethany (see Luke 10:38-40).

Jesus seemed to enjoy attending dinner parties with his friends, but he told his disciples that another kind of food was more important to him. Once, when they urged him to eat something, he told them, "My nourishment comes from doing the will of God, who sent me, and from finishing his work" (John 4:34). Earlier in his ministry, when Satan tempted Jesus to use his power to turn stones into bread, Jesus told him that people don't live by bread alone, but by the words that come from God's mouth (see Matthew 4:4).

Sometimes when we crave a snack, it's not physical food that we really want. We may have a hungry heart rather than an empty stomach. We might benefit more from filling up with some quiet time alone with God or by opening the Bible and asking him to speak to us. God's words are calorie free, they satisfy our souls—and they're much more nourishing than Cheetos.

> *When I discovered your words, I devoured them. They are my joy and my heart's delight.*
> *Jeremiah 15:16*

December 10

Unashamed Love
THE WOMAN WHO ANOINTED JESUS' FEET

Luke 7:36-39

I set the tray on the table, passed out the food, and then paused. At home, I always prayed with the kids before meals, but the fast-food restaurant was especially crowded today. I couldn't help wondering what the group of boisterous teenagers next to our table would think if they saw us bow our heads. As I unwrapped my burger, my preschool daughter and two little boys followed my lead without saying anything. Eating lunch at McDonald's that day may have been a treat for my children, but for me it was no happy meal.

Today's Bible passage tells of a woman who put serving Jesus before other people's opinions. When Jesus was invited to a dinner party, uninvited people showed up and stood to the side to listen to the conversation, as was the custom. It may have been hard for this woman to enter the house, knowing that the host and the guests despised her for her immoral reputation. But at the sight of Jesus, she immediately forgot her self-consciousness. As she wept over his feet and dried them with her hair, she was oblivious to the others' outraged stares and murmurings. Her mind was focused only on the Man who taught about God's love and mercy.

It's easy to get caught up in what other people think about us and forget that God is the One we really want to please. Even when we're afraid of looking silly to others, he deserves to be honored and adored. This sinful woman's love for Jesus drove out any embarrassment she may have felt about being the center of disapproving people's attention. Her example encourages us not to be afraid to express our faith, even when we feel intimidated about praying in public.

I am not ashamed of this Good News about Christ.
Romans 1:16

December 11

Forgiven
THE WOMAN WHO ANOINTED JESUS' FEET

Luke 7:40-50

This is going to be one special anniversary dinner. She smiled as she marinated the beef tips. She'd made his favorite cheesecake and picked up the bread he liked so much. Hard to believe that just over a year ago, it had looked as if their marriage was over. *How could I have been so selfish and stupid?* she wondered. Although she hadn't expected him to stay after what she'd done, he had agreed to counseling. It had been a long, hard road, but she would never forget the day that he held her hand, looked in her eyes, and said, "I forgive you."

The immoral woman in Luke 7 also knew how it felt to be forgiven. Everyone looked down on her—especially the religious leaders. She hadn't expected this new Rabbi to be any different, but he was. Through his teaching, she heard about God's forgiveness and mercy. At the sight of Jesus, her tears started flowing and she couldn't hold them back. Lavishing kisses on his feet and anointing them with costly perfume seemed like nothing compared to what he had given her. She was grateful for the opportunity to express her love.

Jesus praised the woman's behavior but scolded his self-righteous host, who had not even offered him the common courtesies usually extended to guests. Many of us are like Simon—we regard ourselves as moral people who love God. But we can't have a deep love for God until we understand the depth of our sin and how it hurts him. Once we see how much God has forgiven us and how little we deserve it, no expression of love for him seems lavish enough.

> *God made you alive with Christ, for he forgave all our sins.*
> *Colossians 2:13*

December 12

Beautiful Women
SARAH, REBEKAH, ESTHER, BATHSHEBA

Tonya Ruiz began modeling at age fifteen and soon signed with a prestigious modeling agency in Paris. She spent the next two years traveling the world to pose for magazine covers, billboards, and posters and appearing in commercials and movies. In her book, *Beauty Quest: A Model's Journey,* Tonya admits that she got caught up in the ugly side of the beauty and fashion industry, with alcohol, drugs, and eating disorders. At age eighteen, she decided to end her life, but God had other plans for her.

Being beautiful doesn't guarantee happiness, and the Bible includes stories of women for whom great beauty caused serious problems. Twice, when Sarah and Abraham traveled to a new place, Abraham feared that someone would kill him in order to get his beautiful wife. He asked Sarah to pretend that she was just his sister, which led to tricky difficulties. Abraham's son Isaac repeated this scene with his wife, Rebekah. As a young Jewish girl, Esther's beauty caught the attention of Persian officials who were gathering girls for the ruler's harem. A bathing beauty named Bathsheba caught King David's eye, prompting an adulterous affair that caused both of them much heartbreak.

Our society tries to convince women that we would have better lives if we were beautiful, but that's not true. The Bible teaches that true beauty comes from who we are on the inside, not from being overly concerned with our outward appearance. God wants us to develop a pure heart, a gentle, loving attitude toward others, and a spirit that quietly trusts in him at all times. When we allow the Holy Spirit to control us, we display the kind of beauty that catches God's eye. Through Tonya's new relationship with Christ, she discovered the true beauty that never fades away and never causes problems.

You should clothe yourselves instead with the beauty that comes from within, the unfading beauty of a gentle and quiet spirit, which is so precious to God.
1 Peter 3:4

December 13

Imprisoned
WOMEN GOING INTO EXILE

Psalm 137:1-4

As the guard slid the heavy metal door closed, Jennifer felt as if she were shut away from the rest of the world forever. Would her friends forget her as they went on with their lives? Would the number on her jumpsuit make her forget her own name? *The hardest part is knowing that I chose this,* she thought. Jennifer knew that she'd had plenty of warnings from her friends and family, and also from the judges. The first time, she had been given probation, and the second time, she did community service. Now Jennifer couldn't deny the fact that she was in prison because of her own poor choices.

The people described in this passage from Psalms also went into captivity because of their choices. They couldn't claim ignorance of God's laws. As the people turned away from God to worship idols and imitate the evil practices of the surrounding nations, God repeatedly called them to return to him. He had given them written warnings in the Law and sent prophets to remind them of the penalty for disobedience and idolatry. When the people continued to reject him, God allowed them to be taken captive. As they were led away to exile in a strange land, the women must have thought that they would never feel joy again.

When we turn away from God, he calls us back to him in all sorts of ways, but he never violates our right to choose. If we continue in sin, we eventually pay the price of ignoring his warnings. Sometimes we suffer temporary consequences, and sometimes the effects of sin are irreversible. When we feel we're in a prison of our own making, God still waits for us to call on him in repentance, and he promises to be with us. Even if we're shut away from the rest of the world, we are never shut off from God's love.

> The LORD is close to all who call on him, yes, to all who call on him in truth.
> Psalm 145:18

December 14

Set Free
WOMEN RETURNING FROM EXILE

Psalm 126:1-3

As Jennifer got in the car, she looked back at the prison and felt as if she were in a wonderful dream. Her time there had not been wasted. She had taken several computer classes along with practical courses, such as budgeting and nutrition. Her parents had agreed to let her move back in with them while she attended the community college and worked at the part-time job the social worker had helped her get. She had also attended a Bible study and now looked forward to getting involved in a church. Jennifer didn't feel that she was returning to her old life; she had found a new and better one.

When the Jewish people mentioned in Psalm 126 came back to Jerusalem, they also felt as if they were in a wonderful dream. They laughed and sang for joy because God had brought them home again. The years spent in captivity as judgment for their sin had given them a renewed appreciation for God's love and mercy. After they repented of their idolatry and rebellion, God eventually restored them to their former homeland. The women must have felt that they had found new lives.

Even when God disciplines us for rebellion and sin, he longs for us to return to him so he can heal our wayward hearts (see Jeremiah 3:22). If we repeatedly ignore his warnings, we may have to "do time" and pay the consequences of our ungodly choices. But God doesn't want the time to be wasted. He wants us to humble ourselves before him, examine our lives in the light of his Word, and turn away from wrongdoing. As we accept his discipline, he will draw us into closer relationship with him until we have a new understanding of the amazing things he has done for us.

> *Yes, the LORD has done amazing things for us! What joy!*
> Psalm 126:3

December 15

New Life for the Dead
WIDOW OF NAIN

Luke 7:11-17

Joanne fought back tears as she hung up the phone. She remembered how her little boy used to talk about loving Jesus, and how much he enjoyed Sunday school. By his teen years, Justin wanted nothing to do with church. As Joanne watched her son grow more hostile toward spiritual discussions and become trapped in an ungodly lifestyle, she felt as if her heart would break. Once again, she closed her eyes to pray for Justin in spite of her feelings of hopelessness. Her son's faith seemed to be dead.

The widow from Nain also grieved over her son. Her only son and her sole means of support and protection had died. Without a close male relative, she would probably end up as a beggar. Besides grieving the death of her dearly loved son, she must have felt as if her own life were over. Jesus saw her sorrow and her need, and "his heart overflowed with compassion" for her.

Jesus touched the coffin and told the young man to get up. The boy sat up and began talking, and Jesus gave him back to his overjoyed mother. The widow must have been amazed when Jesus restored life where there was only death and replaced despair with hope. He did this out of love and mercy, without being asked.

Jesus always sees our grief, whether we're heartbroken over the death of loved ones or over their spiritual condition. We can trust him to bring hope into hopeless situations. Jesus always spoke directly to the person he raised from the dead, and he can speak directly to hardened hearts that resist God. The same Savior who gave new life to a widow's dead son can surely renew the faith of a twenty-first-century mother's prodigal son.

> *"Young man," [Jesus] said, "I tell you, get up."*
> *Luke 7:14*

December 16

Unequally Yoked
EUNICE

Acts 16:1-3; 2 Timothy 1:5

As Melody watched her children singing in the Sunday morning Christmas program, she wished that her husband sat beside her. Melody longed with all her heart for him to share her faith in Christ, but he made it clear that he had no interest in anything spiritual. Although she tried not to preach at him, sometimes her frustration got the better of her, like this morning. Melody couldn't help wondering what effect his attitude would have on the kids. Would they imitate their father and refuse to go to church when they got older? Would they ever worship together as a family?

The Jewish woman in today's verses probably experienced some of the same feelings and questions as Melody. Eunice probably became a Christian through the apostle Paul's early preaching. Although her husband was a Greek and apparently not a believer, Eunice, with the help of her mother, trained her young son in the Scriptures. As a result of her faithfulness, Timothy became a godly man much admired for his exemplary lifestyle. He became Paul's protégé and, later, his trusted coworker. Eunice had the joy of seeing God use her son in powerful ways that influenced countless lives.

Christian women who are married to unbelievers struggle with unique questions, problems, and anxieties. In addition to the typical pressures of marriage, they are unable to share the most important thing in their lives with their spouses. Some women become overbearing or preachy out of a desire to encourage spiritual interest in their husbands. The Bible encourages Christian women who are married to unbelievers to concentrate on being loving and godly wives. Such pure lives will be more powerful witnesses than any spoken words and will be more likely to influence unbelieving husbands and children.

> *You wives must accept the authority of your husbands. Then, even if some refuse to obey the Good News, your godly lives will speak to them without any words.*
> *1 Peter 3:1*

December 17

Shining Stars
ESTHER, DEBORAH, RUTH, HANNAH

As I stepped into the crisp, cold air that night, my eyes were immediately drawn upward. Out in the country, away from city lights, the sky appeared to wrap the earth in unbroken blackness. Even the waning moon was hidden behind a cloud. Then I saw a single star. How tiny it looked from my perspective, yet in contrast to the darkness surrounding it, the star shone with such brightness that no one could fail to notice it.

The Bible gives many examples of women whose lives shone like bright lights in a dark world. Esther, whose name means "star," became the wife of a pagan monarch, yet she kept her faith in God. Her humility and gentle spirit drew the attention of those around her and made it possible for her to save the Jewish people from annihilation.

Deborah, Ruth, and Hannah all lived during a dark period of Israel's history when the nation had abandoned God's ways. Deborah faithfully served her country as prophet and judge. Ruth left Moab to care for her destitute mother-in-law and to follow Israel's God. After years of praying for a son, Hannah gave her little boy to God for full-time service. In spite of the corruption around them, these women lived moral, godly lives. Through the biblical accounts, their lights still shine for us today.

We live in a world that is growing darker as people turn away from the truth and reject God's standards of right and wrong. God calls his children to shine like stars in such an environment. The power of the gospel should light up our lives so that others can see God's love and truth. Our transformed lives should draw attention to him, not to us. We may not be stars in the worldly sense, but through God's power, we can be lights in the darkness.

> *Live clean, innocent lives as children of God, shining like bright lights in a world full of crooked and perverse people.*
> *Philippians 2:15*

December 18

Opposition
NOADIAH

Nehemiah 6:14

As Martha drove home from the meeting, she thought about the tough decision she faced. Several women had practically begged her to chair the committee for another year, but she just didn't know. Martha didn't mind the extra hours, but there was one problem—and she usually sat at the end of the table. Dee was loud and brash. She voiced opposition to every project someone suggested and made critical remarks after meetings. She seemed to be more interested in pushing her own agenda than in working as part of a team. Martha wasn't sure that she could stand another year of Dee's intimidation.

Only one verse in the Bible mentions Noadiah, but it identifies her as a woman who tried to intimidate Nehemiah, a man who was supervising a project for God. When the Israelites returned to Jerusalem after seventy years of Babylonian captivity, God appointed Nehemiah to oversee the rebuilding of the city walls. Nehemiah faced stiff opposition from Israel's enemies and from some of his own people. Of all the false prophets who threatened and schemed to stop the rebuilding, only Noadiah is specifically named. She must have been loud, brash, and bold in her antagonism toward Nehemiah, but her efforts did not succeed against the God-ordained work.

We can feel intimidated when we have to interact with loud, pushy people. It may seem easier just to avoid contact with them when that's possible. But sometimes we face criticism or opposition because of our faith. Satan often uses other people to interfere with our witness or our work. Some people who claim to be believers are actually antagonistic toward God's truth. But although Satan wields a powerful evil influence in the world, God's power is far stronger. When we remember whose Spirit lives in us, we never need to feel intimidated.

> *You belong to God, my dear children. You have already won a victory over those people, because the Spirit who lives in you is greater than the spirit who lives in the world.*
> *1 John 4:4*

December 19

God's Waiting Room
EVERYONE

I tossed the magazine down. What a waste of time! This car repair was taking much longer than the mechanics had estimated. I began to mentally calculate how much time I'd spent in waiting that day. First, there was the time on hold waiting to speak to a customer representative, then the long line at the supermarket checkout, followed by the slow-moving line of cars at the fast-food drive-through window, and now this. *Hmm,* I thought, *if I could get someone to pay me for the waiting that I do, I could probably earn my living at it!*

Women in the Bible knew about waiting. Sarah waited until she was ninety years old to have the son God promised her. The nation of Israel endured four hundred years of slavery while waiting for God to deliver them from Egypt. The break between the Old and New Testaments represents a period of silence on God's part because his people had rejected his prophets. For four hundred years, the Israelites waited for word from God until he sent the angel Gabriel to announce John the Baptist's birth. Six months later, he announced the coming birth of the Savior, whom the world had really been waiting for since the Garden of Eden.

Waiting is an unavoidable part of our lives. We wait for appointments, we stand in lines, and we wait for other people. As uncomfortable as it is, God also makes waiting a part of our Christian lives. We all experience times when God seems silent and unresponsive. Despite all our prayers, we feel stuck in God's waiting room, wondering when he will act. Although it's an uncomfortable spot, God uses his waiting room as a classroom for teaching us to trust him. As our faith grows and deepens, we discover that waiting on God is never a waste of time.

Let all that I am wait quietly before God, for my hope is in him.
Psalm 62:5

December 20

Everyone Is Invited
WOMEN IN JESUS' ANCESTRY

Matthew 1:1-16

Although Jewish genealogies didn't typically include the names of female ancestors, five women are specifically named in Jesus' genealogy in Matthew. Except for Jesus' mother, Mary, all the women were probably non-Israelites. From a human standpoint, some of these women had shameful blots on their life stories that made them unlikely candidates for being included in the ancestry of God's Son.

Tamar was probably a Canaanite. When her father-in-law, Judah, failed to arrange her marriage with his surviving son as the Law required, she pretended to be a prostitute and had sex with her father-in-law. God allowed Judah's line to be traced through one of her twin sons. Rahab was a prostitute in the city of Jericho, which God destroyed because of its wickedness. When she chose to believe in God, she married an Israelite and their descendants included Boaz.

Ruth came from Moab. According to Deuteronomy 23:3, no Moabite could be "admitted to the assembly of the LORD." When she settled in Israel, Boaz married her, and their son was King David's grandfather. Because Bathsheba was originally married to Uriah, she may have been a Hittite. The child born from her adultery with David died, but they later had Solomon, who succeeded his father in ruling Israel.

God included these women in the Messiah's line despite their backgrounds and mistakes, which reveals something about his character and his mercy. God did not choose the Jewish nation as his special people to exclude anyone, but to draw the entire world to himself. Nothing can keep us from being a part of God's family if we choose to believe in him. Our family background or past mistakes are neither hindrances nor excuses. No one is outside God's grace unless he or she chooses to be there.

Everyone who calls on the name of the LORD will be saved.
Joel 2:32

December 21

From Ordinary to Miraculous
MARY

Luke 1:26-33

I scanned the brochure for the upcoming women's conference with mixed feelings. Although I looked forward to the fellowship, encouragement, and inspiration, the lineup of speakers intimidated me. Reading about the successful recording artist, the former Miss America, and the internationally known Bible teacher made me feel so—ordinary. *Oh well,* I told myself, *I guess I don't have the kind of life that will ever get me into a brochure.*

Outwardly, there was nothing special about a poor, ordinary young woman living in an obscure village, yet God chose Mary to be at the center of one of the greatest miracles of all time. The angel Gabriel's visit on that seemingly ordinary day changed Mary's life *and* the rest of the world. He told Mary that she would give birth to the Son of the Most High. Every Jewish woman dreamed of giving birth to the long-promised Messiah, but the sudden announcement startled and confused Mary. At first, she couldn't grasp what Gabriel meant, but she knew this was no ordinary day.

At times, our lives may seem so mundane and inconsequential that we can't believe God would ever use us for some great purpose. But God has plans for each of us to accomplish things with eternal value. He desires to use our lives in such miraculous ways that we can't even imagine them.

Gabriel told Mary that she had "found favor with God." That same wording is used in only one other place in the Bible. In Ephesians 1:6, Paul refers to God's acceptance of believers through his gift of unearned favor (often translated as "grace"). If we know Jesus Christ as Savior and Lord, then we are "favored" women. He has already done something miraculous in our lives, and his presence within us makes all our days extraordinary.

> *[Gabriel said,] "Greetings, favored woman! The Lord is with you!"*
> *Luke 1:28*

December 22

Unconditional Surrender
MARY

Luke 1:34-38

"Kids! Come downstairs!" Leanne called. "I've got a surprise for you." They had balked and argued when she'd assigned their Saturday chores, but they had soon buckled down. Now Leanne wanted to reward them. "We're going out for hamburgers!" she said.

"Now? But I'll miss SpongeBob!"

"Can't we get pizza instead?"

"Mom, I'm expecting a call from Jenny this afternoon. What time will we be back?"

"I want to stop at the video store, too."

"I call shotgun!"

"That's not fair—it's my turn!"

When the angel Gabriel told Mary that she would give birth to the Son of the Most High, she didn't protest or argue. She had only one question: How will this happen since I'm a virgin? Gabriel explained that God would perform the impossible through the power of the Holy Spirit. Mary didn't try to figure out the mystery of a virgin birth. She didn't stop to ponder how this would affect her life. Mary's response reveals her heart for doing God's will: "May everything you have said about me come true." God had a special assignment for her, and that was all she needed to know at the moment.

Most of us have a tendency to argue with God. If he allows suffering to come into our lives, we ask, "Why me?" When we sense him calling us to do something difficult, we ask "Who, me?" We may want to weigh all the pros and cons before we commit to an answer, but God wants us to demonstrate a steadfast faith and submit to his will even when our minds are full of questions. When it comes to obeying God, the only real question is, Am I willing to fully surrender my life to God's purposes, as Mary was?

> *[Mary responded,] "May everything you have said about me come true."*
> Luke 1:38

December 23

Exalting God
MARY

Luke 1:39-56

A few days after Gabriel visited Mary and announced that she would give birth to the Messiah, Mary went to visit her elderly relative Elizabeth. As soon as Elizabeth saw the young woman, God's Spirit revealed to her that Mary was pregnant with his Son. Elizabeth cried out that God had blessed Mary above all other women. Mary responded by bursting into the song of praise and worship that we call the Magnificat.

Mary rejoiced in God and praised him for taking notice of her, a lowly servant girl. When Mary said that all future generations would call her blessed, she wasn't boasting but humbly acknowledging the incredible privilege she had been given. People would call her blessed not because of anything she had done, but because of what God had done through her. Mary praised God for sending the Messiah to fulfill his promises to Israel.

Throughout Mary's song, she emphasized God's glory and the great things he had done. She sounded as if she were filled with awe and wonder that God would graciously choose her for such a special purpose through no merit of her own. I can only wonder how shocked Mary would be when some people understand her role to be that of a co-redeemer. Mary came to understand that her Son would be the "one Mediator who can reconcile God and humanity" (1 Timothy 2:5).

God entrusted Mary with the honor of being the mother of the Messiah because of her humility and her readiness to obey his will. Although Mary would nurture and train Jesus until he grew to manhood, she regarded her privileged position as a way for her to serve God, not a road to self-glorification. Mary would gladly have echoed the words of John the Baptist, who pointed his own followers to Jesus as the Messiah.

> [John said,] "He must become greater and greater, and I must become less and less."
> John 3:30

December 24

A Christmas Mess
MARY

Luke 2:1-7

I lugged box after box down our attic stairs that December afternoon. My two youngest children immediately began opening the cartons to look inside. Before leaving the room, I instructed them to look, but not to take anything out yet. I planned to decorate the tree and the house in an orderly, logical manner, one step at a time. When I returned several minutes later, it looked like a fully loaded Christmas tree had exploded all over the carpet. "Just look at this mess!" I scolded. "Yes, but Mommy—isn't it wonderful?" five-year-old Holly exclaimed. "It's a Christmas mess!"

Mary knew about a Christmas mess. As her due date drew near, a royal decree forced Joseph and Mary to make a long journey to Bethlehem to register for a census. When they arrived, they weren't able to find lodging in the crowded town. The Bible says that Mary laid her newborn son in a feeding trough, indicating that she may have given birth in a cave or stable used to shelter animals.

Instead of being surrounded by women relatives to help out, Mary gave birth to her firstborn far from home. Although she longed to give her baby the best, she could welcome him only into a dark and dirty environment. Mary's normal maternal instincts must have conflicted with anxiety over the chaotic events surrounding the birth, but she clung to the belief that God would work out his plan.

Just because we're following God doesn't mean that things will be easy, comfortable, or even tidy. Sometimes our plans disintegrate and events seem to spiral out of control, but God is always in charge. Our role is to concentrate on obeying him and trusting him to work out the problems. God looked at a world in a mess caused by sin and sent the Messiah. When our lives look like a mess, we can remember why Jesus was called Immanuel.

> *They will call him Immanuel, which means "God is with us."*
> *Matthew 1:23*

December 25

Treasures of the Heart
MARY

Luke 2:8-24; Matthew 2:1-12

I opened the Christmas present and thanked my son warmly. What made the gift so special was a recent conversation we'd had about music. I told Eric that in college I'd liked the music of the band Chicago, and he had bought me a two-CD set of its greatest hits. As thoughtful as that gift was, I remembered another one from long ago. I still had it in one of the "treasure boxes" under my bed. When I came home from a meeting late one evening, I found a note on my pillow that said, "I love you Muthr."

All mothers have special memories tucked away in keepsake boxes, in scrapbooks, or in their hearts. Mary was no exception. The circumstances around Jesus' birth were difficult, but God sent some unexpected visitors to help celebrate his birth. Mary must have been surprised when a group of poor, weather-beaten shepherds showed up to gaze upon her baby. Her heart surely thrilled as she listened to their story of the angel's announcement that the Messiah had been born. Later, wise men followed a star so they could worship and present precious gifts to Jesus. Mary stored these and other signs from God in her heart. She must have thought often about them as the years passed.

Sometimes we get so busy that we neglect the treasures tucked away in our hearts. An important part of prayer is a quiet time of reflection on what God has done for us. Instead, we often plunge straight into our list of needs and wants, as if we were talking with Santa Claus. Every good thing in our lives comes from God. When we rehearse our memories of his goodness to us, we develop an attitude of gratitude and joy, and our faith in his character is strengthened. Then we remember that we're sitting on our heavenly Father's lap, not Santa's.

Every good thing given and every perfect gift is from above.
James 1:17 (NASB)

December 26

Bitter and Sweet
MARY

Luke 2:21-35

One year, after we trimmed our Christmas tree, my husband and two young sons went off to watch television. I sat alone in the living room and stared at the twinkling lights, sobbing quietly. Soon my younger son, almost three, wandered into the room. "Why are you crying?" Kevin asked, with a look of concern. We had recently moved four hundred miles from our families, and I explained that I felt sad that we couldn't celebrate Christmas with the grandparents, aunts, uncles, and cousins. My son put a hand on each side of my damp face and pulled it close. "Don't cry, Mommy. Jesus loves you, and I'm here for you!"

Even on the first Christmas, Mary's joy must have been mingled with sorrow. Although she joyfully received the news that she had been chosen to deliver the Messiah, at some point she must have been struck with the horror of what her pregnancy would mean. Later, when the couple took Jesus to the Temple to be dedicated to God, they marveled at Simeon's words. The old man proclaimed that Jesus would make salvation possible for the entire world, not just the Jewish people. Then he told Mary that she would experience grief like a sword piercing her soul. She must have remembered Simeon's bittersweet prophecy many times as she witnessed her son being rejected, unjustly persecuted, and finally crucified.

Since we live in a world marred by sin, our joy will always be mixed with sorrow. The relationships that bring us the greatest happiness also can cause us the most grief. Even in the best of times, we live with the possibility of loss and tragedy. We will know pure, untainted joy only when we get to heaven. Then all the bitterness and sorrow of our earthly lives will fall away and be replaced by the sweetness of Jesus' presence.

> *[Jesus said,] "You have sorrow now, but I will see you again; then you will rejoice, and no one can rob you of that joy."*
> *John 16:22*

December 27

True Family
MARY

Mark 3:20-21, 31-35

When Mary and her sons became worried about Jesus' mental condition, they tried to interrupt his ministry and take him home. The crowds of people surrounding Jesus had grown so large that he and his disciples couldn't always find time to eat. Some people came to listen and learn; others came hoping for a miracle or out of curiosity; and some religious leaders came to criticize, even accusing Jesus of being possessed by Satan. Jesus' family didn't fully understand what he came to do, but they were concerned about his well-being.

Someone told Jesus that his family stood waiting outside to speak with him. His response may have surprised his mother. Jesus looked at those around him, and said, "Anyone who does God's will is my brother and sister and mother" (Mark 3:35). Did Mary remember the time when she and Joseph searched for Jesus for three days and finally found him sitting in the Temple with the religious leaders? "Didn't you know that I must be in my Father's house?" Jesus had asked (Luke 2:49). Perhaps Mary felt a pang as she began to understand that the Son of God was now independent of earthly relationships and focused on the world he came to save.

Jesus never denied the importance of family, but he did point people to a higher, more important relationship—our place in God's family. We don't become Christians by being born in Christian families or nations. Our relationship with God doesn't depend on our membership in a church or our impressive Christian service. The only way to enter the Kingdom of Heaven is by doing God's will. We all begin by answering God's invitation to believe in Jesus' death and resurrection as the only payment for our sin. Then we become true members of God's family.

> [Jesus said,] "Not everyone who calls out to me, 'Lord! Lord!' will enter the Kingdom of Heaven. Only those who actually do the will of my Father in heaven will enter."
> Matthew 7:21

December 28

Scandalous Behavior
JESUS' ATTITUDE TOWARD WOMEN

Author Dan Brown revived ancient legends as the basis for his worldwide best seller, *The Da Vinci Code*. The "secret" information supposedly suppressed by the early church includes Jesus' marriage to Mary Magdalene and the children they are said to have had. The book also claims, among other things, that the idea of Jesus being divine was invented by a meeting of church bishops in A.D. 325.

Christians with knowledge of the Bible found the material in *The Da Vinci Code* scandalous, and rightly so. During Jesus' ministry, many people found his behavior scandalous, but for a different reason. His dealings with women especially must have shocked people in a culture where the men prayed in thanksgiving to God that they were not born as women. Although rabbinic teachings held that it would be better to burn the words of the Law than to teach them publicly to a woman, Jesus willingly taught God's truth to the women among his followers. Jesus allowed women to support his ministry and to travel with his disciples. He initiated a conversation with a Samaritan woman with a questionable reputation (see John 4:6-26) and shocked dinner guests by allowing a repentant sinful woman to touch him (see Luke 7:37-50).

Jesus went against social norms to demonstrate that men and women are equally valued in God's sight. We are all born as sinners in need of a Savior. We will never be able to comprehend fully the anguish and suffering that it cost a holy God to become a human and come to a world infected with evil. We will never know the pain that Jesus experienced in his agonizing death on the cross to pay the price for our sin. And we will never know the immensity of God's love for us that broke through time and space, scandalized a world caught in sin's grip, and wouldn't let anything keep him from reaching us. But we can spend the rest of our lives thanking him for it.

With all my heart I will praise you, O Lord my God. I will give glory to your name forever, for your love for me is very great.
Psalm 86:12-13

December 29

Righteous Anger
JESUS CLEARS THE TEMPLE

Mark 11:15-18

April's friends couldn't believe it when they heard the news that she had attacked a man. How could such a quiet, gentle woman go berserk and hit a man with a baseball bat? It was totally out of character. They later heard the full story. April had moved her car from the parking lot to the edge of the field to load up the Little League equipment. She drove up just in time to see a strange man forcing her son into his car.

The women who didn't know the full story must have felt shock as they witnessed Jesus clearing out the Temple. They had seen Jesus holding children on his lap and blessing them. He had treated the needy with compassion and healed the sick. How could such a gentle man knock over tables and chairs and stop those who were selling the animals needed for sacrifice?

If the women knew the extent of the corruption involved, they knew that Jesus did the right thing. The money changers cheated the people by charging a fee to exchange their currency to the special Temple money. Then merchants who sold animals for sacrifice inflated the prices. God's house had become a hotbed of extortion and commercialism instead of a place for prayer and worship.

Most people reading the Old Testament have a difficult time with the accounts of God's destroying entire cities as punishment for sin. The book of Revelation reveals God's plan to pour out his anger on the earth and finally wipe out all those who persist in rejecting him. Although God is patient and delights in showing love and mercy, his holiness requires that he eventually judge evil. His anger is always righteous and justified. If we think otherwise, we don't know the full story of his character.

> *The LORD is slow to anger and filled with unfailing love, forgiving every kind of sin and rebellion. But he does not excuse the guilty.*
> *Numbers 14:18*

December 30

Saving the Best for Last
JESUS' MIRACLE AT CANA

John 2:1-11

Many people think that the best holiday on the calendar comes in the last month of the year. Most people would agree that the best part of a meal is served last, at least during holidays. But sometimes we get the best first and the worst later, especially in the world of advertising. What seems like a great deal may turn out to be only an introductory offer, with the price going up later or with additional fees and charges tacked on.

In Jesus' time, the Jewish people had a custom similar to an introductory offer: A host normally served the best, most expensive wine first and then served the cheaper wine later in the evening. By then, the guests had already drunk enough that they were unlikely to notice the poor quality. But when Jesus turned water into wine at the wedding in Cana, it was of exceptional quality even though the celebration had been going on for a while.

If the bride heard the remarks made to her groom by the master of ceremonies, she and her husband must have been pleasantly surprised. The master of ceremonies marveled at the superior quality of the wine, not knowing that it had been water only moments before. He told the bridegroom, "A host always serves the best wine first . . . but you have kept the best until now!" (John 2:10).

When we read the end of the Bible, we see that God is saving the best for last. He tells us up front that when we accept Christ, we can expect trials, sorrows, persecution, and hatred from God's enemies. Being a Christian means taking up our own cross and dying to ourselves. Although we experience incredible joys from our relationship with him now, the best will come later. Someday we will live in the perfect place he's prepared for us, and we will enjoy his best forever.

> *No eye has seen, no ear has heard, and no mind has imagined what God has prepared for those who love him.*
> *1 Corinthians 2:9*

December 31

Anxious Bridegroom
BRIDE OF CHRIST

Revelation 19:6-9

The young woman smoothed her gown as she waited for her entrance. The last several months had seemed like a countdown to this very day. Now she couldn't believe that the moment had finally arrived. Questions darted through her mind. *Does my hair look okay? Did the makeup cover my blemishes? Am I really ready for this? I wonder if he's having any doubts right now.* Suddenly she took her father's arm and stepped through the doorway. She looked toward her groom and her anxieties vanished. In that moment, she saw a reflection of her beauty in his eyes and his intense longing to claim her as his own.

In the New Testament, believers are pictured as the bride of Jesus Christ, made pure and unblemished by his blood shed on the cross. The passage in Revelation paints the scene of the union between Christ and his bride. Everyone who has believed in the gospel will enter into a new relationship with God and enjoy an intimacy that was impossible before. This wedding feast will be the pinnacle of human history, the event that all creation has been groaning for (see Romans 8:22).

Understanding the sacrifice that Christ made to pay the price for our sin is enough to motivate us to live godly lives. Knowing that one day we will be claimed as Christ's bride puts the temporary troubles of our earthly lives in perspective. Looking forward to our "wedding day" helps us to resist sin's pull and to do everything we can to get our hearts ready for our groom. When that day comes, we'll understand that our entire lives have been a countdown to that glorious event. And in that moment, we will see our beauty in his eyes and his intense longing to be with us for all eternity.

> *He who is the faithful witness to all these things says, "Yes, I am coming soon!" Amen! Come, Lord Jesus!*
> *Revelation 22:20*

Topical Index

Do-able. Daily. Devotions.

START ANY DAY THE ONE YEAR WAY.

Do-able.
Every One Year book is designed for people who live busy, active lives. Just pick one up and start on today's date.

Daily.
Daily routine doesn't have to be drudgery. One Year devotionals help you form positive habits that connect you to what's most important.

Devotions.
Discover a natural rhythm for drawing near to God in an extremely personal way. One Year devotionals provide daily focus essential to your spiritual growth.

For Women

The One Year Devotions for Women on the Go

The One Year Devotions for Women

The One Year Devotions for Moms

The One Year Women of the Bible

The One Year Daily Grind

CP0145

For Men

The One Year Devotions for Men on the Go

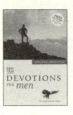

The One Year Devotions for Men

For Couples

The One Year Devotions for Couples

For Families

The One Year Family Devotions

For Teens

The One Year Devos for Teens

The One Year Devos for Sports Fans

For Bible Study

The One Year Life Lessons from the Bible

The One Year Praying through the Bible

The One Year through the Bible

For Personal Growth

The One Year Devotions for People of Purpose

The One Year Walk with God Devotional

The One Year at His Feet Devotional

The One Year Great Songs of Faith

The One Year on This Day

The One Year Life Verse Devotional

It's convenient and easy to grow with God the One Year way.

CP0145

THE ONE YEAR WAY

Teach Truth.

MEET JESUS EVERY DAY THE ONE YEAR WAY.

For Kids

*The One Year
Devotions for
Girls*

*The One Year
Devotions for
Boys*

*The One Year
Devotions for
Preschoolers*

*The One Year
Devotions for
Kids*

*The One Year
Make-It-Stick
Devotions*

*The One Year
Bible for Kids:
Challenge
Edition*

*The One Year
Children's Bible*

*The One Year
Book of Josh
McDowell's
Youth Devotions*

The ONE YEAR® MINI

The Perfect Gift

THOUGHTFUL. PRACTICAL. AFFORDABLE.

The One Year Mini for Women helps women connect with God through several Scripture verses and a devotional thought. Perfect for use anytime and anywhere between regular devotion times. Hardcover.

The One Year Mini for Students offers students from high school through college a quick devotional connection with God anytime and anywhere. Stay grounded through the ups and downs of a busy student lifestyle. Hardcover.

The One Year Mini for Moms provides encouragement and affirmation for those moments during a mom's busy day when she needs to be reminded of the high value of her role. Hardcover.

The One Year Mini for Busy Women is for women who don't have time to get it all done but need to connect with God during the day. Hardcover.

The One Year Mini for Men helps men connect with God anytime, anywhere between their regular devotion times through Scripture quotations and a related devotional thought. Hardcover.

The One Year Mini for Leaders motivates and inspires leaders to maximize their God-given leadership potential using scriptural insights. Hardcover.

CP0161